Personal Souths

Personal Souths

Interviews from the *Southern Quarterly*

Edited by Douglas B. Chambers

UNIVERSITY PRESS OF MISSISSIPPI ∾ JACKSON

www.upress.state.ms.us

The University Press of Mississippi is a member of the Association of American University Presses.

First printing 2012

∞

Library of Congress Cataloging-in-Publication Data

Personal souths : interviews from The Southern Quarterly / edited by Douglas B. Chambers.
p. cm.
Includes index.
ISBN 978-1-61703-290-5 (cloth : alk. paper) —ISBN 978-1-61703-291-2 (pbk. : alk. paper) —
ISBN 978-1-61703-292-9 (ebook) 1. American literature—Southern States—History and criticism.
2. Authors, American—20th century—Interviews. 3. Authors, American—21st century—
Interviews. 4. Southern States—Intellectual life. 5. Southern States—In literature.
I. Chambers, Douglas B., Ph. D.
PS261.P47 2012
810.9'975—dc23
[B]   2011039250

British Library Cataloging-in-Publication Data available

Contents

Part III ᕔ 1990s

Part IV ᕔ 2000s

Acknowledgments

First and foremost, I thank the contributors for choosing to publish their literary interviews with the *Southern Quarterly*. Peggy Prenshaw deserves special recognition for encouraging this kind of work in general, and for providing a welcoming publishing venue in particular. In producing this volume, I am proud to acknowledge the diligent efforts of Elizabeth Simmons, who, while serving as the *Quarterly*'s graduate assistant during 2010–2011, worked her digital magic to rescue these published interviews from the journal's bound reference collection. The current managing editor, Ann Branton, has always been a supportive and reliable exemplar of professionalism, for which I am grateful. As editor it has been my privilege to work with her and her staff on the twenty-four journal issues we have produced together. I also thank Craig Gill of the University Press of Mississippi for seeing the value in publishing this collection of literary interviews, in honor of the journal's fiftieth anniversary, and I extend my thanks to the Press's anonymous reviewer for the excellent suggestions that were provided for improving this volume. As the *Southern Quarterly* approaches its golden jubilee, I dedicate this volume to the past and *future* editors of the journal.

Introduction

Personal Souths and the *Southern Quarterly*

DOUGLAS B. CHAMBERS

In 1962 Mississippi Southern College, which had been founded a half century earlier as a state teachers' college, transformed itself into the University of Southern Mississippi. As an integral part of this new vision of Southern Miss as a comprehensive state university, then-president William D. McCain (1907–1993) established the *Southern Quarterly* in the same year, under the editorship of James L. Allen Jr., a professor of English.

Allen's inaugural editorial introduced the *Southern Quarterly* as "a scholarly journal of studies done in the humanities and social sciences by members of the faculty of the University of Southern Mississippi," and specifically as "a journal of articles grounded in research and scholarship rather than a magazine of book reviews, creative writings, or essays of mere opinion." Furthermore, the founding editor asserted, "the completely scholarly orientation and the broadly humanistic scope of our publication give it, we feel, its *raison d'etre* in an age of journalism increasingly characterized by magazines of opinion and review and in a social and academic age where technology and science threaten to overshadow all unless the voice of humane learning speaks out and makes itself heard."[1]

Professor Allen closed his inaugural statement with the point that the founding of the *Southern Quarterly* was one of the institution's three "milestones" of 1962:

Actually, however, the relationship between these three milestones in the school's academic development—designation as a university, granting of doctoral degrees, and inauguration of our own scholarly publication—really goes much deeper than mere proximity in chronological sequence. For the latter two are unmistakable manifestations of the increasingly evident fact that Southern has come into full maturity as an institution of higher learning, that it has become an institution actively involved in all the broad academic and scholarly interests consonant with the name and state of university.[2]

With the development of the University in the 1980s and 1990s into a reputable regional university, and the university's investment in the journal under the presidency of Dr. Aubrey K. Lucas (1975–1996) and the longtime editorship of Dr. Peggy Whitman Prenshaw (1973–1991), who also served as a professor of English and as dean of the Honors College, the *Southern Quarterly* earned a solid regional reputation in southern literary and cultural studies. Some fifty years after the journal's founding, the University of Southern Mississippi has evolved into a truly comprehensive research university, and today recognizes itself as "the premier public research university in the Gulf South region." Likewise, the *Southern Quarterly* has been transformed from a modest publishing venue for the university's humanities faculty to a member journal of the Council of Editors of Learned Journals (one of only two such academic quarterlies in Mississippi). With a contributing staff of ten and a cumulative annual budget of $70,000, today the journal has a distinguished editorial advisory board and an international subscription, and is collected in nearly five hundred libraries worldwide.

One of the ways that Peggy Whitman Prenshaw developed the *Southern Quarterly* during her editorship was to publish interviews with noted southern writers. A scholar of southern literature and a recognized authority on the work of Elizabeth Spencer (b. 1921), Professor Prenshaw had recognized that thoughtful conversations with top-tier southern writers constituted a useful form of literary scholarship. To its credit, the University Press of Mississippi agreed. In the past quarter-century the Press has published over a hundred books in its highly regarded *Literary Conversations* publication series, with Prenshaw as the series editor.

As part of the celebration of the journal's fiftieth anniversary in 2012, we have selected a number of literary interviews from the *Southern Quarterly*, which are collected in this volume. The twenty interviews in this golden jubilee collection represent a wide variety of southern writers, all of the first rank. They range from Erskine Caldwell, Eudora Welty, and Tennessee Williams, who were interviewed in the 1970s, to a veritable *Who's-Who* of southern literature in the second half of the twentieth century. All of these interviews were originally published in the journal in the 1980s, 1990s, and 2000s.

The diversity of these interviews is impressive. Men and women each make up about half of the collection. The South is represented broadly, with writers from at least ten states (Arkansas, Florida, Kentucky, Louisiana, Mississippi, North Carolina, South Carolina, Tennessee, Texas, Virginia). A least five (Donald Harington, David Madden, Bobbie Ann Mason, Robert Morgan, and Lee Smith) represent the "mountain South"; and another four (Reynolds Price, Mary Lee Settle, Elizabeth Spencer, and Tennessee Williams) typify a "cosmopolitan South." The greatest number of voices, about half of our authors, speak for or from what one may call the "poor white South," in one way or another: Brown, Caldwell, Crews, Harington, Madden, Mason, Morgan, Shores, Smith. Of the seventy literary interviews which were published in the journal in the past thirty years, only one was with an African American writer, Ernest J. Gaines (2006), which we include in this volume. Several other interviews (Larry Brown, Ellen Douglas, William Styron) comment significantly on issues of race, and Styron (the Pulitzer Prize–winning author of *The Confessions of Nat Turner*) focuses on a conversation about African American literature. And in a departure no doubt from what would have been deemed publishable in the earliest years of the journal, we also include a recently published interview with an openly gay Southern writer, the contemporary Texan playwright Del Shores. The Shores interview is also notable for being the only one in this collection produced via the new medium of email.

The interviews were conducted in a variety of contexts, which themselves are interesting. Many of the interviewers held their conversations in southern settings, sometimes at literary events, such as the contribution by Jere Real from a 1979 Tennessee Williams Festival in Lynchburg, Virginia, or Ashby Bland Crowder's interview with Reynolds Price during a visit to Hendrix College in Arkansas in 1988. Others were done in more intimate settings. Martha Van Noppen sat on Eudora Welty's sofa in her home in Jackson in 1978; Susan Ketchin joined Larry Brown for catfish at a country restaurant in Taylor, Mississippi, in 1991; Larry Vonalt met with Donald Harington twice (1998, 1999) in Harington's living room at his home in Fayetteville, Arkansas; Linda Byrd Cook was invited to interview Lee Smith on the front porch of her mountain cabin near Hillsborough, North Carolina, on a spring day in 2008. Other interviewers were good friends. For example, David Hammond, who interviewed Elizabeth Spencer in 1994, had directed the premiere of one of her plays at UNC in 1989. Virginia Gunn Fick, who interviewed William Styron on the back porch of her home in High Point, North Carolina, in 1995, had been classmates with him at Duke some forty-nine years earlier, and they were lifelong friends.

The interviews are all fascinating. Not only do they reveal the personalities of these southern literary stars, but they represent a self-conscious community of writers. It is surprising how often they mention each other. Or rather, it is a testament to the quality of the journal that many of the writers, when discussing their most important contemporaries, often reference other writers whose interviews are in this collection. For example, in 2000 the North Carolina poet and novelist Robert Morgan, who has been called the "poet laureate of Appalachia," was interviewed. His best-selling novel, *Gap Creek*, had just been chosen for the Oprah Book Club, but he was interviewed about a 1977 PBS-TV film, *The Gardener's Son*, for which Cormac McCarthy had written the screenplay. When asked about how he would rank McCarthy in the pantheon of twentieth-century American writers, Morgan's reply included mention of three writers whose interviews we include in this volume: Lee Smith, Doris Betts, and Reynolds Price.

Q: *Where would you rank McCarthy among American writers, particularly those of the twentieth century?*
MORGAN: My sense is that some of the writers of the last half of the twentieth century and the beginning of the twenty-first are as good as the great writers of the earlier twentieth century. In the future, writers like Cormac McCarthy, Tim O'Brien, Louise Erdrich, Lee Smith, Doris Betts, Reynolds Price, Alice Walker, will be seen as great writers the way Faulkner, Hemingway, and Fitzgerald are.[3]

There are a number of common themes in this collection of interviews. The interviews of Caldwell, Crews, Douglas, Madden, and Welty provide in-depth discussion of the writer's craft, and of the relationship between author and reader. For example, Eudora Welty was asked a complicated question about the relationship between writing fiction and reading it as literature:

Q: *In the relationship of the reader to the work of fiction, I often find readers who don't trust themselves to have an understanding of the work, particularly what was intended by the author. Students often turn to interpretation and scholarly criticism. Perhaps that's part of the reason some of us are fortunate enough to have interviews with writers.*
WELTY: Well, every writer takes a chance with everything he writes that it will be understood. Also, a writer is learning all the time he's writing, and things are being suggested to him in the work. Everything I write teaches

me how to do it as I go. All kinds of things open up. Something I write today, I didn't even know about yesterday. I don't mean a fact in the plot, but just an insight into something, and so it's a constant learning process with me when I write. I'm not surprised what any reader may go through, just as I feel when I read something.[4]

Many of the authors discuss their own work in remarkable detail, giving personal insight into the fictional characters they created, and telling us how they interpret their own creations (see Douglas, Harington, Madden, Mason, Price, Shores, Smith, Spencer). Others (such as Betts, Brown, Gaines, Shores, Smith) emphasize the importance of spirituality and religion, both as foundation and as obstacle in their own journeys as creative writers. Many of the interviews offer remarkably honest personal accounts of their sources of inspiration, both in general and for particular characters and stories (see especially Crews, Douglas, Gaines, Harington, Hoffman, Humphreys, Mason, Shores). These discussions will continue to animate and inform scholarly appraisals of their work.

Quite by accident, several of the interviews serve as thematic pairings: Doris Betts and then Larry Brown on spirituality, death, and religion; William Styron and then Ernest J. Gaines on African American literature and history, including how their earlier work had each been criticized as not sufficiently "black" or insufficiently "political"; and lastly, Del Shores and then Lee Smith on issues of homosexuality or sexual orientation, with Shores as an openly gay writer and Smith as a female writer who included lesbian characters in her fiction. Though Smith is not a lesbian, she had been recently publicly criticized for including what she calls "kinds and kinds of love" in her novels. In an interview that specifically focuses on the importance of an inclusive, sensuous, humanistic spirituality in Smith's work, she explains why she, though herself not lesbian, does not shy away from the issue of homosexuality in her fiction:

Q: *I wondered if you ever resisted this before, if you ever had a story going in your head that homosexuality could have been a part of and you edited it out.*
SMITH: I don't really think so, I guess because of my sense of my own sexuality and so on. I haven't ever had any lesbian experience and therefore I have felt unqualified to really write about it in depth and the way I like to do my characters. Several times in short stories, I have had lesbian

characters and gay characters, but in terms of major characters for these long novels, I just haven't felt like I knew enough exactly.

Q: Of course, with Miss Torrington (Fair and Tender Ladies)*, that's never developed, but that's a good example.*
SMITH: Yes, she is definitely a lesbian character.

Q: You know, her comment to Ivy that there are kinds and kinds of love, and Ivy, of course, doesn't understand that until she's much older.
SMITH: And then Ivy *does* understand that there are kinds and kinds of love. But *I* believe that there are kinds and kinds of love.[5]

When I was appointed editor of the *Southern Quarterly* in 2005, I accepted a mandate to revitalize the journal. Since Peggy Whitman Prenshaw's departure in 1991, the journal had gone through a period of transition, with several different editors and institutional reorganization, culminating in a year of publishing hiatus (2003–2004).[6] My tenure as editor concluded in 2011, but one hopes that the succeeding editor will maintain this longstanding *Southern Quarterly* tradition of literary interviews as the journal continues to develop in the coming years. That the journal continues as strong today at its golden jubilee as ever in its fifty years of existence, with a renewed focus on the many Souths, personal and collective, literary and historical, and scholarly all, is a matter of great pride.

We hope that you will join us in celebrating the golden jubilee of this learned journal. The University Press of Mississippi also will be publishing a second fiftieth-anniversary volume, a companion to this interviews one, of selected literary and historical essays from the *Southern Quarterly*.[7]

Other compilations of interviews of southern writers have been published during the decades covered in this volume.[8] However, this *Southern Quarterly* collection is unique in gathering in one volume literary interviews conducted by a variety of contributors for a single scholarly journal during the whole span of the past four decades.[9]

In reading these collected interviews, and in sifting the many personal Souths evoked in these literary conversations, we hope that you will be inspired, as am I, to read more of these exceptionally accomplished writers' novels, short stories, poems, and plays.

Notes

1. J.L.A., "An Inaugural Editorial," *Southern Quarterly* Vol. 1, no. 1 (1962), p. iii.
2. *Ibid.*, p. iv.
3. See Morgan interview, *infra*. The *Southern Quarterly* has twice featured Cormac McCarthy in a special issue: Vol. 30, no. 4 (Summer 1992) and Vol. 38, no. 3 (Spring 2000); and recently also featured a special issue on Robert Morgan (Vol. 47, no. 3, Spring 2010). Other special *Southern Quarterly* issues on authors featured in this collection of interviews include Erskine Caldwell (Vol. 27, no. 3, Spring 1989); Harry Crews (Vol. 37, no. 1, Fall 1998); Donald Harington (Vol. 40, no. 2, Winter 2002); Lee Smith (Vol. 32, no. 2, Winter 1994); Eudora Welty (Vol. 20, no. 4, Summer 1982) and (Vol. 32, no. 1, Fall 1993); and Tennessee Williams (Vol. 38, no. 1, Fall 1999) and (Vol. 48, no. 4, Summer 2011).
4. See Welty interview, *infra*.
5. See Smith interview (2008), *infra*.
6. The *Southern Quarterly* editors are, respectively: James L. Allen Jr., English (1962–1963); Arthur H. DeRosier Jr., History (1963–1965); William H. Hatcher, Political Science (1965–1973); Peggy Whitman Prenshaw, English (1973–1991); Stephen Flinn Young, Art History (1991–2000); Noel Polk, English (2000–2004); Douglas B. Chambers, History (2005–2011); Philip C. Kolin, English (2011–).
7. *The Past Is Not Dead: Essays from the Southern Quarterly*, edited by Douglas B. Chambers, with Kenneth Watson, and foreword by Peggy Whitman Prenshaw. Featured contributors include D. C. Berry (1974) on James Dickey's poetry; Thadious M. Davis (1981) on defining southern writers; Manning Marable (1985) on W. E. B. Du Bois; Harriett Pollack (1990) on Eudora Welty's fiction; Don H. Doyle (1991) on Faulkner's use of history; and more recently, Randy J. Sparks (2006) on antebellum white evangelical culture, and Joseph Millichap (2010) on *Let Us Now Praise Famous Men*; as well as other essays by Willie Morris (1979) on the Americanization of Mississippi, and Margaret Walker Alexander (1991) on Richard Wright and Natchez.
8. See for example John C. Carr, ed., *Conversations with Twelve Southern Writers* (Baton Rouge: Louisiana State University Press, 1972); William Walsh, *Speak So I Shall Know Thee: Interviews with Southern Writers* (Jefferson, NC: McFarland & Co., 1990); Dannye Romine Powell, *Parting the Curtains: Interviews with Southern Writers* (New York: Anchor Books, 1994); and Ernest Suarez, T. W. Sanford, and Amy Verner, eds., *Southbound: Interviews with Southern Poets* (Columbia: University of Missouri Press, 1999).
9. We have included as an appendix a comprehensive list of all literary interviews published in the *Southern Quarterly*.

PART I

1970s

Erskine Caldwell ❧ 1971

JAC THARPE

I interviewed Erskine Caldwell ten years ago, in August 1971, for the Mississippi Oral History Program at the University of Southern Mississippi. He was very pleasant throughout the two afternoon sessions, though he warmed somewhat on the matter of truth in art. I don't know whether he felt strongly or had often replied to such a question. I regret that I am unable in these excerpts to convey his personality as well as his opinions.

These remarks are published with his permission and that of the Oral History Program, and I am grateful to both for the privilege of the interview. Tapes as well as a transcript of the complete interview are available in the Cleanth Brooks Reading Room of the William D. McCain Library at the University of Southern Mississippi in Hattiesburg.

QUESTION: *Do you object to the use of the term social critic in describing you?*
CALDWELL: I've never had the ability to be a social critic. I'm only a story-teller. And what I do, or have done, and tried to do is tell the story of people and the life they live, which may produce some sermons in stones. I don't know whether it does or not. But I have not consciously and knowingly set out to be a social critic. It just happens that the life of people in the lower echelon does appeal to me, not because it's a curiosity but only because I have sympathy for life that is deprived. I grew up in the same way myself.

Q: You think of writing as working at a career?
CALDWELL: When I say working, what I mean is that I have done many things like radio, television, journalism. But even beyond that, I like to take part in the distribution of what I do. I'll go to a sales convention with a publisher, for example, and spend a week there talking to people in the business, make a little speech to salespeople.

Originally published as Jac Tharpe, "Interview with Erskine Caldwell," Vol. 20, no. 1 (1981), 64–74.

Or I'll go on a lecture trip. I did that for a couple of years because I felt I didn't have enough to do. I was writing books, of course, all the time; but then I would have three or four months in the year with nothing to do. So I went on lecture tours around the universities and colleges for about two years, spending two or three months at a time. So that's what I call working.

Q: *The Weather Shelter, I gather, is proposing with some seriousness that miscegenation might be a solution to the whole racial problem. That is one of the reasons I wondered if you are a social critic.*
CALDWELL: It's not that I advocate anything of the sort. This amalgamation of races is a distinct possibility whether I have anything to do with it or not, or whether anybody else has anything to do with it. So if it is going to occur, that's nature's way, so to speak. I don't think anybody is going to change it by making any pronouncement or by criticizing it or by praising it. That's always been my feeling about the mixture of races, about the socializing between whites and blacks and others. Maybe it's going to end up where you have a race of people like Brazilians who claim that there is no racial distinction—that the white and the black in Brazil are all the same thing and that the shades of color between black and white make no difference whatsoever to the true Brazilian. Whether it's going to be, I won't be here to find out myself.

Q: *Have you had objections to the rather intense move to integrate the South?*
CALDWELL: No, though I understand what you say. I haven't been pressured in any way. I have had criticism from people who accused me of being in favor of integration, people whom I'd call professional Southerners, but nothing from the Northern point of view. People in the South have criticized me for feeling that nobody should be penalized for associating socially, sexually, economically.

Q: *When you were writing back in the thirties, were you particularly conscious of your colleagues?*
CALDWELL: Well, you see, I never got associated with other writers. I still am not familiar with other writers personally. When I came out of Georgia, the Carolinas, Tennessee, there were no writers around. I didn't know any. I thought they all lived in New York or Paris or someplace, which was true. There weren't any. The first writer I ever saw probably was in New York. I had to go that far to see what one looked like.

Q: Was he anyone we would know?
CALDWELL: Well, I guess I could name a few people. Thomas Wolfe, for example.

Q: You met him?
CALDWELL: In New York. I think he probably had the same experience. He had to go to New York to see a writer like me. I knew quite a few writers in those days, in the thirties, in New York because we had to associate in order to help each other out in the way of survival. If someone knew a certain place you could go and get a book review and get paid two and a half or five dollars that was something to pass around.

Q: Would you just name the others who occur to you?
CALDWELL: I don't know what their reputations are now. There was a chap by the name of Robert Cantwell, who was writing novels in those days, and now he's an editor of *Sports Illustrated*.

There was a fellow by the name of Charles Henri Ford, out of Mississippi, who was in New York trying to scrape up enough money to run a magazine, as I recall, and I think he—every time he'd get enough money, he'd go back to Mississippi and get out another issue.

Who else can I think of right now? Norman McLeod. He was trying to write a little magazine too. Everybody in those days either wrote for a little magazine or tried to edit a little magazine. There were dozens of them, dozens of them. That's how I got started getting published. There happened to be a magazine in Paris called *transition* that did it. That was the first one. That was the only way to get published in those hard times.

Q: Were you aware of other figures who have become famous, like Dos Passos or Steinbeck?
CALDWELL: Well, not in those days, no. It was only later that I ran into Steinbeck, and I ran into Faulkner, to name two. That was much later. Not in the thirties, because in the thirties, I was either grubbing it away in New York, trying to make enough to pay the room rent, or else I was out somewhere else, like Maine, away from writers. So I never got involved in the coteries of literature, so to speak. That's one of the things Malcolm Cowley criticizes me for, for not associating more with the élite in the field. Jokingly, of course, he's saying that. Well, Cowley is a real good critic, no doubt about it, but I have no

inclination to move to Connecticut to live next door to him, just because he is a good critic, and become friendly with him. I'd rather stay miles, hundreds of miles, away from people than become obligated, in a sense, to be friends.

Q: Did you actually meet Steinbeck and Faulkner?
CALDWELL: I got to know Steinbeck quite a while ago. Let's see, this was way back when he had a play on Broadway just about the time *Tobacco Road* was there. Our wives got to be friends, and they write occasionally now.

Q: Did you think he deserved the Nobel Prize?
CALDWELL: Well, no. I remember I was in Yugoslavia when I heard about that, heard about them awarding the Prize to him, and someone asked me why he was given the award when there were other great writers about the world. Well, I think he deserved it in a way, but I was surprised at the time that other people were passed over.

Q: Would you feel that Hemingway or Faulkner deserved it more than Steinbeck?
CALDWELL: Yes, I would say certainly Hemingway, because I think he had the ability to produce what other writers could not do. I didn't always like what he wrote. After he began writing novels, I sort of lost interest in Hemingway because I'm an aficionado of short stories. But just for his short stories, I would say he was deserving of any award. I never knew Hemingway, I knew one of his wives, who at one time was a correspondent in Europe when I was there, but I never had the opportunity to meet him.

As for Faulkner, I thought Faulkner was a choice that had to be made worldwide, for the fact that he had a lucidity, an ability to make clear through a very dark screen, make a clarity that you would never get just by a bland looking at people or looking at life. You had to look through this screen.

Q: You admired Faulkner then?
CALDWELL: Yes. He and I a lot of times were writing the same thing. I didn't know until it was too late, and he didn't know.

Q: When did you first become aware of Faulkner's work?
CALDWELL: Oh, this was way early, way back in the thirties. I remember I was living in Maine at the time when some of his first books were done, and I read one of his first. What it was, I don't know. But this was way back in the early thirties.

We were once at a banquet in Paris when he was on the way back from receiving the Nobel Prize. He didn't say anything. Mostly the conversation around the table was in French, and I don't understand French. So I didn't know what was going on, and I don't think he knew either.

Q: After you read his first book, did you keep up fairly well with his career?
CALDWELL: I know what it was. *As I Lay Dying*, which I thought was a great book and still do. Well, no, not especially. I would hear about him. People would talk about him in New York.

Q: Would you say that Faulkner's work is a true picture of the South?
CALDWELL: Let's put it this way. You see, I don't think there is a true picture of any region, South or otherwise. It's the interpretation of truth or reality that really makes a work outstanding. It's the interpretation that the writer gives to it; and whether it's true to the South or not, I don't think really matters. That's not the point. The point is: What interpretation does he give of life in the South?

Did Faulkner write about life as it was? Sure he did. But it was not a re-production of life. It was a creation of life, and therefore it was much sharper, much more true than the reality of it would have been. I think any great writer has that same ability.

Q: Do you remember what authors influenced you or those you would have been particularly conscious of when you started writing?
CALDWELL: Probably the only writer that interested me was Sherwood Anderson. I read all the short stories of Anderson I could find, along with every other short story I could find in the little magazines. (I do remember Anderson had—I think it was *Winesburg, Ohio*.) Anyway, I got interested in the fact of writing, and I wanted to do the same thing. I wanted to be a writer. I wanted to tell stories.

Q: Had you wanted to be a writer before, or do you mean reading actually made you want to be one?
CALDWELL: I'd wanted to, but I didn't know how to because I had never been able to go to writing school. I began reading magazines. I found a whole new world which was contemporary, up-to-date, rather than something out of the past. I had no interest in reading anything about the past. I wanted the present, and here it was in these small magazines.

That was my hardship in life, so to speak, to learn to write as rapidly as I could and the best I could under the circumstances. I think that's what influenced me to leave school, leave college, and go to work on newspapers, because I thought I had a better opportunity to learn to write on a newspaper than I would by staying in college, so I left.

Q: Does that mean that you consider you are self-taught as a writer?
CALDWELL: Yes. I had accumulated so much. I think, in those prior years, living all over the South, that I had all the material I could use. I didn't have to be influenced. I didn't have to be inspired by anybody else, by a tall story of anybody else. I didn't know what these guys were writing or had written. It didn't interest me what de Maupassant had written; I wasn't interested in what he had done. I wanted to know what I was going to do, what I was trying to do, so that's why I say I never read books. I still don't read books.

What interests me as a writer is having an idea that's based on some solid, factual incident, but has no suggestion how it's going to do in the middle, or anything of the sort.

In the South the small town is always alive, not only with gossip, but with stories and anecdotes and talk and conjecture about other people—next door, across the street, around the corner, on the other side of town. Then of course the more cohesive this life is, the closer they live together and the more intimate they are, the more they know about each other. All these things I think are conducive to Southern writing.

You contrast that with New England life where everything is remote. You can live in a rural area of Maine or New Hampshire and live across the road from somebody, and you may never know what that person's first name is even, or else you won't call him by his first name. You'll call him Mr. So and So as long as you live. That remoteness and that isolation are imposed by that life, whereas in the South there is no compulsion to be remote. The more friendly you are, the better you're going to enjoy yourself and the more friends you're going to make and so on.

The person who is raised in the Southern atmosphere, I think, has more freedom of feeling about life around him, and therefore he can project himself into other people better, to know what they are doing, saying, thinking or have done or might do in the future.

I think it opens up a little more for a writer to have been born and raised in a small Southern town. What it's going to be in the future, I don't know, because the towns are getting larger, and there are very few small towns left.

Q: *Was it that kind of thing that made you like Sherwood Anderson?*
CALDWELL: In a way, except that Anderson's attitude and approach to the story were so much more interesting to me. He didn't have that stiffness and tightness that a New England writer would have, for example. He was more fluid; there was more activity in his words and in his sentences and in his speech and dialogue. I had a feeling of more activity and more life than I would find anywhere in, say, Theodore Dreiser.

Q: *Are you familiar with Dreiser?*
CALDWELL: No. I knew him when he was working in Hollywood, and I was too. I only read one or two of his books in my whole life, so I don't know much about him.

Q: *Could you expand the comparison between you and Faulkner?*
CALDWELL: I haven't read enough of Faulkner to make any great comparison of what he did with certain situations and things of the sort, but I know he must have been dealing with the same kind of people I was dealing with, all the way through. I don't know how many books Faulkner wrote. I have no idea; I guess everything he wrote was about Mississippi.

Q: *Were you ever consciously sensationalistic in your writing?*
CALDWELL: No, no, because I never had any control over the things I was writing about. It goes back to the fact that I never knew how anything was going to end, so I couldn't consciously manipulate.

Sensationalism, if it existed, would have to come out of the people and things themselves rather than being imposed upon the story. It would have to be a logical outburst of the character. It would have to be true to their nature, to whatever it was they were doing. If they were cruel, then that was their nature, and I could have nothing to do about it. I couldn't change their nature; otherwise, it wouldn't be true to their character.

Q: *Did anyone ever call you a Communist?*
CALDWELL: Yes, I was listed in the *Red Book*—what was the name—the woman who got up this compendium of names? Dilling! Mrs. Dilling. *The Red Network.*

Q: *Was that because you were in Russia?*
CALDWELL: I don't know. I don't think so. No, that was before. That was

before Russia, I think. I think it all started because I went down to Washington one day with Rockwell Kent, who called himself a Communist. He had a project in mind that had something to do with welfare. I was involved in a few things like that inadvertently, but I was never deeply involved enough to contribute any money to these causes and didn't get into any membership of anything. I was just on the fringe of Communism, I suppose you would call it.

I did write short stories that were published in *New Masses*, which in those days was considered violently Communist, and maybe it was. I don't know. But that was about as close as I got to Communism. Then I had gone to Spain during the Spanish civil war and on the Loyalist side, which was labeled the Communist side.

I was interested in writing, and it just happened that in those days around New York most writers were involved in some way in a poverty program. The only people who were actually trying to raise any money for people to survive on, writers especially, I guess, were those Communist-affiliated or Communist-tainted groups.

I was involved just like anybody else around New York in those days. Nobody ever asked me to join the Communist Party, and I never paid any dues or anything of the sort. It was just in the atmosphere of the time. I have a very good friend who was a Communist. Mike Gold was sort of the leader of the young American writers in those days. He was the editor of *New Masses*, I guess—one of the editors.

Q: *Was there any particular ideological reaction associated with your rebellion? Did you reject religion, for example?*
CALDWELL: Yes, I did. That was one thing I was going to say. When my father, who was a minister, gave me the choice, he said it was my privilege to decide whether I wanted to go to church or not. I chose not to, and I told him so, and I didn't go. I didn't want to go and didn't need to go.

I thanked him for giving me the privilege of making the choice, so I never went back to church again after that. I didn't become violently anti-religious or anything of the sort; it's just the fact that it doesn't interest me to take part in it. Religion is fine for other people that want to engage in it. They're welcome to it.

Q: *Were you aware of Maxwell Perkins?*
CALDWELL: Yes, I was aware of him because he was real good to me, in a way. He never helped me in any way as a writer other than to publish some

things I had written, but he was the only commercial publisher, or the first commercial publisher, who ever did. So I did appreciate the fact that he saw something that he found publishable. These were short stories that interested him at the time.

I guess he had seen some I had written in little magazines, and that's how he got in touch with me—or the reason he got in touch with me—because he read some of my little magazine stories, which paid no money. So he comes along right in the middle of the Depression and wants me to send him some short stories, which I did and which he paid for with money. Of course I was so encouraged and enthusiastic and grateful that I was almost like William Saroyan. I'd write a story a day and send it to him until he told me to quit—said he had enough—don't send anymore.

Q: Were you familiar with Nietzsche?
CALDWELL: No, no. About the only philosopher, I think, who has ever influenced me is Henry Mencken. He was a little sharpster, you know. He was a little sharp boy, and I admired him because he was contemporary in a sense. I liked the way he presented his ideas, in modern dress, so to speak. I always admired Mencken.

I only knew him by correspondence. He had published some stories of mine in *American Mercury.*

He disregarded the conventions of life. He would throw out new ideas and reject whatnot; and I admired him for going up to Boston to sell *American Mercury* on the Common and getting arrested. I thought that was a great publicity stunt, and he wasn't too dignified to do it. I admired him for doing that.

Q: Will you talk about what you are doing now?
CALDWELL: I never talk about what I am doing. Once you have created the thought into words—put it into words—you have lost the whole essence of what you're doing, because then you cannot re-create the oral substance of it and put it into words. I don't want to talk about it, and I don't know myself what I'm doing most of the time. I have to wait and see what comes out on the printed page.

I never wanted to have a bestseller, because I hoped to keep on writing the rest of my life, and I didn't want to fade away at any point along the way. I don't expect ever to have a bestseller. Over a period of time, some of my books, over a period of fifteen, twenty years may have achieved the figure of what might be a bestseller.

Q: Korges persistently talks of you as having a comic vision or of writing comic scenes. Does this seem accurate?

CALDWELL: I can only say that consciously I could not write anything that was comic or humorous, if you want me to use that word. To me, there is comedy in tragedy and tragedy in comedy; they are inseparable; they're interchangeable. It's like the old saying you hear sometimes, "I couldn't laugh for crying; I couldn't cry for laughing." To me, they are such interchangeable things that it's all one. It's life. It's a person's life that you are writing about, and he's going to have tragedy. He's going to have comedy in his existence. It's inescapable.

I wouldn't set out to try to write a comic or a tragic interlude. By the time I got halfway through the chapter I still wouldn't know whether the effect was going to be funny or sad.

Q: Are you acquainted with any figure you consider a neglected writer?

CALDWELL: No. But I have always had a great admiration for a certain writer—to continue his work over a long period of time and to make it fresh and interesting over the years, and that's William Saroyan. He is what's would call a natural born writer. He has never lost the instinct, I think, that he had in the beginning.

Q: Could you name anyone else you consider a natural born writer?

CALDWELL: I think Sherwood Anderson, by all means, would fit into that classification. I don't think I am influenced by the fact that I knew him slightly, because I admired his work long before I ever met him, and I have read him since, after having met him. I think he would be one of the candidates in my mind.

Eudora Welty ～ 1978

MARTHA VAN NOPPEN

The following interview is part of a taped conversation with Eudora Welty at her home in Jackson, Mississippi, on August 9, 1978. I arrived at Welty's Tudor-style home at 1:30 in the afternoon, after receiving perfect directions from her over the phone, and was warmly greeted and shown to a sofa in front of a large window. Miss Welty, sitting in a wing-back chair, immediately put me at ease with her lyrical, distinctly Southern voice. Beginning the interview with a reassuring "Don't worry" she generously discussed her work and beginnings as a writer. Excerpts from that discussion follow.

QUESTION: *In* The Optimist's Daughter *you've used the limited omniscient narrator, through Laurel's point of view. Did that story give you any trouble, as far as viewpoint or narration is concerned?*
WELTY: No, because the whole story's conception was in the character of Laurel, so I didn't have to work to get it into her point of view. I thought of it and wrote it out of that point of view. It was my given—my set of circumstances out of which I wrote it, so it didn't cause me trouble. It was my real method of working it out . . . It's told through her point of view and there's no other point of view.

Q: *Does that mean that Laurel's a totally reliable character?*
WELTY: What do you mean by "totally reliable?"

Q: *Can we believe her perceptions?*
WELTY: Well, I certainly intended for you to believe her. She may be mistaken in some things, but the whole story is a growth of her understanding, so she understands much more at the end than she did at the beginning. But there isn't any lying going on. She is writing, speaking in good faith all the way

---

Originally published as Martha Van Noppen, "A Conversation with Eudora Welty," Vol. 20, no. 4 (1982), 7–23.

through. It all depends on what your intention is. I wasn't trying to play tricks. I've seen that used in the detective story; the narrator who may be a villain is consciously trying to trick the reader. Well, that has nothing to do with the kind of thing that I was doing in this novel. I was writing with a passionate conviction on the part of one who is telling it that she was trying to get at the truth, so it was the complete opposite of any chicanery.

Q: *I particularly like the way Laurel is revealed—slowly.*
WELTY: It is gradual. I think some people said that it was a surprise to find her emerging as she did, but naturally I wanted her quiet in the beginning before the situation was revealed. She was present and tense, and you knew that it all mattered to her. But she herself didn't move into a prominent position until the story progressed.

Q: *Would you call the scene with the breadboard the epiphany of that story?*
WELTY: Well, I don't use such terms to myself much. I mean, it's a Joycean term. It's much more dramatic in the sense Joyce uses it and has more reverberations. I suppose you could call it that, but I don't like pretentious words. I suppose it was more of a means of revealing what I was trying to do, and in a sense it was symbolic in the gesture, but also it was a very real material thing, and everything was sort of brought together, into focus, with that. In that sense, you could call it, I suppose, "epiphany." If you wanted to force a word on it, you could call it that. I didn't call it that to myself.

Q: *We, the reader, know from Laurel's memory in the course of the novel that she has lived through the deaths of her husband, mother, and now father, but we aren't actually present with her husband and mother, as we are with her father. I thought that the moment with the breadboard, when Laurel says to Fay, "I see the whole solid past," was the point of recognition or self-realization for Laurel, when everything comes together for her.*
WELTY: Yes. Exactly. That's what I was trying to do. That describes it much better than a word like "epiphany." Really, it was a focusing and bringing together and revelation—self-revelation—when everything cleared for her. She realizes a great many complicated things at once about herself and her parents, and about Fay—all together.

Q: *In "Place in Fiction" you say that place lies in the fact that it has a more lasting identity than we have and that we attach ourselves to it. I believe this, and also believe that's how we come to understand who we are in all our connections in the world. But doesn't there come a time in some people's lives when they no longer want to be attached to the very things that helped shape their identity, a time when they want to create new identities? I'm thinking now of Laurel, who at the beginning of* The Optimist's Daughter *has already been away from home for some time.*

WELTY: No, because what meant the most to her, I think, was her identity down there. That didn't mean that she couldn't fall in love and marry and live somewhere else, but that wasn't breaking with her family. I don't think that one means denying the other. I think there are people such as you describe, but it was not true of Laurel.

Q: I meant to suggest that, rather than breaking with anything, Laurel might have needed to see herself identified with something else—particularly for the reasons that her own community in Mount Salus sees her differently. Mrs. Pease says, "If you come back you'll be a stranger."

WELTY: People always say that. But she knew where she was—her identity was always clear . . . If you go away, you know, people always think you must be somebody else if you come home again. At least they used to. You used to always need to explain why you'd been away. But I think that's a Southern small town characteristic. She herself was quite secure in her identity, and she did have a definite, strong sense of identity with family and place.

Q: Laurel gave her mother so much credit—sometimes more than herself, it seems, for that kind of strength. Even though Becky's not present, except in Laurel's memory, I felt that Laurel has as much strength as her mother.

WELTY: Well, I don't know. I think she was getting ready to have it, anyway. She was learning to have it because she'd had to be strong for her mother and for her father. In the end, she had to support them with her own character, although she was taking support from them too. In this three-way interchange of everybody giving everybody something—some taking something just when they all were by Becky's bed, all holding each other's hands—I tried to give that feeling of support and dependence that just ran in an endless line among the three of them.

Q: Walter Sullivan, in A Requiem for the Renascence, *says that when a writer's society becomes fragmented, an uncertain moral vision is reflected in the writer's work. Speaking about the South, he suggests that Laurel has an excess of*

virtue for this reason, and that she has nothing to sustain her. Did you mean to suggest that Laurel represents the decay of moral certainty for the South?
WELTY: No, that never occurred to me. I wasn't using her as a figurehead. I wasn't writing anything about the South. She is a person, a human being.

Q: I wonder if you would mind saying anything about the role or the function of "memory" in The Optimist's Daughter?
WELTY: I've said all this the best I can, and I've already written it, you know, in the novel. I worked so hard on what I said about memory . . . I can't put it into words in a spontaneous conversation in a way that says something I worked very hard to make clear and plain in my work. It's just not easy to do. I do think memory is of the essence—it's the organ that accounts for our continuity of feeling and understanding.

Q: I brought up the subject of "memory" in The Optimist's Daughter *because I think that some of the things you do with memory in that novel are similar to what Shakespeare does in* The Tempest.
WELTY: Oh, my.

Q: I remember that somebody compared Losing Battles *to* The Tempest. *For me, the comparison can be made for* The Optimist's Daughter.
WELTY: I don't know—that just leaves me floored. Thank you for your generosity. I appreciate that very much.

Q: It's just such a magical kind of thing. Much of what Shakespeare uses Prospero for, with respect to "memory," is very much like what you do.
WELTY: Following through on what you said—the end, with the bubble, is like a memory, which is like a bubble that holds all this. Well, it's a form of not only storing things, but of cherishing things. It's the organ for all of that, so it's connected with—
Q: Preservation?
WELTY: Yes, preservation, and with love. Also, with patience and endurance. With all those things.

Q: I want to ask about Laurel's parents in The Optimist's Daughter. *Both had eye problems, but Laurel suggests that there was a difference. She says to Miss Adele in the kitchen, after her father's funeral, "It wasn't like it was with Father," that is, her mother's death, I think you meant.*

WELTY: I think she was referring to her mother's mental wanderings and troubles, which were connected with her lack of vision, you know. She got confused and distressed. Her father didn't have that ... Where a quotation comes in a story means everything—it's all interlaced with the whole story. It has all these other meanings, too, that come through the context ... They were two different kinds of deaths, both with the eyes and so on, but her mother died in distress of thinking she'd been betrayed. Her father was just patiently enduring it, and dying, you know. There are a lot of differences.

Q: Did he actually die from the retina problem?
WELTY: Well, it was so complicated. You can't just say it was this, that, or the other, because the way Fay treated him also had something to do with it. She came in and tried to jerk him off the bed. And in those days, when you operated for cataracts, you couldn't move the head for a long time. You can now. I mean people get up and walk out, more or less. He also was old and he made a mistake, I think, in his marriage, and he wasn't too ready to go on with everything. I think it was a whole lot of things together.

Q: Did his realization of what he had done in marrying Fay bring on his death?
WELTY: I didn't want it to be just absolutely arithmetical, you know, like this plus this plus this equals that. I did want to suggest all kinds of complications. I don't want to say it's this either, or that, because I wanted to suggest.

Q: Fay didn't intend to kill him in her selfishness. I didn't think the novel said that.
WELTY: No. But her whole attitude—like "Get up"—was enough to shock and to hurt. No, she didn't physically attack him.

Q: I loved the irony of Judge McKelva's remark when Dr. Courtland is showing Fay something on the wall chart about the eye. Judge McKelva looks at Laurel and says, "That eye wasn't fooling, was it?"
WELTY: (Laughs.)

Q: Did you mean to suggest something symbolic about the birds in this novel— the pigeons and the bird in the house during the storm?
WELTY: Yes, I did mean to suggest. In the case of the pigeons, of course, this very young child was really horrified by all the acts that pigeons went through—regurgitating and reaching down each other's throats. You know how pigeons do.

Q: *No, I didn't. Is that how they eat?*
WELTY: Well, they feed each other, and especially when they're courting. Oh, their acts are really just revolting to the aesthetic sense. It would be very startling to a little girl.

Q: *Laurel drew a connection immediately from what the pigeons were doing to what people do.*
WELTY: Yes. Her mother, the grandmother, said, "They're just hungry like us." It's all nature and so on, and then in the end, when the bird does come in the house, it's just like a return of everything to her. It is terrifying to think of anything with wings that can't get out—the caging of anything, a spirit. I have a terrible panic in a crisis when a bird gets in this house. That was written out of real fear. And, it's also a superstition that a bird in the house means death. Did you ever hear that?

Q: *You said it was more than a superstition, but, yes, I have heard of that superstition.*
WELTY: Oh, it was. I mean, there are all kinds of things you could bring to bear on it. Again, I've tried not to be too specific, but just to suggest the menace of things, and the presence of something, and the difficulty of an imprisoned spirit. She herself was trying to get out.

Q: *At the end of the story, when Laurel releases the bird, sets it free, she sees, we are told, not the body or tail of the bird, but the shape of a crescent moon. I really like that.*
WELTY: I'm glad you liked it. You try to make anything you use suggest lots of things, you know, not just one thing, but a whole lot of things.

Q: *I felt that in this novel more was given to the memory of Laurel's mother than to her father—that I knew more about her mother, even though the part about her mother came from her memory, and her father was an actual character in the book.*
WELTY: Well, I think the mother was the one who influenced both Laurel and her father. So they both referred back to her. We don't know what Laurel and the father meant to her firsthand. We could tell her effect on his life and her effect on Laurel's life. It was sort of the focal point of the influence. So, it was more important to the novel to have the strength of that understood. I hadn't thought of it in that respect, but you're right. So much went back to Becky.

Q: You wrote The Optimist's Daughter *first as a short story?*

WELTY: *The Optimist's Daughter* was very close to me personally. It meant a lot to me in a way that some of the others hadn't, and when I sent it to the *New Yorker*, I stipulated from the beginning that I didn't want it to come out in book form until some time had passed, and I could revise it as I wished to. That's what I did. I just went through on the typewriter, and I typed and changed as I went along. I did change it and enlarge it a little bit. I guess there are many small changes that probably no one but me would notice. But it was important to me to get another chance to shape it and sharpen it. In fact, I think I deepened it in some ways. I tried to because things happened to my thinking in the meanwhile and I could see it more clearly.

Q: You added something toward the end.

WELTY: I added that part about the "confluence" of the waters. I love that part.

Q: When Laurel and her husband were crossing the bridge, on the train?

WELTY: Yes, crossing the bridge at Cairo, Illinois. I wanted to have a meeting of everything.

Q: That is a wonderful word confluence. *I love it.*

WELTY: I love it too. I'm crazy about that word.

Q: When Laurel says that Becky "predicted" Fay, and that what Becky had been afraid of might have existed in the house all along, could you say what it was that Becky was afraid of, or was it anything in particular?

WELTY: She distrusted because her mind began to be suspicious and distrustful. She had predicted nothing definite, like "You'll fall for somebody" or something like that, or "You're not true to me." Nothing that literal . . . The judge couldn't have been truer to her, at the time. He was always true to her, but he was seeking solace. She had predicted that he would. "You'll all go off, you'll all desert me." That's all I meant. She didn't predict Fay herself.

Q: That comment shouldn't be construed, then, as a social commentary, something about social change, since Fay did represent a displacement of the established order?

WELTY: No, I don't think so. It's just her distrust of the whole world, that she couldn't count on anything anymore, that nobody was true to her.

Q: *It was attributable to her condition?*
WELTY: Yes, her distress. And, of course, it was completely unfounded at the time she said it.

Q: *When Judge McKelva was at a loss for any way to answer—*
WELTY: He would walk out. That was just to get his mind cool again, obviously, but he was not in any way unfaithful. I didn't mean to suggest that.

Q: *Laurel said he needed spiritual guidance.*
WELTY: Well, he was in distress, too, you know.

Q: *This story, in particular, sparked my interest in the writing process, I think because of the poetic reverberations. In one of your essays about writing, "Writing and Analyzing a Story," you refer to your own story, "No Place for You My Love," and discuss the creation of a "third character." You say that between the writer and the story he writes is the undying third character. You're not talking about the narrator here are you?*
WELTY: No, I was talking about the relationship between the characters in that story.

Q: *At one point you refer to your having to say "they" instead of "he" or "she."*
WELTY: Yes. Of course that was a story unto itself. I don't do that in all stories. I was using that in that story because I wanted to indicate that this relationship was a presence to these people who were strangers.

Q: *In the relationship of the reader to the work of fiction, I often find readers who don't trust themselves to have an understanding of the work, particularly what was intended by the author. Students often turn to interpretation and scholarly criticism. Perhaps that's part of the reason some of us are fortunate enough to have interviews with writers.*
WELTY: Well, every writer takes a chance with everything he writes that it will be understood. Also, a writer is learning all the time he's writing, and things are being suggested to him in the work. Everything I write teaches me how to do it as I go. All kinds of things open up. Something I write today, I didn't even know about yesterday. I don't mean a fact in the plot, but just an insight into something, and so it's a constant learning process with me when I write. I'm not surprised what any reader may go through, just as I feel when I read something.

Q: You do bring things to the reader that you're probably not even aware of.
WELTY: Yes, I'm sure that happens.

Q: Would you say that most of your revisions are extensive?
WELTY: I'm a heavy reviser. I guess I am. I don't know. I never have com-pared my revisions with other people's. I do revise a lot. I work out a lot as I go, and then I go back and type that up, and then I tear up as I go, too, so I won't have these things reproaching me lying around, and also so nobody else can read them.

Q: And you use pins too?
WELTY: I don't know. I write with anything.

Q: I mean pins, instead of paste.
WELTY: Oh, P-I-Ns. Well, that's an easy way. I never heard of cut-and-pin. I just made it up for myself, but I suppose a lot of other people must have thought of it too. Have you ever worked on a newspaper?
Q: No.
WELTY: When you throw something away, you just tear the strip off across the bar at the top and throw it away. I got in the habit of tearing off the strip, both what I wanted to save and what I wanted to throw away; so that I ended up with strips—paragraphs here, a section of dialogue, and so on. I pin them together and then when I want to cut something, I cut it with the scissors.

Q: I really like that idea of pinning. That means you can move it around.
WELTY: You can move it, you can transpose. It's wonderful. It gives you a feeling of great moveability.

Q: How did you get the idea? Were you ever a seamstress?
WELTY: Oh, I have cut out things with patterns. No, I'm not a seamstress, but I have made things, and that is the way you make things, of course. On a dining room table, too.

Q: I thought you used to do that with your mother.
WELTY: Yes. Both of us used to cut out, back in the Depression. When you grew up in the Depression, you learned all kinds of tricky sorts of things. I mean, I made my clothes. They must have looked like the end of the world, but that was a good way to do.

Q: In your essay, "Writing and Analyzing a Story," you say that fiction writing and criticism travel in opposite directions and involve different choices. You chose "No Place for You My Love" to discuss in connection with analyzing a story, and you call what you did with that story "a piece of hindsight from a working point of view." Did you feel that you were in the position of the writer analyzing her own work?

WELTY: What can I say to that? I wasn't really criticizing my story, which I wouldn't attempt to do. It's like people telling you to review your own book, which I'm often asked to do—of course I've never done it—like estimate your own character. I was trying to analyze it, and the only reason I chose one of my own was that it was the only one I felt that I really knew the answers to. I could really give a first-hand account of it because I didn't believe that we could tell very much about another writer's work through analysis. Therefore, I used my own. It wasn't because I thought my story was a glorious example. It's just because I had first-hand information about it.

Q: What do you think the critic's role should be, and how is it an art?

WELTY: I do think criticism is an art. I don't claim to have it. I like to read good criticism, you know, by marvelous critics. I think criticism is very valuable and that it is an art, and what makes it valuable to me when I read criticism is simply the enlightenment that it gives and its quality of suggestion. It opens your imagination; it gives you a new insight into what someone has interpreted from a person's work. You may or may not agree, but it adds another peephole into a writer's work, which is always interesting. And some of it is inspired. Some of it is a brilliant work of art in itself. I do not mean book reviewing and so on, such as what I did, which is just to take something and write about it as well as you can—a specific work—but, I mean real criticism, and I think it is very valuable. I don't think it is like writing fiction. It doesn't attempt to be, and it's wrong for people to confuse them. You know, a lot of people nowadays who don't really understand much about fiction because they haven't read very much can't even tell the difference between fiction and fact. They often believe that a story that's written is something true and condemn a character because he has ideas that are not in accordance with what they think, when the whole reason for having put a character like that in was to show that point of view. I think it's extremely hard for non-readers, which a lot of students are—non-readers of fiction—to comprehend what fiction is.

Q: *I think that's especially true when they're just learning to read it themselves, with a critical eye—something beyond reading for pleasure, or even reading for pleasure. If they miss things that might have to be looked for, it might be because they're not getting a lot of guidance in the schools.*
WELTY: Well, I expect not. I think really the best guidance you get is the way I did and probably you did—just by reading, growing up reading.

Q: *Do you think critics can influence a writer's success, harm her reputation?*
WELTY: Do you mean by something unfavorable?

Q: *Yes.*
WELTY: I hardly see how it can be harmful unless it would serve to destroy someone's reputation for good, which I don't think could be very frequent. A critic can hurt your feelings, but I don't know that anything else can be done. It usually is not the only voice speaking of you, you know. I suppose what could really hurt a writer worse than unfavorable criticism—I'm talking now about book reviewing—that would be the only cases I think in which this would apply—would be the ignoring of a book, saying nothing. If there's no notice taken, it's as if a book sinks without a ripple. That's often happened. A book may come out in the year that war was declared, when no one is thinking about new fiction. If it had come out the year before, everybody would have been in an uproar of excitement about it. There are some books that have come out during the newspaper strikes. They never get reviewed. And those things can really hurt later. Much worse than an unfavorable review.

Q: *I've been told that there are critics who don't look favorably on Southern writing in general. Do you believe this, and what do you think about such critics?*
WELTY: I suppose so. They expect a certain thing. I remember that review of Reynolds Price's *The Surface of the Earth* in the *New York Times Book Review*, which angered me so that I wrote a letter to the paper. The reviewer didn't actually review the book. He reviewed the fact that a family novel had been written in the South, and he said that was antediluvian, that no one could possibly be interested in the family anymore, and that this kind of writing just ought to be buried and forgotten. That's a case of what you mean, I think, a perfect example of it. I think they're—fairly rare. Those things are a matter of fashion. When I was growing up, it was the same way with Southerners' being popular as Southerners in the North. When I first went to New York to

school, Southerners were just thought to be the most attractive, cutest things in the world. You know—"Oh, she's a Southerner, ask her." Great heyday. Then afterwards, it got to be, "Oh, watch out, you know they're from the South." Well, all those things are frivolous and passing. Neither one means anything.

Q: *I think there are places where Southerners, particularly women, Southern women, would not be expected to do anything with any validity.*
WELTY: That's too bad. I don't think serious people, no matter where they live, hold it against any other person for where they come from.

Q: *But I have been shocked at the number of educated people—*
WELTY: Yes, exactly. I've been asked the most astounding questions from very educated, worldly people. Astounding.

Q: *Do you generally read the critical articles on particular works of yours?*
WELTY: There are a lot of critical articles that are written about my work, and I have read some that are very valuable to me. There are a lot I have not seen, and some that I've been sent that I keep that I haven't yet read. I appreciate the critical attention. A lot of it is very helpful to me. Yes, I do read them. I don't read some of the very technical, analytical things that seem to me far afield. At least I read part of them—enough to see that I don't really understand them. But it's all right with me if that's what they want to do.

Q: *Do you ever feel compelled to answer a critic?*
WELTY: I never have done it. I would like to write an appreciation to some people who have said some good things. That's what I ought to do. But, I would never argue with their judgment on something. They're perfectly welcome to their judgment, and it's their valid judgment, and what good does it do to object to a review? I can't see the point in that.

Q: *Do you think that luck or good fortune, or a "break" played any part in your getting started with your writing career, or anywhere along the way?*
WELTY: Oh, sure it did, because I had good luck getting things published from the start, not in selling things which took quite a while, but in getting accepted by small magazines which did not pay, but which published. That was very lucky. Then to run into *Southern Review* down in Baton Rouge with Robert Penn Warren and Cleanth Brooks and Albert Erskine, who took my work almost from the start and published it. That was wonderful luck. What

could be better? I also was lucky in my agent, who sold my work to begin with to the *Atlantic Monthly*, the first paying magazine with national circulation. *Southern Review* paid, you know, a lump sum—twenty-five dollars, or something—but it was not a national magazine. It was a university quarterly. I had a lucky editor for my first book, John Woodburn, who persuaded Doubleday to publish a book of short stories by an unknown writer, a first book, which was almost unheard of. What could be more lucky?

Q: So you feel fortunate?
WELTY: I certainly do. I know to what I owe a lot. All those people were of the greatest help, not only for publication but by their encouragement, you know—liking my work and thinking well of it. Making me feel that I was professional.

Q: In the beginning of your career, did you seek out any of these people, or did they seek you out?
WELTY: Well, that kind of thing wasn't done in my day. Now everybody looks up people and wants to see them and all that. I was very close, from here to Baton Rouge, but it wouldn't have occurred to me to go down there. Later, I was invited to come and see Katherine Anne Porter, which I did, and I met them, but it wouldn't have occurred to me to write. Nothing was wrong with that, but it just wasn't the way it happened with me. It wasn't the way I did, and I don't think it was the way they did.

Q: Do you think a lot of gifted people fall by the wayside because they don't have lucky breaks?
WELTY: I happen to believe that most people that really have what it takes to be a professional writer are going to do it. If you're easily discouraged, it's not a very strong gift, I feel. When I wrote six years before I was published in a national magazine, I wasn't discouraged. Of course, I had things to encourage me. But I loved to write, and I was determined to do it. So, I wasn't to be discouraged by being constantly turned down by the national magazines all those years.

Q: When Tillie Olsen came to the State University College at Brockport, N.Y., to do a reading, she talked about the real hardships in people's lives, in women's lives particularly, that prevent them from writing. Did your own environment make it easier for you to be able to write?

WELTY: I've heard her speak on that—at a writer's conference. I was on the panel with her at the University of North Dakota. She's so absolutely in earnest, and she has suffered so much. She's very touching, but she will brook no disagreement. Well, she has got a point, she certainly has. I have her new book, *Silences*. I know it's part of her passionate advocacy.

Q: She makes the plight of women, particularly, who would be—or would have been—writers seem very real to me. The kinds of responsibilities and commitments women have believed themselves to have—
WELTY: Well, I've had plenty of responsibilities—always have had. And I've had, mostly, a job to support myself. And although I didn't marry, I had a family that I was working with and helping to take care of, and people who were ill, and different things, and it didn't occur to me to mind this, you know.

Q: Or that it took anything away?
WELTY: No. My own feeling is that human responsibilities come first. That would be blaming another person if you didn't get your writing done. I'm speaking absolutely personally. My life was easier than hers [Tillie Olsen's], I'm sure, but I grew up in the Depression, which wasn't too easy, and my father died the year I got out of college, which wasn't too easy, but that was just all in the way life was, you know. I think you can write no matter what goes.

Q: A lot of people would agree with you, but, whereas I don't think everybody in the world is gifted or is an artist, I do believe, as Tillie Olsen does, that women have always been at a disadvantage.
WELTY: I do too. I certainly do, but what I mean is, it needn't paralyze you.

Q: I believe it can, that it's a very real thing. It must just depend on the circumstances.
WELTY: It depends on the circumstances, on the person, on the degree of talent. I mean by degree, on the *vitality* of the talent.

Q: I think it took Tillie Olsen a period of twenty years, writing on little scraps of paper which became her first and only novel.
WELTY: Well, *Losing Battles*, which I wrote among difficulties, took about ten years, and it was written—

Q: On scraps of paper?
WELTY: On a combination of scraps of paper, and on different things. You can write in any way. At the same time, I was doing lecturing to earn money. I just take for granted you have to manage, you have to learn some way.

Q: I think of Laurel McKelva in The Optimist's Daughter *as a "liberated" person, woman. Do you? And what sympathy do you have for the Women's Movement?*
WELTY: Oh, well, I didn't mean Laurel to sound—I know you didn't mean that, but I have been asked that, believe it or not. I get asked that at least once a week. I don't mean in that particular case, but, "Do your characters stand for—"? She just stood for herself. I've never met, so far as I know, with any prejudice from editors because I was a woman—with the one exception of my story, "Petrified Man," which was turned down by *Esquire* magazine because I was a woman. I didn't send it to them to test them, because I was too ignorant to know they didn't take stories by women. I was sending it to everybody. But, in the way of being paid what I was worth from an editor—of course, I've had an agent. So, I've never met with any prejudice. In fact, the other way. I was treated with so much consideration and kindness and politeness. I think in the publishing world, at least most of the time that I can think of most people who are interested in the books—editors and publishers and so on—are also courteous people. They would treat each other just the way you and I would expect to be treated in a civilized room of people. I've also had jobs with salaries, and I know I've gotten this money that the man doing the same work—and I don't like that and nobody in their right mind would want or like that. I think in some of the movements women are making fools of themselves, and I'm sorry for that, because it's cast a wry sad light on the real facts of the matter.

Q: In some ways, I think so too, but they are doing something for us all, and I believe it's necessary, and think it's something we can be thankful for—for the ones who are out there, in the streets, so to speak.
WELTY: I suppose so. I hate the grotesque quality of it. And you see, if you are a woman and making your living as I am in the world, where you're on the list of everybody that sends out questionnaires—I wish you could see some of the things that you get asked and that you're asked to do. I was asked to sign something saying, "I too have had an abortion and would like to establish something." They sent a note, "Even if you haven't had an abortion, we think you owe it to the movement to sign this."

Q: To lie?
WELTY: Yes. A lot of it is done in this kind of show biz kind of way, you know. "Just come on out, be all out for this." Say "Sure I've had an abortion!" Well, all of that is the most boring thing in the world. Also, I think it's the most fantastic course of events, and I don't believe in encouraging that kind of thing. I have answered some questionnaires to some extent, what I can answer factually, and something I know about, but I believe at least half the questions are nobody's business.

Q: I didn't know they were doing things just like that.
WELTY: Oh, they are, I can tell you. And, like you, I think it should be done, but if it's making comedians of all of us, I don't know that it's worth it. It can be done another way.

Tennessee Williams ～ 1979

JERE REAL

*"Just introduce me as the world's oldest promising playwright from Key West, Florida!" he had told his hosts. Tennessee Williams at age sixty-eight was in Lynchburg, Virginia, making a rare college campus appearance as part of a month-long Tennessee Williams Festival in September 1979. His personal appearance was the capstone of an event that included screenings of the major films based on his plays (*A Streetcar Named Desire; Sweet Bird of Youth; Sud- denly, Last Summer; Cat on a Hot Tin Roof; *and* Night of the Iguana*), a dra- ma department production of his* Summer and Smoke, *special lectures about the playwright, and assigned readings in all literature classes of his work, all at the central Virginia campus of Lynchburg College. Williams's three-day visit to the campus was highlighted by an hour-long question-and-answer session in the college's Dillard Theater, by the playwright's swimming with members of the school's water polo team in the college pool and, finally, by an evening reading and commentary session before 2,300 spectators in the college gymnasium.*

At the informal question-and-answer session held in the college's theater at midday, Williams sat in a chair wearing a grey suit and holding a driving cap in his lap as he fielded questions. He wore his usual dark sunglasses to shield against the bright stage lighting. Behind him loomed the set for the upcoming production of his Summer and Smoke—*dominated by a large statue of an angel.*

In response to a student asking how he became known as "Tennessee," Wil- liams launched into a lengthy account of his Tennessee relations and ended with, "I enjoyed that."

The playwright was asked, too, about his writing practices and he replied, "I get up before daylight each day to write. The hardest part of my day and night—since I do get up before daylight—is when I sit down at the table

---

Originally published as Jere Real, "An Interview with Tennessee Williams," Vol. 26, no. 3 (1988), 40–49.

to write. My hands shake when I start to write. It doesn't get any easier in advancing years, and what's particularly discouraging is that the critics are always comparing you to yourself . . . and you have to ignore that. They're always comparing everything I write to *Streetcar* or *Cat*."

When asked about the fame, celebrity, and monetary reward that had come from a successful writing career, he said, "As I told Dick Cavett on his show recently, the only reward that's worthwhile for a successful writer is a good morning's work."

And monetary success?

"Well, I'm not as successful as Doc Simon! When I was first successful, I wrote a piece called 'The Catastrophe of Success,' and in it I suggested all of the pressures that go with success . . . and they are many."

Had he always wanted to be a writer?

"I couldn't imagine *not* being a writer. When I was a child, I wanted to be a railroad engineer. But I have to make a living, and writing is all I know how to do.

"My mother once suggested to me that I give it up. It was just after the highly unfavorable reception of *In the Bar of a Tokyo Hotel*. She said to me: 'Tom, I think you may have to find another occupation.'" Williams paused and smiled, "But it's the only one I know."

Williams also responded to inquiries about current work and work in progress: "I have a new play going into rehearsal after the first of the year. It's about Scott and Zelda Fitzgerald, *Clothes for a Summer Hotel*." Asked about casting of the new production, he commented that "It's always dangerous to talk about casting, since there's always the possibility things may not work out. We're hoping to get Gerry [Geraldine] Paige for that, but I don't know yet.

"My new play on which I'm working is called *Masks Outrageous and Austere*, and it'll be one of the wildest things in the current American theatre, I think. I'm even surprised at how wild it is."

The plot?

"It's about a woman—Babe is her name—who has three billion in trusts and who has bought two husbands. She is living with the younger of the husbands and with a male student from Harvard. It's a kind of triangle.

"The title comes from a line in a poem by Elinor Wylie. Along with Hart Crane and Edna St. Vincent Millay, she is one of my favorite poets."

Was there a relationship between his work and his own emotional state?

"The impulse that generates a new piece of work reflects the emotional climate in which you exist. I have a nervous breakdown about every ten years

... I had one in 1969 and in 1959." Then, as if considering the year 1979, he added, "Perhaps I'm safe now.

"I spend most of my time now in my Key West compound . . . You can hardly see it from the street. I still spend several weeks each year in New Orleans, but that's because I have some property there. My sister, Rose, lives near me in Key West. I just bought her a house at a highly inflated price."

How did Williams view the various film versions that had been made of his plays?

"I'll tell you about Hollywood. They'll tell you it'll be done the way you want it . . . They'll wine you and dine you and promise you all sorts of things, and then proceed to do exactly what they want to do."

Was the happy ending tacked onto Sweet Bird of Youth *in the film version simply the result of the old Hollywood production code?*

"It was a pretty good film until the last five minutes, in which they managed to completely destroy the point of the play. (Chance Wayne, who has lived off his sexual prowess and good looks, is castrated in the play while in the film he is only beaten up and rides off to happiness with the girl he has always desired.) No, the code was not responsible for that. No, by then, some people in Hollywood had begun to buck the code. It was simply a matter of wanting to have a happy, a more commercial, ending to the film.

"I'll tell you which is the worst of all the films they did of my plays, and that was *The Glass Menagerie*. Thank Goodness, they've stopped showing that."

Could Williams comment on Noel Coward, the playwright-actor who had appeared in the film version of Williams's The Milk Train Doesn't Stop Here Anymore, *the film titled* Boom!*?*

"By the time they were making that film, Noel was having a lot of trouble remembering his lines, but in his long scene with Elizabeth Taylor he did the speech beautifully. Coward is a much underestimated playwright. He has written some of the best comedies since the Restoration. Certainly, *Private Lives* is the best play of its kind since *The Importance of Being Earnest*. Coward's great achievement was his impeccable sense of timing. There's never . . . well, almost never . . . a long speech in a Coward play."

(Later, in private conversation, Williams elaborated on Coward as playwright: "Coward once had dinner with Gore Vidal and me in Rome, and during dinner, Noel began to go through an elaborate explanation of his career, year by year, explaining all of the problems he had had with the critics. He was very sensitive about never having been taken seriously by them. But it was kind of sad for this man to be there explaining all of the things in his career to us when it really wasn't necessary. It was sad, because it really wasn't necessary."

Was Coward's homosexuality at all evident in his work?

"Yes, there is sense of that in his plays, as an undertone. Noel used to come see me when I was living in Rome, and he always wanted me to take him cruising, to find him a boy for the night. I had a Jaguar then and we used to go out in that, and I am such a terrible driver. Well, we would usually drive out along the old Appian Way, and Noel would see someone and he'd get out of the car. Noel was very funny, because he would never want to take anyone back to the Grand Hotel, so he'd go off in the ruins with the boy. And I'd have to sit there and wait for him. Sometimes he'd be off in those ruins for an hour or more, and it would get pretty boring sitting there in the car.")

Why did religion as a subject figure so prominently in Williams's drama, particularly in such plays as Night of the Iguana *and* Suddenly, Last Summer?

"You know, I'm a profoundly religious man, although most people don't realize it. I feel most religious when I go into a church that's completely empty. You know, there's a woman in Key West who is extremely religious—a *religieuse*, do you know that term?—who is always trying to get people to pray for my salvation. She's a *religieuse*, although that's a term usually used for Catholics, and she's a Baptist."

Why don't you pray with her?

"I find her intolerable. The very religious are often coldhearted people, I find, don't you? They think found religion is the true faith."

At another point in private conversation, Williams was asked about his native South, and why he had such a fascination with the place Moon Lake in Mississippi, a locale that appears frequently in the plays and which also has been the name of his film production unit.

"Well, there really is such a place. Part of the use of the name was the suggestiveness of the name itself."

Why did he have Blanche Dubois's young husband kill himself there in Streetcar?

"When I first went to Moon Lake, I heard of a young man killing himself there, and that gave rise to its use in *Streetcar*."

Eudora Welty also has made use of the locale, Williams was told.

"Really? You know I met her years ago in the 1940s at a very bohemian party in Greenwich Village, but I don't know her very well. We see each other across the room at the American Academy and wave. I remember that party well. Someone asked me if I had left my broom on the landing! And I wasn't even riding one."

That evening—September 24, 1979—Williams appeared before 2,300 persons in the Lynchburg College gymnasium where he gave a public reading and answered questions. Periodically during his reading, he took a bottle of California red wine from under the lectern and poured himself a glass. He sipped it between the various reading selections. At one point in the reading, he told the audience that it had been provided "by some of the more decadent members of the Lynchburg College English Department." Then he turned to the audience with a toast, saying, "Here's to you, ladies and gentlemen!" which brought a roar of approving applause from the crowd.

Williams began his reading by apologizing to the crowd for failing to have matched his coat and trousers. ("I forgot the pants that go with this jacket, and I didn't get to the bootblack.") Then he explained his approach for the evening:

"I'm only going to read a few poems, and then I'm going to read some prose that is cadenced a little better. I don't think you will know much difference."

Among the works he selected to read were "Old Men Go Mad at Night," "Apparition," "The Ice Blue Wind," "The Bean Stalk Country," "Faint as Leaf Shadow," and "Intimations." As he began to read "Intimation," he explained that he thought it was "particularly appropriate to the occasion," a statement that caused the audience to break into laughter when he read the first line: "I do not think I ought to appear in public below the shoulders . . . " Similarly, there was laughter when he reached the later line, "I have received no serious wound as yet, but I am expecting several."

Williams also read passages from his play, *Summer and Smoke*, and from his novella, *The Knightly Quest*, and he spelled out "knightly" for the listeners. "Now I consider this to be my best piece of prose writing; it's a novella called *The Knightly Quest*. It's spelled K-N-I-G-H-T-L-Y, knightly quest. I'm going to read a section from it which is cadenced prose, and I hope it won't be too distinguishable from verse. I hope I can get through it. I have no voice tonight, unfortunately."

Before his reading of a passage from *Summer and Smoke*, he explained to the audience: "I'm going to try to read my favorite speech from it without mutilating it too terribly. Uh, John Buchanan, the young doctor in the play has just become engaged to a young singing pupil of Miss Alma's. She's found out about this, and she's come to his office in a desperate mood which will soon be disclosed in the speeches that follow." Williams then read most of scene eleven, Part II, of *Summer and Smoke* (from a text that corresponds with that used in the Signet Modern Classics edition of 1976).

Completing the reading of prose, Williams then asked his audience: "Now, what would you like me to do? I'll do anything but a tango with a kangaroo. I'll answer questions of a reasonably polite nature, anything but how I got the name 'Tennessee.' Now, I can put on my dark shades again."

In the question-and-answer which followed, Williams accepted one question, then interrupted the question period to read Hart Crane's poem, "Cutty Sark." Before that interruption, however, he took an initial question from his audience. (Written questions were submitted from the large audience and read aloud.)

QUESTION: *How did you come about the selection of the unicorn as the symbolic figure in* The Glass Menagerie?
WILLIAMS: Oh yes, Oh, that's an easy one. You see, the unicorn doesn't . . . he's . . . there's no such thing as a unicorn [giggling]. Laura is actually somebody who is totally out of the world, and the unicorn is sort of a symbol for her strangeness being in the world. She's totally unsuited for the world, much too shy to exist in the world.

"And now," Williams said, interrupting the question-and-answer session that had begun, "I'm going to read a poem by my favorite poet, Hart Crane. It's a poem that's supposed to be read when you're slightly inebriated, which will be to my advantage."

As he prepared to read the poem, Williams then took another drink of wine, commenting, "I have to get in condition for it."

"Now this is a difficult poem. Probably a lot of you don't know Hart Crane. He is, in my opinion, the most important American poet since Walt Whitman, Emily Dickinson and, well, he ranks, I think with such poets as Keats, Shelley, the greatest. He killed himself at the age of thirty-two, I believe it was. He had gone to Mexico on a Guggenheim Fellowship. He was going to write a long epic poem on the conquest of Mexico by Cortez. He succeeded in writing only one poem in Mexico, and it had nothing to do with the conquest of Mexico. It was called 'The Broken Tower,' and it was one of his most beautiful poems, but he had no faith in it because he had submitted it from Mexico to *Poetry* magazine, and for some reason or other, they had not acknowledged the receipt of the poem. And, having no self-confidence whatsoever, he thought it was a total mess, like his life had become. And one day north, just a day's sailing north of Havana, he came out at noon, wearing just an overcoat over his pajamas. He went to the stern of the ship, the *Orizaba*, it was called, and jumped overboard, vanished almost immediately, and they assumed he was snatched by sharks. That was the end of Hart Crane. He frequently went to bars on the Brooklyn waterfront, and this poem is apparently about one of his encounters in one of those bars."

After his reading of "Cutty Sark," Williams then resumed his question-and-answer session with his audience:

Q: *Since you have had an impact on the theatre in the past few decades, could you give us your view on how reality has come to imitate art, including such things as space travel or the Three Mile Island disaster?*
WILLIAMS: Not my reading? Well, that's rather a large question . . . a philosophical question. Some people are walking out on it, and I think they anticipate the fact that I can't answer it. I really think that art is supposed to interpret life, not imitate it. That's my feeling.

Q: *There are a couple of questions relative to* Summer and Smoke: *Does the stone angel of your play have any relationship to the stone angels of Thomas Wolfe?*
WILLIAMS: Thomas Wolfe! You know I've always suspected that man died of paresis. Have you? No? Well, now he was a wonderful southern writer, but I think it was, you know, well, his brain disintegrated completely [laughter]. Does that answer the question?

Q: *Who would you say are your favorite playwrights if you exclude yourself?*
WILLIAMS: Must I exclude myself? [laughter] No, I'm one of my least favorite, but in America, I would think Edward Albee [applause]. In England, certainly Harold Pinter. He's the greatest. Harold Pinter is the greatest living contemporary playwright in my opinion. Yeah. Now, Tom Stoppard, I'm allergic to Tom Stoppard, but it may be because he has four plays running at once in London [laughter].

Q: *Several people have asked which of your own plays is your personal favorite, and this was a question asked and answered by you earlier in the day.*
WILLIAMS: Which of my own plays? I answered *Streetcar* because it was the seminal one, the one with the seeds of all my themes in it.
Q: *As a playwright, how do you feel when you finally turn over a play to the eccentricities of directors and actors?*

WILLIAMS: Ah, the actors! The directors. I leave the casting of plays usually to the director. The most important decision you make is about your director because he determines the cast, and if the cast cannot interpret the play, it's usually the fault of the director. Well, there was a very dear lady involved in *Summer and Smoke* who is no longer with us—Margo Jones, she died quite early—but she directed *Summer and Smoke* and I must say that despite our strong friendship, I did everything possible to dissuade her from continuing directing after the play opened in Buffalo and went over like Niagara Falls . . . I mean downward. Well, at rehearsal, actors would come up to poor Margo, and they'd say, "Miss Jones, how are we, how am I supposed to play this?" And she'd say, "Honey, don't *play* it, just *feel* it!" [laughter]. Which sounded like an obscene suggestion, you know?

Q: You have created a number of strong female characters in your plays, and a questioner would like to know if you have a favorite among those characters or would care to comment about those strong female characters.
WILLIAMS: [Laughing] My female characters have gone through as long a transmutation, as long and as preposterous a transmutation, as my own personality. They range from Laura in *The Glass Menagerie*—who is the true heroine, was meant to be the true heroine of that play—to Babe in the play I'm now working on, uh, the old bitch with the three billion dollars in trusts . . . [laughing] who had purchased two husbands (laughter from audience).

Q: What do you think of Elizabeth Taylor's interpretation of your characters?
WILLIAMS: Ah, politicians can say no comment, but I think one can make a comment here. I think Richard Brooks got out of her a very good performance as Maggie the Cat in the film *Cat on a Hot Tin Roof*. But it's necessary to work very hard to get a performance out of Miss Taylor. I think she grew up being chased around Louis B. Mayer's desk. That's not the best dramatic training [laughter].

Q: At this particular perspective on your life and career, how would you view your own opus—
WILLIAMS: [Interrupting] Don't they call it *oeuvre*? Oeuvre means open, doesn't it? Like *Ouvrez la porte*? You mean the totality of my work?

Q: Yes, the body of your work?
WILLIAMS: Oh, well. Thank God I got most of it done . . . Yeah! [laughter and applause].

Q: To clear up a controversy that has come up in some classroom discussion of Cat on a Hot Tin Roof *someone has asked if you would explain more clearly the relationship that exists between Skipper and Brick.*
WILLIAMS: Skipper and Brick? Obviously it is in the play a sublimated homosexual relationship. It was not, I mean . . . Skipper was thoroughly willing to have come out of the closet, but Brick, no. He couldn't, although I think the homosexual element in his nature, although repressed violently, was as much there as it was with Skipper, yeah.

Q: Have you any advice for young aspiring playwrights?
WILLIAMS: Well, I don't want to say "Drop Dead!" [laughter]. No, I want to say, just be prepared. I believe that's the Boy Scout motto, "Be Prepared."

Q: If you had any one thing
WILLIAMS: If I had what?

Q: Any one thing that you—
WILLIAMS: I have two of most things that you're supposed to have two of . . .

Q: Any one thing you would go back and change in your life or in any of your works, what would that be?
WILLIAMS: If I had any one thing I wanted to change? Well, I don't want to change my sex or I would've . . . No, I wouldn't have gone through all that. Nor would I have changed, uh, my apparel? I would have gotten the right pants on tonight, yeah. Any one thing I would have changed, yes. Yes. I . . . I would have won my father's affection when I was a child. He wanted to win mine, but . . . my mother turned us against our father, and I regret that, I think, and of course, my sister's mental collapse, but I couldn't help that. I had nothing to do with that.

At that comment, the moderator closed the evening's program to a standing ovation and applause.

PART II

1980s

Harry Crews ᛋ 1981

DAVID K. JEFFREY AND DONALD R. NOBLE

Harry Crews was born on June 7, 1935, in Bacon County, Georgia. The son of a tenant farmer, he was raised in poverty; violence and disaster were common-places in his early years. He was the first in his family ever to graduate from high school. He then enlisted in the Marine Corps and served for four years. After attending the University of Florida for two years on the GI Bill, he quit to roam the country on a 650cc Triumph Champion, taking whatever odd jobs and experiences presented themselves. Eighteen months later, he returned to the university and completed his B.A. He took a position at Broward Community College, teaching in the English department for five years. In 1968, the year he published his first novel, The Gospel Singer, *Crews joined the faculty of his alma mater, where he is now a full professor of English.*

Crews is an industrious and prolific writer. After The Gospel Singer, *the novels come in rapid order.* Naked in Garden Hills *(1969) is the story of a 600-pound Metrecal addict;* This Thing Don't Lead to Heaven *(1970) is set in a rural Georgia home for old folks;* Karate Is a Thing of the Spirit *(1971) is a tale of sex and the martial arts;* Car *(1972) features a hero who eats an automobile piece by piece;* The Hawk Is Dying *(1973) is a study of the mystical relationship of man and nature;* The Gypsy's Curse *(1974) is a tour de force told from the point of view of a legless deaf-mute acrobat;* A Feast of Snakes *(1976) is the bizarre tale of a rattlesnake rodeo and a former high school football hero. Crews has recently published a memoir of his first six years,* A Childhood: A Biography of a Place *(1978).* Blood and Grits, *a collection of essays, the bulk of which first appeared in* Playboy *and* Esquire, *was published in 1979.*

A physically imposing and energetic man, Crews has a deep voice that still carries a strong south Georgia accent, and his conversation is animated and entertaining. He spoke freely and without reserve throughout the interview. We selected the following material from a transcription of the tape-recorded

Originally published as David K. Jeffrey and Donald R. Noble, "Harry Crews: An Interview," Vol. 19, no. 2 (1981), 65–79.

interview. Crews did not ask for any editorial privileges, nor did he ask to see the interview before it was submitted for publication.

QUESTION: *When do you write? when you have a story? or every day?*
CREWS: I write every day of my life.

Q: *How many hours a day?*
CREWS: I can work about three hours, sometimes four, on first written stuff; you know, the page is blank, and you're trying to kind of find out which way you're going.

Q: *Do you write at home or at your office?*
CREWS: My office.

Q: *Do you look forward to it? Is it fun for you to write?*
CREWS: No. There are times when things are really going well and you know where you are and you know what you're doing; you have a sense that you know what it means. Those times are pretty good. But the real satisfaction is when you get it done and say, "Before me, this was not; because of me, this is." That's a little like (how's it go in the Bible?), "Before Abraham was, I am." I suspect that's why people have told stories from the beginning.

See, you don't want to go there. You say, "I don't know what to write! I don't know the next paragraph!" The Hemingway thing—always stop when you can write another five hundred words—well, that's real nice advice, if you can follow it. But sometimes, you know, you can't follow it. So you say to yourself, "I can't write today because I don't know anything." Then you say back to yourself, "I'll tell you what you do: you go there and you put it on the chair. You get to the chair and you just stay there three hours. And you can't write letters, and you can't clean your fingernails, and you can't pick your teeth or anything else. You just sit there. You don't have a window to look out. You look at the wall. And then in three hours, get up, and you're cool. You've done your best." Well, three hours is a long time. After about twenty minutes, you'll say, "Hell, do something, if it's wrong."

I'll tell you something else. When I start writing, I say to God, "God, give me five hundred words. I don't want to be greedy, although I am at times a very greedy person; but I'm not greedy today. Give me five hundred words and I'll be satisfied. I don't want to know the whole rest of the book. All I want to know is the next five hundred words. Thank you. Amen." And then, do it. Five hundred words, after all, isn't much. If you double space and you've got good margins so you can make notes to yourself, you're only writing two hundred fifty words a page. That's two pages. And, as the young Jules Verne said to the somewhat older Alexander Dumas, "How do you write so much? How do you turn so much out?" Dumas said, "A page a day gives a book a year. Two pages a day gives two books a year!" Now, that's going to sound very mechanical, very arbitrary but that's the way I do it. That's the way I think. Many times those two pages go somewhere else, usually the trash basket or the furnace. Andrew Lytle used to say, "Fire is a great refiner." And it is.

Q: *Do you know when you start them how your novels are going to end?*
CREWS: Never.

Q: *The ending is decided as you move along in the writing?*
CREWS: I move toward where the story seems to be going. You don't make up a story; you discover a story. Robert Penn Warren says a writer does not need to know his story; he only needs to trust his knowledge of craft and technique to discover the story. And the bottom line is what Flannery O'Connor said, you never do really discover it. She said that no matter what the subject, the writer is interested in the mystery of that subject, which he cannot hope to solve but only to deepen. Ain't that fine? That's fine!

Many times you start a novel or a short story or whatever from the wrong point of view. You don't know that then, but as you move it becomes clearer and clearer. *A Feast of Snakes* was about five times as long as it is now. I wrote it all the way to the end, and I saw that I had done it wrong. I'd put it together wrong. So then I just had to go back and do it again. In *Naked in Garden Hills* the first line I ever wrote was "Where ever he was, he looked as though he had been there forever." I was talking about Fat Man—Mayhugh. That line is still in the book, but it's deep in the book now.

Q: *When you've written a book all the way to the end, do you put it aside for awhile then or not?*
CREWS: Once I start with a thing I like to keep in touch with it. I like to keep on with it. When I've got some words on the page, when I'm rewriting, I can write eighteen hours a day. That's rare, when I work like that; but once I start writing, I don't want to turn it loose.

Q: Do you do a lot of revising? Do you rewrite, or do you tinker with what you've written?

CREWS: I think of changing a word or transposing words, deleting a line, I think of that as polishing, not rewriting. I think of rewriting as touching a book structurally; when you say, "This thing's in the wrong place. I don't know where it goes. Maybe it doesn't go anywhere. It doesn't belong here." So you move it. You change the structure. That's rewriting. I do rewrite a great deal.

Q: How do you feel when you sit down to start something new?

CREWS: The fear that I think many writers live with (maybe even all of them; certainly I do), the fear that I live with is that I won't ever be able to do it again. I mean anything—a novel, a story, a thing like *Childhood*. This is not false modesty. When I sit down to write, I sit down with an absolute terror that it's not going to work. I also think that in every book you write, in the middle of the thing it looks like it's not going to work. Because most of the time, as I said, you don't know where you're going. Mr. Lytle, who took me in like a lost dog and was as much a father to me as any man, except for my Uncle Alton, ever was, told me, "Son, the middle of a place, the middle of a thing is no place to judge it from. Suck it up and go on." Well, I'm sure Mr. Lytle never said, "Suck it up." He's a very formal man and a gentleman.

Q: Mr. Lytle, of course, encouraged you while you were a student here at the university, and you've also quoted Robert Penn Warren and Flannery O'Connor admiringly. Are there other writers you've learned from?

CREWS: I think I've learned more from Graham Greene than I've learned from any other writer. To the best of my knowledge I've read everything that he's ever written. I like *The Power and The Glory* an awful lot. But, you know, there are no perfect books. Faulkner said, if I remember correctly, that he read *Madame Bovary* every year; it's a fine book, but it's not a perfect book. For starters, the beginning is very, very wrong. But I love it. I love that book, and I read it quite a bit, too. André Gide, I read and think I've learned much from. I could go on. As everybody knows, people who write more often than not are voracious readers. If I get caught in a house where there are no books, I go nuts.

Q: Do you read Faulkner much?

CREWS: I've read him all, but I never read him when I'm writing. There are a lot of writers I don't read when I'm writing. I think Thomas Wolfe was the best writer this country ever had because he took the greatest risks and made the greatest failures, but I wouldn't touch Wolfe when I was writing.

Q: Any others you admire?
CREWS: James Agee. He was born a prince of the language, and so he remains. And Capote. I don't care what kind of stupid ass remarks he makes, he can write; he really can. When he's on, he's really on. Updike would be twice the writer he is if he weren't such a hot dog. God knows, he's a word man. Eudora Welty, great writer. Erskine Caldwell, by the way, is a helluva lot better than he's ever been given credit for. But if you ask me, "Who's your favorite writer?" there's no answer to that. That's like saying, "What do you like best for breakfast?" Some mornings you want a beer; some mornings you want strawberries; some mornings you want, God help us, Frostie Crispie Flakes with a lot of sugar, and some mornings you want your old lady.

Q: Did you ever feel you'd outgrown a writer you'd once admired?
CREWS: My first hero in letters was Somerset Maugham. I outgrew that. When I was a freshman I thought that Ayn Rand was a hell of a writer, and unfortunately I read all of her books. By the time I was a sophomore I knew she was no good. She's a tract writer. The theme, that the English teachers love so much, comes first and the characters come later. It's something that people have said about me. They're wrong, of course. That's what's wrong with Sartre's fiction: every character has to come in bearing the burden of his peculiar, or particular, brand of existentialism. It constitutes a flaw in the work he does. To some extent James Baldwin is the same way. I think James Baldwin is one of the best essayists, if not the best essayist, in the country. "The Fire Next Time" is a beautiful essay, wonderful essay. I don't like his novels or his play. I think the preface to the play is marvelous. I would much rather these people write essays. That's an honorable and wonderful and difficult profession. It always seemed to me that, in the novels that Ayn Rand or Sarte write, the subject comes before the people; the subject doesn't come out of the people and their predicament in the world.

Q: You don't think of your novels as novels of ideas?
CREWS: Not in that sense. People have said I write thesis novels or tract novels. That hurts. I'm not ashamed of admitting that that hurts me. Real, honest to God pain. Because I don't believe it's fair and I don't believe it's true. I believe it comes out of a superficial reading.

Q: How so?

CREWS: Well, all books deal with subjects. Every novel will make an economic statement because the people in them have to get their bread somehow. And every novel will make a theological statement, and on and on. It all depends on the characters. Faulkner said, generally, that the characters should be so solid they cast a shadow. I think that the people in my books—I've missed a couple of times; who hasn't—I think that most of the people in them are people, not just names clunking around imitating people. They have substance, I think. I am not, despite what I think of as the tight narrative line of my books driving towards what I at least believe is an inevitable ending, despite that, I'm not a very conscious writer. I don't say, "I've got this character here and this one here, and I'm going to do this with that and that with this."

Any character of mine is difficult for me to talk about, in the same way that anybody—any friend, any enemy, anybody I know—would be difficult for me to talk about in any real depth, because they're complex. You know a lot more about them than you can put in a book, or that you need to put in a book. I think that I talk more cogently and succinctly and sensibly about other writers' work than about my own, and we all know why: you're closer to it, and it is very often a mystery, a mystery that you can't solve, but a mystery that you've been involved in. To ask me to unravel that mystery and elucidate upon its parts or how it got put together is something I don't do very well.

Q: You talk about other writers' work a good deal here at the university.

CREWS: I lecture to freshmen in a course called Introduction to Fiction. And then I work with graduate students who think they want to be writers. I try to do for them what a good editor would do for them, if they had a good editor. They write and I read, that's the name of the game. We do have a class and we read accomplished writers and we talk about them. We discuss the stories that the students write; every student that writes a story has a conference with me in my office.

Q: What do you think about that? Do you think that works?

CREWS: I think if the student's a writer, it works; if he's not a writer, it doesn't work. If you ask me, why is a man or woman a writer, what's in there that makes him that, I have no answer. Unfortunately, most of the people that teach that stuff don't write themselves, and a lot of bad information is given to people who take such courses, because the people giving the information don't know what they're talking about, because they haven't done it. They studied with someone who didn't write.

I read their stories, and I read them very carefully, and then I talk to them: "This transition is too fast," or "You have a mechanical break here." Now, some of the best stories that we know of have mechanical breaks in them: "The Dead," Joyce's story I think has five. There are no Thou Shalt Nots in fiction. A writer can do any damn thing he can get away with; as Flannery O'Connor said, unfortunately, he can't get by with very much. Or I'll say to the student, "Look, this language you've got there. This is rhetoric. This language doesn't do anything. It doesn't carry itself. You're in love with the sound of your own voice" (which, God knows, all of us who write, and some of us who don't, are), "but it won't do." There is a soft spot in all of us who write that's got to be killed, squashed, exorcised, before we can write truly, as Hemingway would say, God love his soul.

Q: Writing the way you do, you must sometimes get stuck or blocked. What do you do if and when that happens?
CREWS: Well, I run a lot. I don't run fast when I run, but I run a long way. It takes a long time. When I run, I think about my stories, and I think about what's going wrong. I think about how things are developing. I think about things I don't know. I think about a lot of things, but it all has to do with writing. I have got unstuck running more than I ever have other ways, because it's almost self hypnosis.

I pretend (and I pretend as soon as I hit the street), I pretend that there is a little man in my forehead who is running this machine, which is my body. I've been hurt a lot, so it hurts when I run. The machine—the legs, the neck, the back, the ribs—sends messages up to the little man behind my forehead. It's like a ship, and the guy down in the engine room is calling up to the captain: "Ah, engine two, in trouble. Engine two, firing badly. Smoke coming out." The captain says, "Never mind. I've checked that out all right. Maintain speed." Hangs up. After awhile, no matter what comes up to the little man, he sends it back. He sends it back to the foot: "Foot is all right." Foot hurts, feels as though it may be fractured again. "We've checked it out fully. Foot is maintaining well." Phone hangs up. So then, after, say, about three miles, your body goes away. I get the feeling of becoming total mind, free mind. You get a focus, a concentration that you can get nowhere else.

Q: Despite your earlier disclaimer, we would like to ask you about your novels. Many of them seem to deal with the nature of man's evil.

CREWS: It is more fascinating, perhaps easier, to write about that which is diabolical and evil. We somehow feel, I think, that we understand goodness and love better than we understand badness and evil. Who would be evil? Why would you be evil? Why would you starve the Georgians in Russia? Why would you shovel people into furnaces? You can't think about that. And yet, my God, my God . . . It is the thing in us that keeps us fascinated with ourselves. It fascinates us with ourselves much more, the animal in us, the flesh-tearing, brutal animal in us, fascinates us much more than the kissing, licking sweetheart who sends valentines, who cares enough to send the very best.

Q: You like to end your novels in the midst of holiday crowds. Do these mob scenes reflect this sense of mankind?

CREWS: It has been my observation, perhaps faulty, that we live for that. We make our bread, we earn our living, we do whatever we do in some form of isolation, and it's highly controlled. We all have these facades, these images of ourselves. But if you go to, say, Fort Lauderdale Beach, that which is in us that we deny, either consciously or unconsciously, seems to emerge; and that seems to me more what we really are than what we would have people believe we are. I'm afraid I don't have a very high opinion of the disguised human being, "disguised" meaning his identity, his family, where he came from, what he believes in. When all of that disguise is gone, he then becomes a thing that none of us can be proud of or pleased with. You can call it a form of mass hysteria, if you want to. But, you know, good men, and I mean large numbers of good men, have done absolutely atrocious things for no other reason than that they were caught up in the frenzy of the lack of identity. And when you get caught up in that frenzy, then you revert to the cutting edge of the front teeth and the grinders in the back.

Q: Is that why you like to use grotesques, freaks, in your works? Because they don't have these disguises?

CREWS: Right. They have to deal with it every minute of their lives. When you're the midget with the biggest foot in the world, there's not much chance that you can hide anything; it's right out there for everybody to see.

None of this was very conscious. I told you before I'm not a very conscious writer. Now, there's a midget in each of the first three novels I wrote. I gave the third manuscript, third novel, to a wonderful lady I was married to, Sally, and she read it (she's a pretty good critic and reader), and she came out and had this look of anxiety and despair and puzzlement on her face. She said to me, "You don't intend to make a career out of midgets, do you?" It was the first time I realized—really; I swear to God—that I had three novels, cheek to jowl, with midgets in them. I don't know where that comes from. I don't know exactly . . . it just seems to help me do what I need to do, say what I need to say, deal with whatever preoccupations I have in the world, to have people such as these in the novels.

Q: Another of your preoccupations, as you suggested a minute ago, is with the family. A Childhood *is about your own family, and each of your novels deals with the families that the characters form after the break-up of their real families. Would you comment on that?*

CREWS: It's a thing that's very much on my mind all the time, the disintegration of the family. I see it everywhere I go. I think about the marvel of growing up in the same house. I think that's a very beautiful thing, to be able to do that. And I think it's a very beautiful thing to have your momma and daddy and your brothers and sisters there.

But we're all so mobile; we're all so . . . voiceless is a real good word, used in that context, because accents have almost disappeared. You can take a disc jockey from Gainesville and take him to Los Angeles and nobody would ever know the difference. They've all got that banana-smooth sameness. When we lose our voices, there's no communicating. When we lose that, then we begin to lose the family. You know, damn little was passed on to any of us—voice, place, manners, customs. When that begins to break down, it diminishes the human family. That's what I think.

Q: Your novels comment, too, on the American preoccupation with the consumer economy, our propensity to devour, to gorge it all in. Do you think of yourself as a social critic, a social satirist?

CREWS: Well, I've certainly never thought of myself as anything like, say, Sinclair Lewis, but I think that any writer that writes about anybody living in any culture is going to be to some extent a commentator on that culture and on that system. Maybe because of how I was raised and where I was raised, I just don't care much about clothes and about food. If a man's got a place where he won't freeze to death when he puts his head down to go to sleep and if he's got enough to eat, well then he's pretty much all right. When I lived out on the lake in Melrose, there was not a bed in the house, I slept on the floor. I wrote *The Gypsy's Curse* sitting on two concrete blocks at a desk made out of a door. You know, if everything has to be plastic and polyester color coordinated, that kind of world, it makes me nervous. I don't like it and I don't want anything to do with it. Such circumstances would diminish whatever intellect or perception of feeling I have about my fellow man. To pile up all that stuff is an effort to resist that fact that someday you're going to lie down and die. I just know that's the way that works. I don't think that not piling it up is going to keep you from doing it, but it just seems to me that you can spend your time in a better way.

Q: *Your novels deal with serious themes, but they're also very funny, particularly the last two.*
CREWS: Well, I've always thought a writer has an obligation to show the skull. This is not original with me; I think Flannery O'Connor may have said it—that if you don't show the skull behind the smile, then you haven't shown it all. That's related, it seems to me, to what Hemingway said—that all stories end in death and that him that would keep you from that is no true storyteller. When I'm writing, I want the novel to be terrifying and beautiful and joyful and full of anguish and laughter at the same time, so that you're thinking, "My God, My God, what are we in here." Now, why do I want to do that? I don't know. It's just part of who I am. I can't explain it to you. It's just the way it comes out.

Q: *But you're not surprised that people find them funny?*
CREWS: No. They're funny books. I never set out to be funny. I've never thought of myself as a funny person. Not many people laugh when I'm around. I walk into the bank and all the guards put their hands on their guns. It's just that that terror and anxiety that we all live with is as necessary and real and important as the joy and the beauty that we live with. And there wouldn't be any joy and beauty and ecstasy and all the rest of it, if there weren't at the end of the road the worms for your eyes. There wouldn't be.

Q: *Douglas Day wrote that* A Feast of Snakes *reveals for the first time your "radical despair." There seems to be some of that here, in your conversation, in your personal life.*
CREWS: My personal life is, and has been, as long as I can remember, a shambles. I don't live, I don't do it very well. But the one thing in the world that I can have some control over and shape and feel good about is whatever I can write.

If you look at any writers, if you really look at them, what you see is a trail of mucus and blood and guts and everything else. I think that every writer of any consequence, or a writer that tries to be of consequence and write something of merit, that it costs him an awful, awful lot. If you're married, what you give to the typewriter, you can't give to the girl. That may be all right for a year or two. It may be all right for eighteen years. But sooner or later, it's going to catch up with things. While fathers are out teaching their sons to fly-fish, you're trying to teach yourself how to do something with your craft. If you're a person of feeling, if you feel things keenly and deeply—and I don't think you can be a writer unless you feel things not just for the moment but they live in you—that costs you. I don't think you can be a writer of consequence and merit unless you have grave doubts about yourself, about what you've done and who you are and whom you've hurt. And that costs you. And so, it all costs you.

But . . . people persist. They do what is in them to do.

Q: We read your novels. We've been reading them for a long time. Do they sell?
CREWS: They don't sell very well.

Q: Well, I'm curious about that.
CREWS: I am too.

Q: Do you have any theories, any notions about why not? and how do you feel about that?
CREWS: I feel bad. I feel bad about that. Because anybody that tells me he doesn't lust for an audience, I think he's crazy.

You may or may not know that this has been said, and you may or may not agree with this, but the audience for fiction in America is suburban and middle class. Suburban housewives, around thirty-five or six or seven. That's who buys the books. Now, are they gonna buy a book with a guy walking on his hands, hitting a lady in the head with a hatchet [*The Gypsy's Curse*]? They gonna buy a book with a guy in it that's got the biggest foot in the world, and he himself is a midget [*The Gospel Singer*]? Practically everybody that's written anything about me maintains that I put that stuff in those books—midget with the biggest foot in the world; guy who walks on his hands, can't talk, can't hear, and the story's told from his point of view, which is a goddam triumph—they say I put that stuff in there to sell books. Well, if they knew anything about selling books, they'd know that wouldn't sell books. I don't put anything in my books anyway. Middle-aged women don't buy those books, and middle-aged men don't buy them. That criticism hurts me.

Q: Have you ever sold any of your novels to the movies?
CREWS: All my books are or have been under option for movies. One of them's sold outright, *The Gospel Singer*. People ask me things like, "Won't you feel bad if they make your book into a movie? You know, the producer does something, the director does something, the actor does something, every-body's screwin' with it ... " I say, No. They haven't done *anything* to my book. My book's in the library. Nobody's touched my book. That's what *they* did.

Q: Do you read reviews of your work?
CREWS: I sometimes read the first lines of reviews. Then I quit.

Q: You mean if the first line isn't good you hate the review?
CREWS: Well, I'm not quite that tender, I don't think. But maybe I am. I can get hurt really quickly and really deeply emotionally, and it hurts for a long time. Nobody needs that. You don't need that very much.

Geoffrey Wolff reviewed one of my books, a two-page review, but, you know, he's gotta start out by saying, "Harry Crews has written eight novels, four of which I have read, one of which I have liked, but if you have come here for me to knock Crews, you've come to the wrong place." And then from then on, all roses, which I didn't read, I'm not gonna listen to somebody tell me he's read four of my books and liked one out of eight of them, and now he's gonna give me a good review. I just don't need that. It's probably true. Maybe they're all bad. Hell, I don't know. Let somebody else decide. I just write 'em. I don't review 'em. I don't ever recall reviewing a book of mine. Well, not in public.

Q: Well, I've reviewed them too, and I don't think they're bad. But you're not exactly getting rich from them, are you?
CREWS: If I wanted to make money writing, or if I wanted my son to make money writing, I sure as hell wouldn't tell him to become a novelist. Not that you can't make money being a novelist, but it's rare that you can make money being a novelist and make it honestly. You gotta be a fraud, a cheat, a hypo-crite. You gotta study the market, what's *in* this year, and go do one of those. I never do that. I write what I write; I write what comes to me.

Q: Are you bitter about reviewers? Do you really care about that?
CREWS: I've stopped reading them.

Q: You've gotten a lot of good reviews.
CREWS: Yeh, well, that's nice to know, but it doesn't help very much.

Q: Reviews don't sell books?
CREWS: Nope.

Q: What does?
CREWS: I don't know. I got a kind of theory about it. "Theory," that's sweet. I got a feeling about it. It's that I go down and buy a book and read it, and then I meet you at the post office. I say, "Hey. Richard Price's *Ladies' Man* that just came out. Get it. It may upset you a lot, but it's a helluva book. You oughta get it, and they've got two left down there. If I was you, I wouldn't mail that letter. I'd go get it right now." And then you go get both of them and you send one to Iowa. And then somebody in Iowa says, "Hey, this is not too bad." Like that.

Q: And then he goes to the post office . . .
CREWS: Yeh. I think that must be the way it happens. If it doesn't happen that way, then maybe some of us just weren't meant to be . . . See, the ultimate criticism, and it's a killer, it is a killer, the ultimate criticism that a writer gets is that what he is, is not worth being. I mean, after all the work is in. Maybe by that time you're dead; hopefully, you're dead.

Q: I asked Truman Capote that question about reviews, and he said that reviews were of no use unless they were so orchestrated that they all came out within about one week. He said if you could get the New York Times *and* Newsweek *and* Time *and* Harper's *and the* New York Review of Books *all to come out with the same thing in about ten days or two weeks, this would create a kind of effect.*
CREWS: Well, if nothing else, people'd be talking about it.

Q: Yeh, it'd be all over New York. But if the reviews come out slowly, one at a time all over the place, then no one review does anything for you. You get raves but they don't have any effect.
CREWS: So much of it's luck. Eudora Welty said you don't just need talent

and hard work and the rest of it. To write a good book or a good story you also need luck. And I think most writers would agree with that.

Q: *I've also heard that something like forty percent of all hardcover novels are sold within the city of New York. That can't help you.*
CREWS: The way I get it is "within an 800 mile radius of New York City." But it could be "within New York City." That's true. Whatever reputation I have does pretty much exist, strangely enough, within the urban North. There is none down here, much.

When *Esquire* asked me to write a column for them every month, I didn't much want to do it because I knew it was going to get in my way.

And I didn't start just to be a columnist. But, I told 'em I'd do it for a year. I wrote as well as I could. I wrote things that I thought were real and of some consequence. But I also thought it might get my name around and might help my books to sell. I want my books to sell. I ain't ashamed of saying that.

Q: *You took the job in order to promote your name, right? Nobody else is doing it, so you've got to do it. Right?*
CREWS: That's right. You got it right. And that does not speak well, I don't think, for a man to admit that.

You know, all we've got is time. I'm halfway to eighty-six and that's getting on. I'm on the downhill side. How damn long do I expect to live? I always wanted twenty titles. I always wanted twenty titles because I thought if you did (hell, this sounds so mechanical and arbitrary to say, "I wanted twenty titles," as though that meant anything) but, if you wrote as well as you could and as honestly as you could and with as much concentration, focus, diligence, whatever, as you could, well, then, out of twenty you might get a good one. You know, you might get a good one.

Ellen Douglas ∾ 1985

CHRISTINE WILSON

I interviewed Ellen Douglas in January of 1985 for a feature in ArtsNews, *a Jackson quarterly, as she was beginning spring semester as Professor of Southern Studies at Millsaps College. Jo (that's what I call her) was in good spirits over the forthcoming publication of her new book,* Can't Quit You, Baby.

QUESTION: Like Eudora Welty, you've been a writer working in Mississippi almost all of your life. What were the forces that kept you here?
DOUGLAS: Well, the main thing that kept me in Mississippi for thirty-five years was that I was married to a man and had three children, and he was making his living in Greenville. I think it would have been harder for us to live in some parts of Mississippi during the sixties and the civil rights struggle, but Greenville was a kind of oasis in that period, and it was a very pleasant place to live and raise children and to write. People in Greenville seemed to tolerate writers. My life was such that I couldn't have left, and also it was such that I was happy to stay.

Q: And when you left Greenville and came to Jackson, what were some of the reasons you chose Jackson?
DOUGLAS: Well, I decided it was time for me to leave Greenville, and I thought about where to move to, and I had a wide choice of places. But at my age and given my life, it seemed to me that it would be a mistake to move away from the state. It's my home, it's where my work originates. I feel very strongly about the landscape and the people, about this world. I couldn't imagine moving to New York or San Francisco at my age and thinking about writing about those people. If I were young, I might, but not now.

Originally published as Christine Wilson, "Interview with Ellen Douglas," Vol. 33, no. 4 (1995), 15–21.

Q: *About the landscape of Mississippi: it has a special appeal for you. Do you think it might hold something of the same appeal to many Mississippi writers as, say, the Irish landscape does for its writers?*
DOUGLAS: I think the landscape is wonderfully suggestive—both the landscape of the Delta and the southwestern part, the two parts where I've lived. There are other qualities that are useful to writers: the very complex human world of this state, the ambiguities of moral positions, the whole business of racial problems. And another thing is that when you stay in a place where you were born, you have a stronger sense of its history, and that informs my fiction and certainly the fiction of other southern writers. And that's true of Ireland, too. All of those things are true of both places.

Q: *William Styron cites, in addition to the literary tradition of the South and its biblical rhetoric and storytelling, the "wonderful material," the juxtaposition of modern life against the rural tradition.*
DOUGLAS: And we have a language—black English and southern English in general are very idiosyncratic and full—it's just rich and wonderful for the writer.

Q: *What particular aspects of the Welty Southern Studies appointment at Millsaps College are you looking forward to?*
DOUGLAS: This is an entirely new experience for me. I've never taught a course in literature before, and I'll be teaching a course entitled "Jews and Southerners," a study of contemporary Jewish American and southern American writers, and what it has meant for me is that I've had to do a tremendous amount of reading over the last year to get ready for it, and I've enjoyed that, and I think it's going to be a lively class.

Q: *What Jewish writers will you be looking at?*
DOUGLAS: Malamud, Cynthia Ozick, Isaac Bashevis Singer, and a couple of the younger writers—Steve Stern from Memphis, who's both southern and Jewish. And then the southern writers will be Welty, Percy, Robert Penn Warren, and Flannery O'Connor and then two or three younger writers. You know, some of the qualities that you were talking about that southern writers share with Irish writers are also seen in Jewish writers, I think—access to a very idiosyncratic language of their own (and Jewish writers have Yiddish), a very strong commitment to family or a breaking away from family, and a

landscape. With Jewish-American writers it's the landscape of the city slums during the period after their immigration to the US.

Q: *Is there also a powerlessness, especially about their land being taken from them?*
DOUGLAS: Definitely—alienation that is a result of being an outsider. The southerner is to a certain extent an outsider in American society.

Q: *Is there a correlation of values there—a traditional appreciation of the arts?*
DOUGLAS: Well, maybe we'll explore that question. That's one of the questions we'll explore. The Jewish tradition is highly intellectual, and that's not true of the southern tradition. It's much more oriented to action and power.

Q: *Do you think that in Mississippi people have more respect in general for writers than in other southern states?*
DOUGLAS: Well, I think we had this spooky thing that happened to us with Faulkner. All of a sudden there was a thriving literary world in Mississippi with Faulkner and Welty and Percy and the rest, so it's stronger here than in other parts of the South, but there have been an awful lot of good southern writers in the last fifty years—to name a couple who interest me enormously, Robert Penn Warren and Katherine Anne Porter—and I think all those writers came out of the same kinds of tensions and pressures and ambiguities that southern life produces. But, yes, after Faulkner got going, everybody in Mississippi thought, hey, you know we've got the greatest living writer in the world, maybe we can do it too.

Q: *Beverly Lowry said that in Texas if you go into a store and somebody asks you what you do and you say, "I'm a writer," they don't listen, aren't concerned, but she says that if you do that in Mississippi, they'll say, "Oh, really?"*
DOUGLAS: I think that's true. I think the climate is very hospitable for writers.

Q: *You will also be teaching a writing course—advanced creative writing. A friend of mine who teaches art says that he likes teaching because, although he has a master's in art, he is learning to paint from his students. Are there any benefits to you as a writer from teaching writing?*
DOUGLAS: Well, for one thing, writing is so solitary. You get up in the morning and you go to your typewriter, and as far as your work is concerned, you'd

never need to see a soul. All the people you need to make connection with are in books. You read their books. So that for me, teaching is a way to make an ongoing connection with the human world, with real, live people, and with real, live young people, which is important to me. I have lots of connections with older people, but once you get to be a grandmother, you have to work a little at connections with young people.

Q: *Do you have a basic approach to teaching writing?*
DOUGLAS: Yes, a couple of things. One, I don't think you can teach anybody to be a publishable writer, and you can't teach anyone to be a good writer. You can teach people how to read, I think, and that is helpful to them as writers, and you can teach people how not to write, what not to do. And so mainly what I do is point people in the direction of work that I think is good and deal with the technical problems.

Q: *Do you "encourage" or "discourage"?*
DOUGLAS: That's a very difficult thing to deal with. I don't think—what right have I to discourage anybody? What if Einstein's arithmetic teacher had discouraged him in the fourth grade? So what I do mostly is deal with the work put before me in terms of the problems involved. If somebody comes to me and says, "Hey, should I keep on writing? Am I going to be a successful writer?," what I say most often is, "I don't know, but if you are going to write, you'll answer that for yourself, because you won't be able to stop—you'll keep on doing it."

Q: *What qualities go into what we call "talent"?*
DOUGLAS: Well, the commonplace answer to that question, and I forget who said it, is that it's "ninety percent perspiration and ten percent inspiration"—work! Work is what makes writers. And the reason for doing the work is obsession. I think if one is obsessed with writing, one works at it and gets better.

Q: *Is there such a thing as beginner's luck with writers?*
DOUGLAS: There is, yes. I had beginner's luck, as a matter of fact. That's one of the things about southerners—they're very lucky. They have an immensely complex world, and that's extraordinarily lucky. On the other hand, look at Emily Dickinson, you know. She just sat in her bed for thirty or forty years and wrote the best poems that anybody was writing.

Q: Proust said, "Intelligence and sensibility are rarely accompanied by will." Do you think that's true?
DOUGLAS: Yes, I do. I suppose that's what I meant about obsession and work.

Q: So maybe intelligence, sensibility, and will are the components of "talent"?
DOUGLAS: But not only intelligence, sensibility, and will, but a kind of drivenness, I think, too. Most artists absolutely have to do what they do. They couldn't imagine doing anything else. You know, Flannery O'Connor, when somebody asked her why she wrote, said, "Because I'm good at it" [laughs].

Q: Do you think part of it is the fact that writers enjoy the solitariness, enjoy the workings of their own brains to a greater degree than others?
DOUGLAS: Yes, and enjoy the craft, putting an order on it. I think most writers really enjoy revising, for example, and most students are just horrified when they discover that that's what most writers do most of the time.

Q: Writers describe the work of writing very differently. Walker Percy calls it "ditch-digging work," and William Styron said, "Let's face it. Writing is hell." But Eudora Welty has something very different to say. What is writing like for you?
DOUGLAS: I write because that's what I want to do. And, of course, it's a pain in the neck when the work doesn't come, when it doesn't go well. But it's not true for me that writing is a curse.

Q: Do you think that's a masculine stance—all that about sweat and hell?
DOUGLAS: Might be, might be. But as for me, if I don't do it, then I'm uncomfortable and unhappy, and when I am working, that's what I want to be doing and that makes my life work.

Q: You've written your version of fairy tales for a volume illustrated by Walter Anderson's fairy-tale prints. In doing that you were deriving inspiration for your written work from his visual art. How do you feel about the interrelatedness of the arts? Your ex-husband is a composer, your son is a poet, another son is a musician and actor. Is there a connection?
DOUGLAS: Oh, I think it really is all connected up. This is not true with me—I work with words and I'm not good at anything else. I can't draw worth a hoot and don't have all that good an ear—but it's extraordinary how many writers also draw with facility, and how many musicians are deeply interested

in literature. I think it's a web, and if you touch any strand of it, the whole web shakes. And I think what it is is a concern with giving form and meaning to human experience, and that's what all the arts do.

Q: *How valuable did you find Anderson's drawings to your work on the fairy tales?*
DOUGLAS: This is a curious thing about working: very often what comes to hand, almost always what comes to hand to do turns out to be valuable. One of my rules of thumb is to do what comes to hand to do, and the Anderson tales came to hand, but at a time when I was very much interested in fairy tales. So that reading was useful to me, but it is also true that I spent an awful lot of time looking at those pictures, and getting to be a little bit at home in the world of those visual images, and in fact I thought to myself after the book came out, if I had hung around with those images for another year, it might have been a better book.

Q: *But you can say that about anything.*
DOUGLAS: Yes, it was great to move around a little bit in the world of Walter Anderson's extraordinary mind.

Q: *Did the feminist thought on fairy tales and myth have any effect on your versions of the tales? Were you especially concerned with female characters?*
DOUGLAS: Well, I had a very strong feeling that I didn't want these stories to become a way of pleading some cause—any cause. But at the same time I wanted to give them whatever my own sense of balance was, so some of the changes I made in the stories and some of the ways I dealt with the characters had to do with my own feeling about the role of women in the world and what I think about passive fathers, and all that sort of thing. At least one of the villains—an evil fairy—was changed into a villainous wizard instead [laughs]. But I was preoccupied immensely with fairy tales at that time because I was using some mythological material and fairy-tale material in a novel I was working on, so it all kind of came together. One contributed to the other.

Q: *Did you ever feel confined, working in that framework of the fairy tale, rewriting specific fairy tales?*
DOUGLAS: No, I don't think I ever feel that a writer is confined by a framework from the past. A writer is confined only by his or her own inadequacies. In fact, I'm going to teach *The Robber Bridegroom* this semester, and if

you want to see a work that's not confined by the framework of fairy tales and myth, look at *The Robber Bridegroom*. So what I felt some time is that I wouldn't be equal to the story. But if you're equal to the story, then you can do anything you want. I felt I did best, really, with "Pericles," "The Golden Apples," and "Androcles," that they were the most my own, but, you know, that's what you do when you write anything—you make it your own.

Q: *Readers of your novels know how fairy tales would appeal to you, that you're interested in the problems of good and evil, dichotomies. Do you think that your work on the fairy tales will affect your future fiction?*
DOUGLAS: Before I started working on the fairy tales I was really profoundly interested in the patterns of the tales; I use the patterns of ancient tales in *The Rock Cried Out*, for example. So, I'll always be interested in that.

Q: *Could you say a word about what constitutes a writer's voice?*
DOUGLAS: Gosh. The voice is the whole person—everything the writer brings to the work informs the voice. What I think is that one writes as honestly as one can out of one's experience, and that is the voice.

Q: *You have a novel coming out . . .*
DOUGLAS: My new novel is called *Can't Quit You, Baby*, and it'll be out in May from Atheneum, and, like all my other books except the fairy tales, it's set in Mississippi, between 1935 and 1970, and it's about the lives of two women—one black and one white—set in a medium-sized city. It has some very strong fairy-tale and mythological structures. The title is from a Willie Dixon song, "Can't Quit You, Baby," and the second line is, "But I might put you down for a while" [laughs]—which strikes me as a very strong commentary on human relations [laughs again].

David Madden ∾ 1984

JEFFREY J. FOLKS

David Madden has authored and edited over twenty-five books. His works of fiction include among others Cassandra Singing, Bijou, The Suicide's Wife, *and* On the Big Wind. *Mr. Madden is writer-in-residence at Louisiana State University at Baton Rouge, a position he has held since 1968. He was interviewed on 11 November 1984 in Athens, Tennessee, following a reading at Tennessee Wesleyan College.*

QUESTION: *Let me start with Henry James, where he says that art lives on discussion, on experiment, and on curiosity. As I read that, I really thought of your work, of some of the things you tried to do, especially with popular culture, television, oral storytelling, stories like "The Singer," as experimental types of fiction. So let me start by asking whether you see your work as experimental in terms of fictional technique.*

MADDEN: Pretty much, but I don't think of myself as an experimental writer who is looking for ways to be experimental. I'm not opposed to that. I think there should be that kind of writer, and I like some people who do consciously and deliberately look for new ways.

Q: Like William Gass or Thomas Pynchon.

MADDEN: Yes, but there are better examples of people who do *a lot* of stuff. Those two guys produce very little, but what they do produce, they do it in an experimental way. But what happens is that when I get an idea for a story, it usually comes as a sort of "story." That's what I call a narrative or a character inspiration, whichever happens to be the focus. Then I either seek or wait for, or *will* or whatever, a technical inspiration, which to me is just as exciting and just as important.

Originally published as Jeffrey J. Folks, "Interview with David Madden: *On Technique in Fiction,*" Vol. 25, no. 2 (1987), 24–38.

Q: *You said somewhere that all of your stories start with a decision about point of view. It sounds like a very Jamesian thing to say.*
MADDEN: Yeah, and an experiment sometimes comes from the point of view. What I ask myself is: technically, what is the very best way to bring out everything I want to bring out, and a lot of things I don't even know I want to bring out? Now I do know certain of the things I want to bring out. By things I want to bring out, I mean *things*, I mean experiences; I don't mean ideas necessarily as ideas but I want to put the reader through the experience. Essentially it's an aesthetic experience; it's not an experience of what it's like to have been a soldier in the Civil War or what it's like to have been a wife whose husband killed himself.

Q: *It's not a subject or theme but . . .*
MADDEN: It's a process, a process in which the faculty which is most exercised is the imagination. I talk about my fiction with students, by saying: I first want to stir the emotions, and if I've stirred your emotions, I've stirred your imagination. But I do certain things *to* stir your imagination, just as I do certain things to stir your emotions. And then last, and usually this comes after you finish writing the story, I want to stimulate your intellect.

Q: *I know you worked with the* Kenyon Review, *and with New Criticism. How do you see your relationship to the New Criticism with its emphasis upon intellect, craft, and shaping of fiction?*
MADDEN: Awareness and consciousness, as opposed to the Dionysian unconscious.

Q: *Did that contact with the New Criticism have a large impact upon the way you developed?*
MADDEN: It came very specifically through exposure to *The House of Fiction*, edited by Caroline Gordon and Allen Tate. Their commentary on those stories. It was like a revelation; it was like Paul on the road to Damascus. There's *before* and then there's *after*, and everything after can be directly related, if not to that experience of reading those commentaries, at least to what I picked up about the New Criticism from various other people; and the next most important thing that clarified everything for me was the essay by Mark Schorer.

Q: *"Technique as Discovery."*
MADDEN: Yes. Then studying in the light of all those things, on my own,

Wright Morris's artistry, the stories and the fiction of Faulkner, of Conrad, of James Joyce, of Henry James, and all of these aesthetic writers—who are also experimental to some degree. And what I am pretty convinced of is that I don't imitate any of them, even though Wright Morris—consciously to this day after thirty-five years—I think of as my main master. I think that a look at the technique I use will show that I have done things that none of them have ever done. None of those writers have done anything like "The Singer."

Q: *It has always seemed to me that what you do with technique, with the craft of fiction, is in a way to introduce a kind of dynamic into the whole concept of crafting fiction that pulls against these ideas of the novel as the Jamesian novel. What about your use of storytelling, or the use of songs, of popular culture?*
MADDEN: Yes, which is not Jamesian, but which I worked into the Jamesian aesthetic, in a sense. Very consciously.

Q: *James argued against the idea of writing fiction as "story."*
MADDEN: That's right.

Q: *You know, he questions the whole concept of a dichotomy between story on the one hand and revelation of experience.*
MADDEN: "The Singer" is a very good example of that, because the "story" which did attract me was a *story* inspiration. You know, what if a girl went to a camp meeting and became overwhelmed and then for forty days and forty nights she wandered over the hills of eastern Kentucky, and whenever the spirit moved her, she sang. What *if*? What would happen? O.K. That story is so sentimental, so shallow, so "folksy" in the wrong sense, that even though I wanted to tell it, I *couldn't* tell it because of my consciousness of art on the one hand and because it wasn't very interesting to me on the other hand. Not until I got the *technical* inspiration of having an unsympathetic narrator, an unreliable and unsympathetic narrator, tell it, did everything really open up, all the possibilities open up, so that it's not a story any longer, but is a process in which our emotions, our imaginations, and our intellect are engaged in a "dynamic," as you said.

Q: *This is the idea behind introducing a frame to oral storytelling, so that we have an oral story which has a great deal of vitality, that's based perhaps on immediate experience, but that's filtered through or framed by a third-person consciousness.*

MADDEN: It gets filtered through three characters who are on the scene, Fred the projectionist, Pete and Wayne, four, if you count me, and a whole bunch of other people who perpetuated the legend of the girl as if she was still alive. It's then filtered through the sophisticated technique of a dialogue and its story frame of being set in the church. There are an incredible number of sophisticated mechanisms at work there, and yet when I give a reading of it, before a live audience, there is a feeling that it's all very, very real, very oral-storytelling, and people get all absolutely into it, and they think that I'm somebody else. I can actually make them believe that I'm not reading, and that is the perfect combination, you see. The whole thing is, as Flaubert said, the artist must be everywhere, he must be very conscious, but nowhere seen.

Q: Yes. Invisibility.
MADDEN: Yeah. You know, you don't see my hand unless you stop and say, "Oh, yes, I see what he's doing," but in the immediacy of reading it or hearing me read it, there's just this impression that it's just this simple story of the girl. And to me it's an incredibly complex story. I've claimed, and nobody's called me on this, that nobody has ever really written a story quite like the way I *do* that; *somewhat* like that, but not really . . .

Q: Somehow the strength of the immediate inspiration of the story, the feeling you had for the girl in the story, required an equal amount of calling forth of craft or distancing from the subject matter.
MADDEN: Exactly.

Q: And it was that balancing of distance, of craftsmanship, and the raw materials that produced the power in the story.
MADDEN: Right. You see, for five years I really wanted to tell that story, but I kept waiting for, consciously waiting for, a technical inspiration to strike me, and it literally did one day. I won't tell you how—it's a long story—but it came out of some practical concern. I said, "Oh, yeah, what if I did *this*?"

Q: Did you play around with different approaches to that story?
MADDEN: I explored it in an essay which is published in *The Poetic Image in Six Genres* along with "The Singer." That essay was a lyrical essay exploration, and I then got into the story. What I wanted to say though about "nobody's ever done it" was that the experimental side of me is a lot stronger than I've been given credit for when people write about my work. I don't know why it

slides by them, because if you really look at it, *The Suicide's Wife* is pretty experimental in the kind of strange style and the use of tenses and so on, jumping back and forth, the leaps that I make, and the opening chapter. And then the story "Looking at the Dead." *On the Big Wind* is the most experimental of all, and everybody just misses that.

Q: *The narrative shifts in* On the Big Wind, *for example.*
MADDEN: You see, my point is that my job in the style is to create a context whereby I imply everything that's important and state only what's unimportant. You create the context with those things that are not terribly important but which are interesting. The superficial reader or even the serious reader enjoys them, but that's not what it's about; and then the reader's participation, cooperation, and collaboration conjures up, given the context, what I leave out.

Q: *The same way that with oral storytelling, you provide the image.*
MADDEN: Yeah, and the same way with radio drama. The thing about *On the Big Wind* is that it's the context of the whole novel. I create a context with the whole novel, and you're supposed to fill in imaginatively the leaps between the episodes, not to mention the leaps within episodes.

Q: *The novel covers ten or twelve years in the life of the protagonist, and you wonder what he was doing in the period when he left Nashville, and went to Camden, and from there to western Kentucky. There are significant gaps.*
MADDEN: It's all implied by the context, not just by some carefully planted facts.

Q: *I've always been struck by what seems to me technically the difference between* Bijou *and* The Suicide's Wife. *I marvel that these two works come out of the same writer. Maybe there's more similarity in technique than I've noticed.*
MADDEN: No, there's not, but that's my point. My point is that people are struck by the difference because they're thinking of subject matter, more or less, and characters, and length and other things like that, and locale, and all the traditional elements of fiction, but if you take the attitude that I take, that what I am doing is producing stories and novels out of a creative process, out of a range of techniques, then there's no surprise whatsoever. It's just that I did *that*, and now I'm going to do *this*. But actually within *Bijou* there are those juxtapositions of rather different kinds of things, like the journal entry, which is a rather traditional element, with the midnight

reverie, which is not so traditional; you know, nobody really has that in a novel, even *The Portrait of the Artist as a Young Man*. You don't have him lying in bed reviewing his life.

Q: *Yes. The ending of* Bijou *seems to be experimental. You may need to explain the ending.*
MADDEN: There the novel is pretty straightforward. I then again relied on the reader to see more than I think any reader is going to see, that at the end of this experience when Lucius ceases to be innocent and to be a child (or doesn't cease to be, but he's about to cross over a threshold) I'm more or less hinting that in his future, he will write the book that you just read. So by having that bed, where somebody has just gotten up, still rising, the mattress still rising—I mean he caught it just at the instant, still rising, and the sheet is slightly rippling—that gets an instant emotional response from him. He feels it in his scalp, like when your hair is standing on end. That's the emotion, imagination, intellect thing. His emotions have been stirred, the novel ends. It's implied that his imagination will be stirred, and it's implied he'll think about this—the intellect will be stirred—and you're supposed to do the same thing about the novel that you've just read, and he's going to do, as a character in the novel, the same thing about the material of his life, you see. That's too much to expect anybody to catch. So that it ends up being a kind of miniature version of my whole aesthetic. But in a sense it's not asking too much to say, "Well, I end it abruptly there as if to say it goes on." By the way, that goes back to Faulkner's story "The Bear."

Q: *Oh, yes.*
MADDEN: You know, the footprint in "The Bear," the water rising.

Q: *Yes, that great scene in "The Bear," with the paw-print filling up with water, implying that a bear has just passed through there.*
MADDEN: You see, I learned more from that one passage about implication, about context and implication, than even from the New Critics, but that's not a thing the New Criticism would talk about.

Q: *I suspect, at least from the reviews I've seen of your novels, that one reason why some reviewers miss the technical or experimental quality of your work is the Appalachia subject matter.*
MADDEN: Yeah. Typing.

Q: *Typing. Or the assumption that the Appalachian novel is always going to be naive in its technical qualities, that we're still writing the local color fiction of Mary Murfree, in 1984. I just wonder whether you would agree with that.*

MADDEN: By the way, speaking of Mary Murfree, I would say that one of the finest symbolic images of the Civil War, for me, is the horse trapped in the cellar in *The Storm Centre*, the Civil War novel. Anyway, yes, I think that's part of it. Why they wouldn't remember the sophistication of Faulkner, who uses equally raw southern material, or of Robert Penn Warren in *All the King's Men*, I don't know, instead thinking of James Still or somebody. But then, you see, the other novels, like *Suicide's Wife*, should tip them off, if they know that novel, and the short stories, "No Trace" along with "The Singer." Some of the things I've written about "No Trace" also apply to "The Singer," in that "No Trace" is incredibly open-ended but also incredibly controlled at the same time, simultaneously very controlled. Absolutely everything in there is very consciously crafted to produce something that is completely open-ended, that cannot be closed up. None of the questions, not a single one of the questions raised by that story in the mind of the character or in the mind of the reader separate from the character, can be answered by referring to the material in the story.

Q: *How much effect does the audience, or your conception of the ideal reader, have upon decisions about the technique? I'm sure it has everything to do with your decision about point of view. As you write, do you sense that you are writing for a particular reader?*

MADDEN: Not a particular reader, but actually here's where the relation between oral storytelling and the literary fiction comes in. No matter what kind of fiction I'm writing, I am imagining or I'm feeling the presence of living human beings listening to a human voice talking to them, which is the opposite of what a lot of writers I talk to do. They say they don't hear any kind of a voice. They hear the voice that's in the story, but they don't feel the presence of people listening. So that when I give a reading, and I see those people *today*, for instance, sitting out there, and I look into their eyes . . . I feel I have to have the eyes of everybody in the room available to me. So it seems only natural to read to somebody, even the most literary story, which in "No Trace" is purely literary, absolutely no oral quality to it; when I read that story to an audience, I don't feel uncomfortable or uptight at all because it seems it's part of the whole process that's been there from the beginning.

Q: But you seem to me, perhaps, further than any writer I know, to be reaching toward an oral audience. Of course, there have been many writers who have. Dickens is another good example with his constant need to feel a dynamic both ways with his audience. Does that alter the technical process?

MADDEN: It doesn't alter the technical process at all except that it seems that every element of the art of fiction like point of view and everything else is a consideration of how you want to affect the reader. You know, everything helps you to affect the reader, everything. It isn't just a matter of telling a story and maybe somebody will read it and be affected by it and maybe they won't, but the reader is built into the process, word by word, phrase by phrase, sentence by sentence, the overall technique and so on. The reason why point of view is so important is because the readers must have a very clear orientation to the source of authority for everything that they're learning, or everything that they're experiencing. So that when students and teachers ask me questions about "The Day the Flowers Came," they say, "Well, how'd this happen?" and "What happened then?" and "Why did this happen?" and "This seems unusual" and so on. I say, well, you can't ask *me*, because it's all through the point of view of this one character. It's how *he* perceives everything.

Q: Right. That's a good example of a story that uses a great deal of implication. We're limited in what we can know about the events.

MADDEN: Throughout the story, he is referring to Carolyn as an empty-headed person, such an airhead, with the pink stove and everything pink, and we, because we're in his point of view, are thinking, "my God, this is a really stereotyped housewife," to the point where some people get really teed off at me, the writer, for portraying women that way. The same people very often miss what I deliberately did, which was, I delayed letting you hear her voice. There are all these references to her, there are even surrogates of her, like the woman from the PTA who is just another one of those people like Carolyn. At the end, near the very end, he remembers what she said as she got on the plane, which is, you know, "Our life, it's the way we live," and she goes on in this very poignant way. She comes alive in the immediacy of dialogue for four lines, in the context of his insensitivity to what she says, and I want the reader who is more sensitive to leap in and say, as if to J.D., "my God, this woman isn't the woman that you have been perceiving and I've been perceiving through your eyes. This passage that you're remembering in one context implies to me that she was a totally different kind of woman." And so what I wanted to happen was this great rush of intuition, for readers to intuit a wholly different story, to run that whole story back through their minds, from *her* point of view, by implication, intuitively, not literally and consciously, but intuitively in one great rush to say, "Oh, my God." So that in a sense you can almost say that the story is about Carolyn rather than about J.D. I mean, in a sense.

Q: I'm not sure I did that in the story, but I did feel a sense of the poignancy. I was struck by the despair that the relationship seemed to conjure up. A lot of your stories seem to me to be about subjects, fragmentation or loss or kinship falling apart, the loss of the community or the oral storytelling. Now I'm not going to get onto that as a subject matter, but I suppose I'm interested in whether that affects the techniques that you use. Is there some kind of a parallel between the theme and what you need to treat that theme?

MADDEN: I don't consciously think very much about theme at the outset, but I can see how the choices of techniques that I have ended up with produce a feeling of fragmentation and alienation because one of the techniques I use is the juxtaposition of fragments, as in "No Trace." "No Trace" is nothing but fragments, using the metaphor of the hand grenade blowing up. Nothing but attempts to take fragments and put them back together again only to have them blow up in your face, in Ernest's face, all over again at the end of the story because they don't really cohere at the end. And so, yes, maybe the techniques do give the sense of things falling apart or of alienation. In a story I just sent off, two lovers meet every once in a while at airports and have quick meetings. It's a story about how they meet over many years. When he takes business trips, she jumps on another plane and they meet at airports, go to a city and have a night or two. It's called "Looking for Pittsburg in Cincinnati" and what is happening is that he's saying, "Well, now, this place I'm going to take you to, honey, this is really terrific," and they drive around and around Cincinnati and he's looking for this little quaint neighborhood and this great restaurant. At the end of the story he says, "Oh my God, that's in Pittsburg." And by this time you have a feeling that this whole relationship is at a point of critical development.

Q: Gurney Norman says something about that, that the reason he places so many of his stories in automobiles is that it's a way to maintain the unity of the story but also to create this perhaps uniquely American experience of mobility. You can have the characters in motion, but also imprisoned together in the automobile.

MADDEN: This business of a character in motion, who's supposed to be a relatively insensitive character like an insurance salesman, does go through several stories. In "Looking for Pittsburg in Cincinnati," he's a computer salesman. In "The New Orleans of Possibilities," he's a salesman again. In "The Day the Flowers Came" he's an insurance salesman. O.K. Now all three of those stories are pretty much about guys who are on the move all the time, and I capture them in the latest story in a car. "The New Orleans of Possibilities" is in a flea market, and then "The Day the Flowers Came" is in that house where he feels quite trapped without the people who are usually there. So there's this great mobility, generally with an occasion where everything is very cramped. So that *we* can focus, and *he* can focus on these things. But you know, I'm inclined to take all those stories, and put in "No Trace," which is sort of similar, and "Frank Brown's Brother" and put them together and make them all the same character, as essentially it turned out to be. But I keep getting these damned critics who will say, as with *On the Big Wind*, "Oh, these are a bunch of stories he put together as a novel," you know. As if I was trying to publish another title, which is very frustrating when you find these patterns after many years . . .

Q: *The father in "No Trace" really is one of these rootless men.*
MADDEN: He's really the same guy. They're all the same guy, and none of them are me. You know, they're all an imagined person who's totally different from me. But I can't do it because I continue to get this damned attitude of, "Oh, yeah, he's trying to put that together as a novel." It would allow the reader the great experience of having this incredibly Kafkaesque focus on this guy who has this really weird life, you know, which the reader would have if you put all those stories together, right?

Q: *Styron took a number of years to write* Sophie's Choice, *publishing portions of the novel in* Esquire, *and could have been subjected to the same criticism.*
MADDEN: Yes, but you see, in my case, it's not a matter of setting out to do something and publishing part of them as you go along. It's a matter of discovering after you've done it *that* you have done it. Now, how can I maximize the effect? Well, bring them together. And you can't do that.

Q: *This is really the natural outgrowth of your technique.*
MADDEN: Sure, it is. I mean, if I carefully worked out the techniques of these stories, and if these techniques happened to interact with each other,

it makes *artistic* sense, not commercial sense, to put them together. But the people who object are the people who say, "Oh, yeah, subject matter." You see, they can only look at the subject matter or theme, and say, "Oh, yeah, he just put all these together."

Q: *One of your comments that struck me was when you were talking about the humanizing effect of the bond between the listener and the storyteller. There's something inherent in the process of creating a novel and having people read it that you see as humanizing. Maybe just briefly, what do you mean by that?*
MADDEN: One way of putting it is—*again*—to put it on the technical level. You use all these techniques solely to have an effect, and the three effects that I've already talked about are emotional effects, imaginative effects, and intellectual effects. Now if you can take a person such as the Ancient Mariner, you know, with that gleam in his eye, then take the other Coleridge poem "Kubla Khan," and the Ancient Mariner with his story puts you under a pleasure-dome and you can get your reader to engage his emotions, his imagination and his intellect in such a controlled and intense and dynamic way, that experience is humanizing to the extent that those are the faculties which make us most human. Not "most human" because we feel emotions (maybe animals do, but I doubt that they can feel emotions because emotions are inseparable from consciousness), but what makes us most human *especially* is the imagination. Well, not especially, I guess, the intellect too, but to me, it's the imagination—that we can imagine being what we're not, and that brings in compassion; you can only be compassionate if you can be imaginative. So all of our finest qualities as human beings cluster around our emotions and the emotions that people have are good emotions even when they're bad emotions. That is, it is good that a human being can feel this way for the sake of a story or for the sake of another character, and it is good that people who don't normally use their imaginations a great deal have an experience where their imaginations are stimulated. It is good that they are able to think about the experience that they've just had, and to that extent I think it's extremely humanizing.

Q: *This can only happen through technique.*
MADDEN: Only through technique. Not through subject matter, not through a "nice" story, a "good" story, an "interesting" story, a "fascinating" story, a "thrilling" story, a "suspenseful" story. You see, none of those things really cause all these three things to click and to interact dynamically, to use

your word back there, unless the artistry is at work. As an example of artistry or what I mean as the artistic effect, I would cite, for me, *The Great Gatsby*. I'm not interested in the theme of "the American Dream," which I wrote a book about. I'm interested in having that aesthetic experience all over again where a guy named Nick runs the experience of somebody else through his consciousness in such a way that he ends up being the character that I'm most interested in.

Q: Is there something about your new novel Sharp-shooter *in terms of technique that you're struggling with? Has your new novel engaged you in terms of technical qualities?*
MADDEN: Oh, yes, very much. One of the technical things I wanted to do which was artificially set up in front of me intentionally, early, was to write the most omniscient novel ever written. To take the omniscient, which I think is the most undisciplined point of view (I'm trying to find a novel that is really omniscient but is extremely disciplined and artistic, and I can't find any examples; I look for them to be sort of inspirations), and to write the most omniscient novel of all.

Q: Middlemarch, *perhaps?*
MADDEN: Yes, right.

Q: It covers everything under the omniscient point of view, but is disciplined.
MADDEN: Yes, except that it wouldn't be me as David Madden coming *in*, the way she comes in as George Eliot and makes comments. It would be impersonal. I guess I'm looking for a god-like omniscience rather than the omniscience of George Eliot who is god-like. I want it to be god-like from the beginning, you know, and I'm not in it. In other words, the way Joyce was able to refine himself out of *Portrait of the Artist* was to use mostly the third-person, central intelligence. I want to see if you can do that in some form of omniscience.

Q: You almost want the Faulknerian The Sound and the Fury, *the different colored prints, which is dramatic but enters every character's mind at the same time.*
MADDEN: Yeah. You mean the last part of it, or the whole design?

Q: The Quentin section, in particular.
MADDEN: Well, that's first person, though, you see. Not omniscient. The whole book is omniscient but the individual parts are not omniscient till you

get to the third, but I found that I couldn't quite do it and do other things I wanted to do. I thought, "Well, I'll have a character, I'll have him be a kind of omniscient author in that he takes an interest in all these other people and tries to become totally omniscient about all these other characters, by an effort of will and imagination, and reading and listening and researching." And what happened was that I began to tell a little about him and I got so caught up with him that he became equally important as a character. However, the effect is exactly what I wanted. He consciously strives for omniscience. Here you have an interesting situation where a first-person narrator in fiction for the first time as far as I know (and he's just an ordinary guy at first, as you know) consciously and deliberately strives for omniscience. That is, he wants to know everything, but he wants to know it not in terms of facts but through a combination of facts and imagination.

Q: This derives from his uncertainty about his own action. He wants to look back and he wants to find certitude about what his role was.
MADDEN: That's a theme throughout the whole thing. You see, did I kill General Sanders or didn't I? Well, by the end of the story he still doesn't know, but in the course of asking questions he asks a hundred about other people. He doesn't answer many of those either, but by the end of the story he realizes, "What I have really wanted all this time is omniscience, is to know everything, and omnipresence as well. To be in the tower, one of the towers, and to be everywhere, to know what went on in the tower—did I shoot him or not?—and also to know what went on everywhere else." And that becomes a conscious thing for him toward the end of the novel. Not in the beginning, of course, and not through most of it. We, I hope, begin to suspect that. You know, this guy thinks he missed the war, but look at all the stuff he keeps bringing in. Look at all he's learning. Look at all he's interested in. How could he say he missed it when he experienced all these things in his imagination?

Q: It sounds like a marvelous character, really. A major fictional consciousness.
MADDEN: I hope so. I hope that's the way it turns out.

Q: Maybe to close, will you ever get shut of Lucius Hutchfield of Bijou?
MADDEN: I'm going to write a whole novel about my little brother Bucky. I can get shut of Lucius fairly easily but it's more difficult to get rid of Bucky. Bucky is the one, the little one, that I want to write about. I'm going to see him tonight. But about Lucius, there is one more thing: Lucius in the army, which

was originally going to be part of *Pleasure-Dome*, but it inflated the book too much. It's going to be about his experiences, that is, my experiences, as a kid nineteen years old in the army who refuses to sign Joseph McCarthy's loyalty oath. But one of the things that has kept me from writing that is this—it's too simple and there doesn't seem to be any opportunity for any technical resonancy.

Q: But again that takes off from "The Cartridge Belt" story. Again you have a novel going there.
MADDEN: Yes, and that was conscious. That's an exploration of the novel, that one story.

Bobbie Ann Mason ∾ 1986

ALBERT E. WILHELM

Bobbie Ann Mason was born in Mayfield, Kentucky, on May 1, 1940. After receiving a B.A. degree from the University of Kentucky in 1962, she worked briefly in New York City as a writer for the fan magazines Movie Stars, Movie Life *and* T.V. Star Parade. *Later she earned an M.S. degree from the State University of New York at Binghamton (1966) and a Ph.D. in English from the University of Connecticut (1972).*

Mason's first book was her doctoral dissertation, Nabokov's Garden: A Nature Guide to Ada *(1974). In 1975 she paid tribute to the heroines of her favorite childhood books by publishing* The Girl Sleuth: A Feminist Guide to the Bobbsey Twins, Nancy Drew, and Their Sisters.

After teaching journalism part-time at Mansfield State College for a few years, Mason began in 1980 to publish stories in the New Yorker *and* Atlantic Monthly. *Her first collection,* Shiloh and Other Stories, *appeared in 1982 and immediately won critical acclaim. It won the PEN/Hemingway Award and was also a finalist for the National Book Critics Circle Award, the American Book Award, and the PEN/Faulkner Award. In 1985 she published her first novel,* In Country, *and she is presently at work on a novella and another collection of stories.*

The following interview took place in Atlanta on November, 14, 1986. Earlier that day Mason had read from her novel In Country *at the convention of the South Atlantic Modern Language Association.*

QUESTION: *Could we begin by talking about some of the influences on your writing? What about your growing up in the South? Was that a significant influence?*

MASON: I guess so. If you're asking about my basic experience growing up that influenced me as a writer, my basic experience was isolation and a desire

---

Originally published as Albert E. Wilhelm, "An Interview with Bobbie Ann Mason," Vol. 26, no. 2 (1988), 27–38.

to get out of the isolation because I lived in a remote region and I wasn't around many people. I didn't have any playmates until I was six years old. I was consequently very shy and always much of a loner, so I think all of that contributed to my desire to express myself by writing. It seemed like a preferred avenue because I was too shy to speak or perform. Writing is a more private thing one can do.

Q: *When did you begin to write fiction?*
MASON: I began to publish in 1980, but I was writing even when I was a kid. I wrote short stories in college about many of the same subjects that I deal with now but I didn't have any perspective on my material and I didn't have any encouragement to write. I was busy with other occupations, so I really didn't get focused on my writing until the late seventies.

Q: *After college you worked for a time in New York City. Was your perspective on life in the South developed in much the same way Willie Morris says his was in* North Toward Home?
MASON: Well, I went away from home, and certainly that was necessary for me to be able to get any clear notion of where I came from. That's a classic sort of experience.

Q: *Your first book was* The Girl Sleuth, *and you have commented in other interviews that your early reading of books like the Nancy Drew series was very influential.*
MASON: Yes. That was my literary education until about age eighteen.

Q: *Do you think those books have also influenced the kinds of characters you create?*
MASON: Probably. There's a basic identification with those characters that I felt and will probably never get rid of. Those books contain very innocent dreams of quests for clarity, solving a mystery, and wanting to go somewhere, do something, and be somebody. The Bobbsey Twins got to go on a vacation in every single book, and that probably influenced me as much as anything ever did in my life. We never got to go on vacations in my family. Most people around me were not ambitious or eager about learning or doing something different. They were willing to accept what was handed them, and that made me very frustrated.

Q: Perhaps girl detectives like Nancy Drew were some of the most independent and resourceful female characters to be found anywhere in the fiction of that somewhat sexist era.

MASON: Absolutely.

Q: Did these prototypes influence your female characters who are frequently more determined and energetic than male characters? I am thinking, for example, about the contrast between Norma Jean and Leroy in "Shiloh."

MASON: There's something about that resourcefulness in the female characters in the girl sleuth books that becomes a quest for the experience of the male—what men and boys experience in our society. That is a great mystery and something we females are not allowed to know about as children or as teenagers. There seems to be a great motivation among a lot of women writers to write about this quest for what men experience. In *In Country*, for example, I have written about it in terms of Sam wondering what it was like to go to war. That's something that women by and large don't have to do. We can't exactly complain about being deprived of it because it's not something we would really want to do. Yet men have to do it. Why do they do it and not us? What can they tell us about it, and what does it mean to us? It's just a source of great mystery.

Q: Is that why you chose a name for Sam that can be used for either males or females?

MASON: No, I had the name long before I knew that this book would have anything to do with war or a quest.

Q: According to an interview in W by Nicky Robertshaw, your novel began as a treatment of the adolescent love affair between Sam and Lonnie.

MASON: Yes, something like that.

Q: Was your own trip to the Vietnam War Memorial in Washington in 1983 what gave the book a new focus?

MASON: That was an important stage in the development of the novel. The Memorial didn't give me the idea of writing about Vietnam itself. I had written almost an entire draft before I went to the Memorial, but I realized that the characters would have to go there, too.

Q: You have used the word "quest" in describing the novel. Is that the basic structure of the whole book?

MASON: I'm sure it is. The classic quest for the father is one of the oldest themes there is, isn't it? Except it's usually the young man looking for his father.

Q: *In addition to the quest or pilgrimage motif, isn't the old motif of the all-night vigil also present in Sam's experience at Cawood's Pond?*
MASON: Do you mean going into the dark night of the soul or something like that?

Q: *Perhaps a little like the isolated vigil before a final test in many traditional initiation ceremonies. As you have structured the book, Sam's vigil occurs just before she, her uncle, and her grandmother take off for Washington to complete the pilgrimage.*
MASON: Maybe so. That's for you literary critics to figure out. I just wrote it. The structure seemed emotionally right to me.

Q: *What about the other literary influences on your work? You wrote a Ph.D. dissertation on Nabokov. Has that work influenced you?*
MASON: I don't feel any real connection to any formal literary training. I didn't know what was happening when I was in graduate school. I didn't have time to write fiction; I was too busy writing term papers. I'm always embarrassed by references to this Ph.D. because I don't relate back to that and I didn't carry forward any particular knowledge about literature that I studied.

Q: *Why did you choose to write on Nabokov?*
MASON: I saw him as someone on a trip through the imagination. I'm interested in stylists, and he is the premier stylist. My favorite writers are those that have a unique style. If they don't have that, then I'm usually not interested.

Q: *What other writers do you admire?*
MASON: People like E. B. White. Certainly there you have your "elements of style." An influence has also been some of the new journalists of the late sixties and early seventies like Tom Wolfe, who has a very distinctive style. I wouldn't say he was one of my favorite writers, but I have admired him. John Updike is a writer I admire who is also certainly a stylist.

Q: *You have continued to do some journalistic pieces yourself, haven't you?*
MASON: A few things. I write some for "The Talk of the Town" in the *New Yorker.*

Q: *You've said that your first real job was writing for fan magazines where you interviewed Annette Funicello and Fabian and wrote features about Pernell Roberts's hairpiece. Most of your stories continue to have numerous references to popular culture. Do you get ideas for stories from things like television or the lyrics to songs?*
MASON: Oh, I just pick up bits and pieces here and there. I take notes on whatever is going on around me.

Q: *I believe the epigraph for* In Country *is from Bruce Springsteen.*
MASON: When I wrote the novel, I was aware that it was taking a long time, and I was writing down allusions to whatever was on the radio. As I drew near to the end, I wanted to set it in a specific time as current as possible, so I brought it all up to date to the summer of 1984. That's when "Born in the U.S.A." came out, and it fit so perfectly, almost like a soundtrack. It reflected the themes of the book, and I just latched onto a lot of things from the album.

Q: *Are some of the popular culture elements in* In Country *more than topical allusions to establish setting? For example, what about the numerous references to* M*A*S*H?
MASON: They seemed to fit the fabric of the novel. For one thing, *M*A*S*H* is not just a casual, throwaway reference. It was a TV show that meant an awful lot to a lot of people and was an important part of their lives. They watch it fondly and nostalgically on the reruns. Sam grew up with it, and Emmett found some sort of connection with it because of his war experience. I think a lot of Vietnam vets do. The show was more real to Sam than what she knew about her father. It has an immediacy in their lives, and if they are going to watch something once a week and think about it and feel strongly about it, then it becomes a significant part of their lives.

Q: *Is it almost a kind of therapy? It strikes me as significant that the M*A*S*H series began about the time our country became deeply involved in Vietnam . . .*
MASON: And then it ended shortly after we got out.

Q: *Were you suggesting that, as the country is finally arriving at some sort of peace with itself after the Vietnam experience, it can put aside its TV therapy, except as reruns which become almost nostalgic?*
MASON: I don't really know the answer to that, but now we have back-to-back, double *M*A*S*H.* When it was new each week, something was always

developing. When Colonel Blake got killed, it was very shocking, but in the reruns it's happy recognition somehow.

Q: A recurring motif in M*A*S*H is some terrible psychic trauma which a character must deal with. Is that not similar to the basic problem you are dramatizing in your novel?

MASON: In one M*A*S*H episode Hawkeye treated a wounded soldier and then had a breakdown of some kind. I can't remember the exact details, but the psychiatrist, Dr. Sidney Friedman, hypnotized him and made him remember. The cause of the breakdown turned out to be the smell of the soldier's clothes that evoked a childhood trauma. When Hawkeye delved into his unconscious and confronted the trauma, the whole problem was solved in just a few lines of dialogue.

Q: Are you saying the TV solution was too easy?

MASON: In my novel Sam says at some point that you have to talk out problems. She is telling Emmett at the swamp that he has to do something like Sidney Friedman helped Hawkeye do—to face the problem and get it out. That's a familiar situation on TV. Characters do that on TV all the time and it seems easy. It occurs to Sam that on TV they have script writers and in real life we don't.

Q: You have sometimes disavowed any conscious knowledge of certain patterns or symbols that critics find in your work. Can you describe your process of creating a story?

MASON: Well, I'll say that if you start with patterns and meanings worked out and set out to write a story to fit them, then it's meaningless. It's not going to get you anywhere. It's only after you work through the specifics of a story that perhaps the meanings emerge. Or maybe not. Maybe something will emerge that you didn't quite see yourself, that you didn't know was there. That happens to me a lot. It's a pleasure to find that a meaning is there and that the story works.

Q: Do you know intuitively when the various details of a story fit?

MASON: Yes, I'm sure I was intuitively aware that in the novel there was a typical classical structure of the quest in going out to the dark night and then the journey culminating in an experience of healing. But I didn't sit down and say that's the way I'm going to do it.

Q: *Only we teachers would do that.*

MASON: Yes, you can because you have a finished product, but the writer can't because there's not yet anything to base such generalization on.

Q: *Unlike most of your stories which have straight time lines,* In Country *begins in* medias res *and then goes back to fill in past action.*

MASON: Oh, yes, but again I didn't say I was going to do that because of the traditional pattern. I did it because I wanted the journey across America, but if I had put all of it after the swamp episode, the book would have dragged. So I started the journey at the beginning to set up a small amount of suspense. Such things are intuitive.

Q: *Well, perhaps that's why Homer used the pattern also. Do you frequently have a specific image in mind when you begin to write a story? You are no doubt aware of Faulkner's comment that his inspiration for* The Sound and the Fury *was the mental picture of a young girl with dirty underpants climbing a tree to peek through a window. Do you sometimes start a story with nothing more than an image like this?*

MASON: Yes, a story can come from as simple a provocation as that. Then a writer would have to find out where the story is going—who the girl is, why her underwear is dirty and where she has been.

Q: *Or at the beginning of your own story "Shiloh," why is Norma Jean lifting weights?*

MASON: Yes, I just started that story right there. I had no idea where it was going. I had two minor characters, C. W. and Betty, in another story called "Graveyard Day." I asked myself what C. W. and Betty would be like when they went home. As I was thinking up some things about them, they evolved into Norma Jean and Leroy. They weren't what I thought of originally at all. They were nothing like C. W and Betty.

Q: *I guess "Shiloh" has now become your most frequently anthologized story. Why did you choose it as the title story for your collection?*

MASON: That story had gotten more attention, and people seemed to like it best.

Q: *I teach that story frequently, but you probably don't want to comment on some of the questions my students ask.*

MASON: Oh, they want to know if Norma Jean killed herself?

Q: Exactly.

MASON: Isn't that strange. Only students ask that. You can't read the story that way because there's nothing to support the idea of suicide. Her life is on the way up. Isn't it funny that a lot of students ask that question. A grownup wouldn't.

Q: Despite your open endings, do you think that many of your troubled characters, like Norma Jean, will ultimately find solutions to their problems?

MASON: Some people, like those in my hometown, would probably say that my stories are very pessimistic. But my attitude toward life is not negative. I'm very hopeful about people like Norma Jean.

Q: The story "Detroit Skyline, 1949" is about the only one of your stories that is not contemporary in its time setting. Was Peggy Jo in that story a kind of precursor of Sam in In Country? *In sending Peggy Jo on a trip to Detroit in the years shortly after World War II, were you also writing about her growing awareness of the social changes produced by this earlier war?*

MASON: That was not my intention when I started writing the story. To reveal all the secrets, the story was motivated by a very slight memory of a similar trip my mother took me on. On the trip I was captivated by the television set, and the story was originally called "The Television Set." These faint first memories of television were the springboard for the story. Since I didn't remember the trip well, in order to find out what was going on in Detroit in the summer of 1949, I got two weeks' worth of microfilm of the *Detroit Free Press.* I found stories about a city bus strike during the time in which I had been there. Lo and behold, I found all this other stuff going on—polio epidemics, the Communist scare in Detroit. The Alger Hiss trial was also taking place, but I didn't work that in because it was too much. Then I invented the story about the mother's miscarriage. I can't say that I intended to write a story about post–World War II traumas. I was just trying to write about television, but it turned out to be about something else. I had a lot of fun with it, but my intention has very little to do with what comes out.

Q: Can you comment on your inspiration or your process of writing with respect to some of your other works?

MASON: I've realized that in most of my stories I start with surface details— something I've noticed, a compelling image, some description. I rarely begin with the emotional center of the story. For example, a new story of mine,

"Bumblebees," is about three women living on a farm together. One of the women lost her husband and daughter in a car wreck three years before. The emotion of the story resides in that situation and those facts. However, I began writing the story with descriptions of the farm and details from nature—bumblebees, fields, a garden. All of the raw material I had was of that sort. It was stuff grounded in reality, in my experience. I started with that and felt my way into the story. So I had certain physical details I knew about, but I had to make up entirely the emotional conflict, their lives, their situation. When I have tried to start with a strong emotional situation—say, a woman whose ex-husband kidnaps their child—I can't find the facts that will fill out that premise. I have to go at it the other way around. So my stories are surprises to me; they lead me, I suppose, into the subconscious. I suppose I'm simply saying what Eudora Welty once said about how in writing you go from the particular to the general, and not the other way around.

Q: *One of the stories that you did not include in your collection is the piece called "Fan City."*
MASON: It was originally called "Fan Mag." The editors changed my title.

Q: *This story, set in New York City, is not rooted in the places you seem most comfortable writing about. Is that why you omitted it?*
MASON: Well, it just wasn't as good as some other stories.

Q: *Speaking of the sense of place in southern literature, William Styron has commented that "the Old South has disappeared—the aspect of it that made it so compelling and dramatic as a source. The enormous tension between the races and the intense parochialism and sense of family roots, community, and religion—these things have become the victims of attrition . . . Younger writers like Barry Hannah and Bobbie Ann Mason do capture a flavor of the South, but I don't know if it makes much difference any longer, whether the voice is so distinctive as to make it peculiarly Southern anymore."[1] Could you respond to this observation?*
MASON: I'm not so sure those qualities of the Old South were all that terrific, and I really don't know what Styron means but it sounds like a lament for the good old days. I'm not nostalgic for the past. Times change and I'm interested in writing about what's now. To me, the way the South is changing is very dynamic and full of complexity. There's a certain energy there that I don't notice in other parts of the country. It comes out of an innocent hope of possibility.

My characters have more opportunities in their lives than their parents did, and even the parents are more prosperous in their old age than they ever were before. That is what's changing the face of the South—that more and more people are getting in on the good life. But many are still left out; the blacks still have not gotten their share, so I wouldn't say that tension is gone.

Q: *Some reviewers of your stories have commented that the individual pieces are brilliantly done but that the themes are always much the same. Do you think that is a just criticism?*
MASON: No, Nabokov had the same one or two themes. That's all you've got; that's all any author has.

Q: *Are you currently writing anything strikingly different from your past work? Do you want to?*
MASON: Of course I would like to, but I don't know if I have the resources. I'm working on more stories, but I don't think of writing in any kind of formal or experimental terms. I think more in terms of subject matter because I have to have some material to fuss over and work through in order to make discoveries about craft. I try to find out what's going on in people's lives. There are whole realms of experience in the particular setting that I'm attracted to writing about—experience that I don't know much about. I'm simply trying to get more into those worlds I don't know. For instance, I understand a lot about what's happening emotionally to the older generation of farm people I'm so familiar with, but it's vital to me to discover what's going on with their grandchildren. For all of them, the oldest to the youngest, the world is opening up in both promising and disappointing ways.

Q: *I trust we can look forward to more fine stories in which you explore those promises and disappointments.*

Note

1. Quoted in Georgann Eubanks, "William Styron: The Confessions of a Southern Writer," *Duke,* Vol. 71, no. 1 (1984), 4.

Reynolds Price ❧ 1988

ASHBY BLAND CROWDER

"Waiting at Dachau" is the fourth story in a volume of Reynolds Price's short stories entitled Permanent Errors *(1970) and is grouped with three other stories—"The Happiness of Others," "A Dog Death," and "Scars"—which together constitute the first division of the book, "Fool's Education." This "fool" is an American living in England working on a university degree and on becoming a writer. The fool, Charles Tamplin, is involved in a relationship with a girl named Sara, and some years after the Third Reich they visit together the Nazi concentration camp at Dachau.*

In a recent visit to Hendrix College in Arkansas, Reynolds Price entertained questions from students and faculty on "Waiting at Dachau." In his opening remarks, Price said, "I had visited myself the remains of the concentration camp at Dachau in the summer of 1956. So there was a gap of thirteen years between my seeing the place and having a strong emotional response to it and having those emotions mingle with a number of other emotions and observations in my life and produce this story." This comment led to the following question, even though in his essay "To the Reader" at the beginning of Permanent Errors, *the author had denied that the stories were autobiographical:*

QUESTION: *Is "Waiting at Dachau" about yourself?*
PRICE: Well, let's say something I think is really basic to understanding all literature, certainly all literature written in the first person. That is, be very careful that you don't assume that the "I" in any story, novel, or poem is the author. Charles Tamplin is by no means me. I just told you that I went to Dachau. I did in fact myself spend four years in England doing graduate work at Oxford—three years doing graduate work just on my own. So Charles Tamplin will embody a number of things that I've thought and no doubt a number of things that I've felt, but you'll have to trust me when I say that he

---

Originally published as Ashby Bland Crowder, "'Waiting at Dachau': An Interview with Reynolds Price," Vol. 26, no. 2 (1988), 12–26.

really is a very different person from me. I don't necessarily subscribe to everything he says, especially not in this story. He's obviously operating in this story under a strong head of quite intense personal emotional steam; and I may, myself, in 1969, have associated myself with some of that steam. But it's been thirteen years ago, and I would find it very hard to remember how much of that material I actually would have subscribed to at the time. I think, when Tamplin deals with that passage about the de Wieks, that he feels that theirs is somehow an enviable and emblematic human relationship; and I, myself, in that particular case, I think, would sympathize with that. I don't think one ought to try to provide any recipes for any two human beings as to how they conduct their own particular emotional relationship, aside from hoping that they won't cause each other unavoidable pain. I think very few human beings are placed, thank God, in the appalling situation in which those people found themselves being transported toward certain destruction. One wouldn't look at them and say everyone should behave like this because, luckily, very few people are ever going to be faced with anything quite that appalling, certainly not that dramatic. It's a very moving episode, and I remember myself when I first encountered that particular passage in some excerpts from a book about Anne Frank in *Life* magazine years ago, I remember being very moved by it. It obviously stuck in my mind so that when I was writing this story I went back and tracked that passage down and quoted it in my own story.

It's been a long time since I've written or read the story, but I think that obviously its major theme is a tormented set of questions about what love is between human beings, what it can be, what sorts of strains it can take and really how the great holocaust experience reflects upon our own cliches about love. I think Charles in the story asks a number of questions about what happens to what we call human love, romantic love, love between men and women or parents and children, when love appears to conflict with individual survival.

One of the most appalling things that one reads in all the vast literature about the Holocaust—whole libraries of appalling, moving books on the subject—one of the most appalling things of all is that thing which I think I included or alluded to in the story: the fact that in the late years of the war, the Nazis were no longer keeping alive any mothers who arrived in the camps with young children because they had a policy of immediately exterminating children; and if they took the child from the mother, the mother then became just a bad prisoner—she was so unhappy. So if you arrived with a baby, they immediately took you and your baby to the chamber, straight from the train to the gas chamber. There are horrible stories of mothers who would disguise themselves and run away from their children just so they could stay alive.

It's absolutely irrelevant to judge anybody in that situation. It would be the height of absurdity for you and me to sit here in this nice parlor and say those women did something wrong because very, very few human beings have ever been faced with that ghastly a choice. It asks all sorts of questions about what happens to something even as allegedly instinctive as maternal love when you find out that that occurred numbers of times, when maternal love ran in direct opposition to the possibility of personal survival. The whole story is a kind of elaborate condensed meditation on what a human experience like the concentration camps does to all of our official views about love and human relations.

Q: Can you tell us what Sara was thinking, why she didn't want to go into the camp?
PRICE: Anybody got any ideas? I don't want to be coy about this, but I'm not sure that I have the complete answer to that. You might read the other stories in this series called "A Fool's Education"; the title is purposely ambiguous: does it mean you take a fool and educate him into something else, or does it mean you educate somebody to be a fool?—which obviously a great deal of education is dedicated towards doing. I myself would vote for the fact that Charles gets a lot of the foolishness educated out of him, not by academic institutions but by his own experience. My guess is that, if you've read what comes before about Tamplin and Sara and then read this, you're faced with several things, one of which is that Sara realizes that Charles is setting this up as some kind of elaborate emotional test, that they really are going to do this pretty awful thing. At the time they go into Dachau—does the story give the date? I said I was there in '56. I think they're there in '55 or '57, a year before or a year after I was there for some reason. At that particular time it was only twelve years after the liberation of the camp, twelve years after the whole world found out really what was going on there. I myself was twelve years old at the time the camp was liberated, so I have vivid memories of suddenly seeing in *Life* magazine or in the newsreels the piles of corpses being pushed together by bulldozers. That was really the absolute first time that any civilians in the western world knew that the concentration camps existed, or at least existed as dead ends for that many Jews and gypsies or other "impure" elements.

I should have brought along my little leaflet that I found in a Holiday Inn day before yesterday. There was an American Nazi group spending the night in the local Holiday Inn in their Nazi uniforms with their swastikas on; and they left little leaflets around the tables, about racial purity and the necessity of exterminating the Jews from around the world, and so on. It's hardly an idea that ended in 1945, as you probably know. This was a group of people in Idaho; I'm happy to say they weren't from Arkansas, but they might get some sympathy in certain parts of Arkansas, as they might get some sympathy anywhere in America for that matter.

Anyway, Charles and Sara were there at a time when the camp was still a kind of physically raw place. The story talks about the fact that literally nothing had been done to prettify it or make it into a kind of national park. Have any of you been to Dachau? A number of American tourists who go to Germany now—especially to Munich, which is only a few miles from Dachau—take a little side trip over there. I myself haven't been since 1956 and don't want to go, but I gather from what students of mine have told me and from photographs I've seen that it has indeed been decorated quite a lot. All sorts of museums have been built, and statues have been put up, flowers have been planted. That's only natural; but at the time I was there it looked essentially the way it looked on the day of liberation, except the bodies were all gone. So you just saw this absolutely stark—and as I say in the story—this surprisingly small thing. You always think that if you hear of some great event, you're going to go there, and the place is going to be physically as grand and frightening as the whole thing has become in your imagination. In 1956 Dachau looked like a little Arkansas brick factory. You couldn't imagine that millions of people had passed through.

So I think Charles in his own rather dramatic, poetic way, has built this thing up in his mind as some sort of symbolic testing of their own love. Sara knows him well enough to resent that, to resent that romanticism in him: and really when the crunch comes, when they get there to the parking lot, she's just independent enough to resist it. It's not some elaborate plan that she's made to stage a refusal at that point; it's just a spontaneous choice. Charles reads it quite correctly. He reads it as some sort of symbolic rejection of their whole relationship, and it does become a sort of watershed that is the end of their relationship. They go on—though actually there is one story that comes after this in the series, called "Happiness of Others"—they go on to England and part there but have essentially parted for good at Dachau, which is what the story says; it invites Sara back, it begs her back, but there's no indication that she's coming.

I just heard yesterday morning on the news channel at the Holiday Inn (everything seems to be happening at the Holiday Inn this week) that the

Red Cross now estimates that about 2,500 Arabs were murdered three or four weeks ago in Beirut, in those massacres. I suppose that's the single most dramatic example of mass murder that we've had that has been widely publicized; apparently there have been other mass murders in the years since 1945—in Indonesia, in Cambodia, in other places—but they've been bottled up and kept from the public eye. But just watching the clean-up operation from those Palestinian camps on the evening news, I've been tremendously reminded of childhood memories of seeing American soldiers with gas masks on, removing rotting bodies around German camps. It's a very heavy piece of information to acquire—that people quite easily do this to one another. I mean the American Nazis were sitting in the Holiday Inn, less than a mile from here, three days ago. I first walked in for breakfast, and I saw these five men sitting at a round table, like the highway patrol. They had on blue uniforms, and they had some kind of round shoulder patches, and I said, "Oh, highway patrolmen," and I sat down. They were all laughing and joking with the waitress. They just seemed like, you know, your Uncle Jim. Most of them, five of the six of them, were men in their late fifties, early sixties, kind of broken-down looking, normal guys that might have worked at the hardware store or sold groceries. They had with them this one rather dazzlingly handsome typical Nordic boy about twenty-two, with blond hair, flashing blue eyes. He was obviously their genetic showpiece specimen. And the name of the group was the Aryan Nation. But surely this was what it would have looked like if you had seen a group of the men who manned Dachau; they would have just been sitting around having coffee or beer, joking with the waitress. They weren't monsters in any obvious way. They were somebody's parents. Somebody loved them. They were somebody's husbands. The great political philosopher Hannah Arendt, whom some of you may know, wrote a controversial book about the concentration camps and one of the great officials of the Holocaust—a man named Adolph Eichmann, a book called the *Banality of Evil*. And that was her whole point, that these people weren't satanic; there wasn't smoke and fire coming out of their eyes. They were just somebody's husband, and somebody's daddy. They were probably good to their wives and dogs. The chief commandant at Auschwitz, the worst of the camps in terms of the number of people that were exterminated, was a great lover of poetry and German music, and he would sit around and play his Mozart and Bach records while the odor of burning bodies was coming into the little house where he and his wife and children lived on the edge of the camp, where six million people were exterminated in about a three-year period.

It's very easy to do. Something just clicks in people's heads. You just turn a little key one turn, and absolute madness sets in and becomes extremely difficult to stop. And when that happens, obviously this elaborate social system of human relations and love that we can sit around the parlor and think is the most important thing in the world, the most important thing in our lives—it vanishes that fast, and people have it no more than dogs in the yard have it, or foxes in the woods. I knew a number of people when I was in graduate school, mostly Poles, who had refugeed to England at the end of the war. They had been in the camps, and I remember once in typical adolescent fashion asking what the sex life in the camps must have been like because I thought, well God, it must have been really orgiastic. And my friend said there was absolutely no sex. He said it was the first thing people stopped doing. Because, he said, if you've been starved for two weeks, sexuality is the first thing that goes; and apparently it's true—if you know anything about behavioral psychology. Hunger becomes the absolute total obsession of your life. Getting food is all you think about. And he said, in fact, it was horribly comic because every now and then the Nazis would let them have Red Cross packages that had come through, and you'd get a few chocolate bars and a few concentrated granola bars, and people would get a quick surge of energy. For a day or two there would be all these horror-comic sex scenes around the camp, and then very quickly everybody would lapse back into appalling fatigue. They really thought about nothing but how to get the next potato peeling out of the garbage bin.

Some interesting experiments were done during the war in America on prisoners in, I think, Montana. They took volunteer prisoners and subjected them to hunger, virtual starvation; and they found that very quickly prisoners would take down pin-up girls off the walls and start putting up pictures of steaks, salads, and things out of *Better Homes and Gardens* dinner menus.

Q: What is the scene in which Charles and Sara discuss the "old chalk fingerprint" in the sky ("the great spiral galaxy in Andromeda") supposed to suggest about them—that they (and all of us) are a part of nature?
PRICE: That and the opposite of that, which is the standard thing you say upon looking up at the stars—"Gee, what am I so upset about my own little problems for, when the whole thing is this big and this grand and this mysterious and this inscrutable? Why am I so depressed about, you know, what Bobby Jo said to me today in the cafeteria?" That, added to the fact that we are all to some extent literally the same *thing* as the galaxy in Andromeda; we're

made out of the same hydrogen and oxygen and carbon atoms; and, I think, any kind of satisfactory human relationship probably needs to have some sort of, not necessarily conscious, awareness of those facts. Yet, in the end, Charles appears to go beyond all that rationalization and all that intellectualization and just says, "Sara, come back." What the hell, what's the point of depriving ourselves of the consolation that personal commitment and personal loyalty can bring, the sort of consolation that presumably the de Wieks got out of being who they were to one another.

And there's nothing at all implicitly or explicitly anti-Semitic in saying that one of the amazing things about the Holocaust is how easy it was for Hitler to bring it off. Certainly the Western European powers and the United States made it a lot easier, for various complicated political reasons that you may or may not know anything about (very fascinating and horrible reasons). But the Jews of central and eastern and Western Europe also made it much easier for Hitler to bring it off by their own refusal to believe that Hitler really meant what he said, that he was really going to do this, and by their refusal to get out. If these guys at the Holiday Inn suddenly became a political majority, would those of us who were running contrary to their program, would we pack up our toothbrushes and our favorite two pieces of clothing and leave the United States and emigrate to Canada or Mexico? It's unthinkable that somebody's going to pull a truck up to your house and haul you away and convert you to ashes just because you're a Jehovah's Witness or a homosexual or a Jew or a black or a gypsy, or whatever the particular program happens to condemn as being racially impure. That's what was happening.

Q: *Would you explain about Sara's writing on the mirror?*
PRICE: That's something that happened to me. I once was with a friend at a bar, and the friend was telling me about the serious problem he was having. The problem didn't involve me; it was a problem with another relationship in his life. He got up and went to the men's room and came back; and half an hour later I got up and went to the men's room, and I saw in his handwriting (he had very distinctive, unmistakable handwriting)—I saw that written on the bathroom wall, and I couldn't resist putting it in the story. So I don't quite know what it's doing there except obviously Sara is at a very serious emotional crisis in her own life. She's deciding whether or not to give up on this relationship that has been the center of her young adult life to this point; and at this particular time in America, the '50s, it was much more fashionable for people that age, in their early twenties, to go steady and get engaged and

have . . . I mean the fashion's beginning to come back but certainly through the '60s and '70s relationships of that sort weren't nearly as common as they are now—these very intense engagement experiences when people were in great detail planning the next sixty years together in their neat little house and their little children and their little car and little jobs and what not. So she's making a very crucial decision that she thinks is of the greatest importance to her future life, and she just phrases that prayer. I don't really mean to imply that she has some sort of mystical experience in the ladies' room. She's just feeling very intense, and she's probably had a little wine, and she just writes it. Do women's bathrooms have a lot of graffiti in them?

Q: Could you comment further on Sara and her relationship with Charles?
PRICE: If you'd read the other stories about them, you'd see that the relationship has altered. She's begun to feel pretty rejected. She's tried to catch up with what seems to be his rejection of her . . . I think she would have been much more willing to try to hold on for the whole trip than he.

If you really want to read a full expansion on a relationship of this sort, you might look at my novel published a few years ago called *The Source of Light*. It really is very much about a young man and a young woman a lot like Charles and Sara. They have different names, but I really think in many ways "Waiting at Dachau" is a kind of sketch for the later novel, *The Source of Light*. It's set in virtually the same time period, and is about very intense, thoughtful young people.

Q: Why do Charles and Sara travel to Dachau in the first place?
PRICE: I don't think they necessarily planned it to produce any great discoveries. Charles is a graduate student in England. Sara has come over there to visit him. They take a trip, just what you do when you're in Europe: you sort of get in a car or bus; you ride around and look at the great scenes. Charles has this rather bizarre idea that they should go and look at this one rather awful scene; most people would not include Dachau on their travel itineraries any more than you would include the State electric chair on your itinerary around Arkansas. Few people would. But Charles did that. As the trip moves along—I don't know whether you've noticed or not, but nothing in the world is harder on a relationship than traveling together; it's the ultimate test of any relationship from friendship to roommates to romance. Sara and Charles experience a lot of that travel abrasion. And then poor old Charles—he's a fool—decides to stage this one big showdown—the showdown at the Dachau corral. Sara

realizes that he is trying to stage a showdown, and she just says, "I'm not going to play. This is some kind of elaborate romantic game. The woman is supposed to be the romantic, and you're the man, and you're not supposed to be; but you've gone a little bananas, and I'm not going to play your game." Then she regrets it and realizes that she's rained on his parade, and that's why that very peculiar scene follows when they're in the restaurant and the lion bites her, which again is something I really saw. Could I ever have invented anything like that? I was once in a restaurant on the French Riviera; and some men came in with a lion, exactly as described in the story. "Does any- body want to have their picture taken with a lion?" This one woman, not with our party, said "sure" and picked it up and held it in her arms; the flashbulb went off, and the lion chomped into her shoulder, and she was absolutely magnificent. The men who owned the lion went absolutely haywire. They were screaming. The woman stood there and kept stroking the lion until he finally turned her loose. She had this row of teeth prints and blood streaming down her arm.

You know if you're a writer, you go through life like a magnet, or an elec- trically charged comb: all sorts of little bits of paper or metal filings start clinging to you; and when you come to write something as complicated as this, you suddenly think, "Oh, there's that whole lion business—that was in- teresting, that was weird. Suppose that happened now in this story."

I like Sara a lot. She's a very strong, admirable character. And obviously so does Charles. She's much stronger and more realistic than he—which is frequently the case in male-female relations. It is our stereotype that men are supposed to be strong, rational people, and women are the weak romantics. But it's almost invariably the other way around, I find. And Charles comes to realize it years later when he writes the story and presumably sends it to her, wherever she is. Maybe I should write a sequel to it. I always wonder what happened, what she does. Does she require a condominium in Florida and live happily ever after? Presumably Sara has gone on about her own life in the interval. Charles certainly doesn't tell us at the end of the story where Sara's been. That's one of the unspoken messages that the story contains—that is, again, that Charles is continuing to think of the world entirely as it relates to him and not as it relates to Sara or anybody else.

Q: Does Sara really want him to read what she has written on the wall?
PRICE: I never thought of that. It's a very interesting idea. Anybody else think

that? I guess it's one of those unisex bathrooms, isn't it, in the story? I forgot. Isn't it called, *Damen*? Why does he go in there?

Q: She won't come out. She locked the door. So does Sara intend for him to read the message on the wall?
PRICE: How do you vote? I vote that she really doesn't do it for that reason. I don't think she's that self-conscious. If she wanted to tell him, she would tell him—not that she'd go through this charade of making him come in the ladies' room to see it on the wall. She probably would be rather embarrassed if she knew he had even seen it. It was almost an admission of weakness on her part that she wouldn't have wanted to concede to him. She's tried to seem very strong at this point. Don't forget she's a bit of a pioneer for this period. This isn't exactly the way women were supposed to behave in the 1950s. Quite a pioneer. But not unique. There were plenty of big tough women around, but their role was expected to be rather different from this.

Q: Did you yourself have such a relationship with such a girl when you were at Oxford?
PRICE: This story really isn't—I'm not denying, I'm not lying to you—this story really isn't about any relationship in my own life. But I traveled in Europe at this period with a young woman that I was very devoted to, and for various reasons we never really made anything permanent of the relationship. I've only recently recontacted her, and she now is crippled with multiple sclerosis after all these years. It would be interesting to know what a character like Charles would do if faced, years later, with a person of Sara's intelligence and practical courage—if faced with someone like that who had taken a terrific tragedy in her own life. Oh, but Charles is such a self-absorbed person; it's not a lot of fun to write about him for long at a time.

We just saw him through a bad period in his life; he probably got a lot nicer later. I mean, most people between the ages of fourteen and twenty-five ought to be chloroformed and kept in a closet. It's the most awful period of your life. Let me assure you; you will get a lot nicer. You will enjoy yourself a lot more once you get into your thirties and begin to accept your limitations. You finally say, "Look, I'm not gonna do XYZ, PQL, and T." And you scratch those off the list of priorities. I'm not very good at C and J, and I'm probably OK at B and M. You begin (unless you're nuts) to get much more realistic about what your priorities are and what you've got the time and the energy and possibility of doing. Charles and Sara both are still in a kind of post-adolescent period, which our society, white middle-class American society, has agreed to allow people to stay in until they're thirty, don't forget—often until they're fifty. But it's kind of amazing when you think that my grandparents got married when they were sixteen and eighteen, and that was just a perfectly ordinary time to get married. Working-class people finished a few years of school, got married, and started working ten hours a day—if you were a man—and twenty-four hours a day if you were a woman raising children. Only in the late 1950s did America agree that people were allowed to be children until thirty. Include the '60s in that. Society agreed that middle-class people could be irresponsible until they're thirty.

In many ways society really did betray an awful lot of young people by leading them to believe that. And Charles and Sara are in their early twenties, going through all these intense, rather humorless trials. I think one of my challenges in these stories was to see if I could write interesting stories about people in what is really the most uninteresting period in human life—adolescence and post-adolescence. If you really think about it, there are almost no good novels about adolescence. There's *Huck Finn*; there's *The Catcher in the Rye*; there are one or two others. But it's extremely difficult to write an extended work of fiction about people, let's arbitrarily say, between the ages of fourteen and thirty. And I think it's primarily because they're like Charles and Sara. They're humorless; they're into all this "Who am I? What am I going to do? I am the most important in the universe, I and my feelings and my desire." I always cringe a bit when I know that some young author is attempting a novel about being eighteen or twenty-four. In fact, I think really your chances of writing something good about actual adolescence, say thirteen to twenty, are better than one about the early twenties. In our particular society, anyway, the most difficult thing of all is young adults like Charles and Sara. I don't mean to say that your lives aren't interesting and worthwhile. But to a bystander, which we always are when we read a story, they're not interesting. They're just very boring.

Q: *Did you ever think about what it was Charles was studying at Oxford?*
PRICE: This story doesn't say? I'm trying to think if this one does, or one of the others. I just assume that since he's very interested in becoming a writer that he's studying English literature in some form. He'd have been studying language in some form or other, either English or a foreign language; or he

could have been studying something like history. He wouldn't have been studying physics or higher math.

Q: You suggest that their life together is boring?
PRICE: I don't want to be too hard on them. Most people's idea of what life together is going to be like is incredibly dull, don't you think?

Q: Oh, yes.
PRICE: If you listen to young people—they all start writing each other Valentines about our lives together, or future together. You want to say, "What will you be doing?" And if you really stop and realize that it's going to be a lot of PTA meetings and TV and TV dinners, then you might begin to say, "Are you sure you want to do this?"

If people could see—I'm not trying to discourage anybody, but luckily most of us cannot predict the future with any certainty or more than one of us would jump out the window in cold winter before breakfast.

We're a country absolutely infected by romanticism; our country is romanticism's greatest victory. Hallmark cards can tell you how healthy romanticism is. Hopelessly unreal ideas. The divorce rate in America is the continuing and appalling testimony to the durability of the romantic myth. People go on with this dream of living together as easily as dogs, though we know that roughly fifty percent of all marriages end in the first three years. People are just standing right up to be mowed down one more time, like the Russian army on the Second Front in 1942. The human race would end if most people got terribly realistic about their chances for living together as easily as dogs.

So, it's not a very good time for marriage. And I think obviously if Charles and Sara came along in the '80s, their own particular views would be conditioned a lot, and Sara would be much more consciously a feminist. She's really a pioneer feminist as it is. But there's no political structure behind her. Gloria Steinem is not back there sending her manuscript newsletters and things that say, "Right on, Sara! Tell this sucker where to get off!" So she's doing this whole thing on her own, which is awfully brave of her, I think, and resourceful. But she really is out at the end of a long, lonely string. She probably would have had very little support from her parents in being as independent as she is. She's expected to get herself a husband who's going to keep her in new clothes, so that Daddy and Mama could sign off and get their little retirement house in Florida.

Q: What was the experience of visiting Dachau like for you?

PRICE: Pretty powerful. It's one of the top five most powerful places I ever visited. One of the strange things, I think, about scenes of great suffering—have any of you ever been to a place where there has been an enormous amount of concentrated suffering over a substantial period of time? There're not a lot of such places in America. God knows there's plenty of suffering; but America tends to be a violent country and, if there's going to be suffering, it tends to happen fast. Somebody gets lynched in an hour, or we mow down X number of Sioux Indians in a five minute encounter. We don't tend to put people in a single place and keep them there. You can say slavery went on for 300 years, but you probably can't quote me one single place where X number of slaves were made to suffer for X number of years.

There's only one place I can think of—it's in the South, Andersonville Prison in Georgia. If you ever go to Americus, Georgia, ride out about ten miles in the country and see the National Cemetery at Andersonville. It was a concentration camp kept by the Confederates. I've forgotten how many people died at Andersonville but far too many, maybe eight or nine thousand prisoners (northern prisoners were kept there). It was not maintained as a conscious extermination place the way the Nazi camps were. It was just largely the result of incredible mistakes. The Confederates got all these people in one place, and the sanitation conditions got so appalling. They were losing the war, and they couldn't feed or take care of these prisoners, so enormous numbers of them died. My point is, if you go to something like Dachau years later or Andersonville or any one of the battlefields of the First World War, almost invariably the scene now has the most incredible peacefulness to it. The birds are singing and the flowers are blooming, and you think: this is unimaginable. What I felt at Dachau is what Charles feels: something's all wrong. He'd read about this place as being the scene of all this concentrated suffering, and yet it seems like the world's nicest picnic ground. Andersonville is one of the loveliest places you'd ever want to go to now. Yet all the photographs hanging in the museum at Andersonville show this appalling hogwallow that it was in 1865 when men were dying like flies.

Q: What is the significance of "waiting" in the title?

PRICE: Well, there's got to be some significance if I put it there, but I'm not sure at the moment I can exactly remember. I think what Charles really means is that in a sense what he's saying in the story is "I'm still waiting. I'm still waiting *for you* to enter this commitment with me." And you see from the end of the story that Charles has changed and matured some, but the old Charles is still very much there. The fact that he calls the story "Waiting at Dachau" means that he still is clinging to this very romantic notion that love is this very titanic commitment—total loyalty, total suffering, total togetherness— whereas Sara has a much brisker, more realistic notion of what they're up to.

Note

1. By the time Price wrote his introduction to the stories published in *Permanent Errors* (New York: Atheneum, 1970), the memories were fifteen years old, as he says (p. vii).

PART III

1990s

Doris Betts ～ 1996

W. DALE BROWN

"I have never found life, faith, nor art really so neat. I continue to outlive many days surveying this world with the suspicion that Deus has really absconded. With the funds."

Doris Betts is an elder, a Sunday school teacher, and part-time organist in the Presbyterian Church. A former chairperson of the faculty at the University of North Carolina-Chapel Hill, she has taught in the English Department for more than twenty-five years. From 1978 to 1981, she served on the Literature Panel of the National Endowment for the Arts and since 1980 has occupied the position of Alumni Distinguished Professor of English. Mother, grandmother, and wife, Professor Betts lives on a farm near Pittsboro, North Carolina.

Since 1954 she has produced three collections of short fiction and four novels. Her most recent novel, Souls Raised from the Dead, *was published in 1993. Betts has been accused of being a gloomy writer because she is preoccupied with the spiritual and with death. She likes William Saroyan's comment, "I began writing in order to get even on death." "That's not a bad reason, really," say Betts, but her Calvinist roots lead her to more than the predictable bleakness of many contemporary novelists. "Deny the metaphysical and the trivial will triumph," says one of Betts's characters, and, although she mourns the visible emptinesses of our time, she continues to believe that "there is a moment in every day that the devil cannot find."*

I spent a day talking with Professor Betts about her writing and her faith and the ways in which they come together. What follows is some of that conversation.

QUESTION: *I remember a review you did in* Southern Quarterly *on an Anne Tyler novel. You said something about a missing philosophical dimension in her work. You wish she had done something more with spirituality?*

Originally published as W. Dale Brown, "Interview with Doris Betts," Vol. 34, no. 2 (1996), 91–104.

BETTS: But she isn't going to. She has a Quaker outlook on people and that will be maintained, but she doesn't want to get into theology and philosophy. And in a way I suppose that's prudent.

Q: *But you do get into theology and philosophy?*
BETTS: Might as well.

Q: *David Holman has an essay in which he says, "Doris Betts characters are always asking unanswerable questions." Serious writing by Christians often, I fear, shies away from the questions. You say somewhere that "Christian spoils to a rancid adjective." Yet we speak of the Christian publishing industry, Christian bookstores, Christian novelists. A current phenomenon in the industry is Frank Peretti who has sold over two million copies of a book called* Piercing the Darkness. *It's full of demons and the like. Popular Christian fiction. And here you are, professing Christianity yourself, and toiling away at a career so very different from one like Peretti's.*

Over a year ago, I attended a church service at a small congregation meeting just off campus at the University of North Carolina. As it turned out, one of your colleagues was doing the sermon that day. I never did hear his name, but he talked about when you were chair of the faculty and Billy Graham had been invited to campus, and you became embroiled in a controversy over whether or not you should introduce Graham. The speaker quoted from the speech that you apparently did eventually deliver. And it was pungent with wonderful phrases. You spoke of "the tribe of Thomas" into which you were born, and I heard echoes of my own journey. So I began to say who is this person?
BETTS: I do remember that speech because it was a kind of turning point on this campus for me. I was not only faculty chairman but very conscious that in a secular, tax-supported institution where you represent everyone from the atheist to the agnostic to the Jew to the Hindu to the Christian to the nothing that some neutrality was required. Also I am not a particular fan of Billy Graham, although I liked him better after he had been here than I did before. He handled faculty questions superbly, I did not know he could do that. But two students came and told me that there was going to be this big thing in the gym, an audience of ten thousand, and they wanted people before he spoke each night, and this is the word they used, *to testify.* You can just imagine! At first I refused; I just shuddered. Then I began to feel guilty. Was this what Paul meant about being ashamed of Jesus Christ? Am I afraid to just come out and declare myself a Christian? Am I worried that I'll lose the respect

of the faculty that has elected me? This is not a campus in which one hears much about religious faith. I finally decided, "Well, if they won't introduce me as chairman of the faculty, if they will just allow me to be a person, a writer, I will do it."

And so I did. Everything that I had thought would happen didn't. On the contrary, two things happened that I found interesting. One was that I did talk about doubts and of being of the "tribe of Thomas," and I said that for me faith was always going to be a pilgrimage. And then Billy Graham arose and spoke after me about how he'd never had a doubt in his life. He had swept through the revolving doors and come out of the other side. It was a large crowd and people whom I had never thought about before would come up days after and say, "I'm a Baptist." It was as if everybody was revealing some shameful secret. That was not the reaction that I had expected. I'm sure there were people who disagreed and didn't like it, but for me it turned out to be a very rewarding experience. That little talk has been reprinted more than anything I ever wrote. Isn't that bizarre?

Q: *You have a character in* The River at Pickle Beach, *I think she's a nun, who says, "Deny the metaphysical and the trivial will triumph." Is that happening in contemporary fiction and contemporary culture?*
BETTS: I think that's a very great risk. It seems to me particularly evident in, say the brat pack writers of New York who have had big successes and are very young. They are extremely clever; not a thing wrong with those brains. But they don't really have very much to say and you can strike only so many poses. After you put them down, you have nothing left on your mind. As the years pass, such writers flicker and go out or they change. I read so much material like that; it's partly just a function of being young and clever and impressed with technique. If you decide to have something to say, you go at it in the worst way and have two people sit down at the bar and discuss life—incredibly boring. But I miss that quality because I'm not going to get it in eighteen year olds, and it is not popular now. So most of the reading that I enjoy doing comes from writers who at least are still questioning.

Q: *I seem suddenly to be coming upon a raft of writers who are, at least, interested in religious questions. Gail Godwin in* Father Melancholy's Daughter *or Anne Tyler with* Saint Maybe. *Even John Irving in* Owen Meany. *There does seem to be an interest in religious issues.*
BETTS: I think that's true. It seems to me that even if it's not conscious that

part of it may be a rebellion, not just against what I might call certain super-ficial fictions but against the prevailing mode of deconstructionist criticism. Sooner or later most writers begin looking at that and thinking, these people are not on my team. At the end of that is a real nihilism and it will all go down. I suspect that a great many writers who keep up with what's going on have begun to look again at deconstruction. How long can you go on telling stories if human beings don't matter? Biography has become almost more rewarding than fiction, because it appears to look at a whole life and perceive some kind of pattern. Some have made a determined effort not to perceive pattern, but I think that is hard to sustain. You can do with only so much razzle and dazzle.

Q: Then there's the romance novels.
BETTS: Yes. People are clearly reading those in the same way they look at television. They are looking to be entertained. Yet those books are almost pi-ously moral for all of the soft pornography in them. I mean the evil get their just desserts. It's pretty much like literature for children in which the villain is always punished and there's not much complexity. More interesting, I think, among writers who are serious, would be disagreements between writers like John Gardner and William Gatz. Gardner got so much flack over that book *Moral Fiction*, and, William Gatz, who is his good friend and a good friend of mine too, is a writer who really does think of writing the way you might think of musical painting. He puts together objects in a way that they haven't been put together before so that the glittering surface is an end in itself. He always says that what he remembers from reading a novel is not the content but the sentences. I think that's the real disagreement in writing. It's the same thing that has happened in art and in music; it just has been slower to get to literature because we still think words are what we use to make sense to one another. I'm inclined to think common sense is not willing to let go of that presumption. I do think that at the other end is an abyss and you need not write at all if you really think that through. But I like content wedded to an excellent style. I think content alone can be like it sounds, like the religious publishing you were talking about, like preaching to the choir. The sentences set your teeth on edge.

Q: I want to ask you about the Associated Reform Presbyterian background. "All the Right People." This is what you were born into and grew up in?
BETTS: Yes. And it's a shrinking denomination. The whole denomination is

20,000–30,000. It is not as fundamentalist as I perceived it when I was a re-
bellious adolescent. It is leavened by some kindness and by the songs, by the
good songs. At the same time, a woman may not be an elder. Its reading of the
Bible is still quite literal. You cannot say "I don't believe this is correct; where
did this come from?" You just may as well not bother with that. Hook, line,
and sinker. You have to take the whole thing.

*Q: Did you reach a stage where you began to wonder where Cain got his wife
and all that?*
BETTS: Yes, when I was very young in fact. At the same time, I was devout
and pious but up and down, up and down—worrisome. As soon as I got away
from it, I really went all the way away. I thought people like Jean Paul Sartre
and Albert Camus had the real answer.

Q: And now you've returned to "mainstream" Presbyterian?
BETTS: Yes. I'm in a small church near Pittsboro—fifteen miles south of Chapel Hill. Pittsboro is beginning to become a big community but it still is a
small southern town. There's maybe one other person in the church who has
anything to do with the university. Most of these people are farmers or people
who do public work or work in factories or are school teachers. They are not
fundamentalists in a way that would have driven me away. The Sunday school
class I find thoughtful. I find comfort in that asking questions is not thought
a falling away from grace. Nobody has to come up with exactly the same
answers. It's really a very loving, small church and I have been very happy
there. I'm very involved. I'm an elder, I'm a Sunday school teacher, I serve on
several committees, and I'm an organist, but I play poorly. In a small church
everybody has to pitch in. This Sunday is the opening of Sunday school for
the season. My job is to cut up fruit for the fruit bowl and help clean up the
dishes afterwards.

*Q: When you're writing and think of audience, do you think of some particular
person or group of people? Or from whom do you hear? Who writes you letters?*
BETTS: I've always agreed with Eli Evans, who says that when he wrote a
book, he had a mental jury for each book of maybe about twelve. They were
the people he wanted to please. Pleasing them would be enough. And he says
that these juries change. He wrote one book that involved his family history;
he wanted his mother and dad on that jury. But he removed them from the
next one. I've always had a sort of a jury. Hugh Holman is a professor here

whom I admire very much. He is someone with whom I've never discussed religious matters but I know that he is a Presbyterian, an elder, and that fact affected his work. He took that duty seriously. He was an excellent teacher. So on my jury there are people like him whose opinions I respect. Many of them are fellow writers but not all. Most of my family are not bookish. So if they are pleased and proud, it has to do with their affection for me. That's not to be sneezed at, but it's not the same thing. They're not critics. They think that if you get anything printed, it must be good. Would that it were true.

Q: *I'm interested in this business that you mention with Hugh Holman. What does being a Christian have to do with being a writer?*
BETTS: For me, the relationship increases. The book that I just sent off to Knopf [*Souls Raised from the Dead*] is more overtly engaged with these questions than anything I have written. Religion is literally in the plot. The book is full of moments when people actually go to church and bury their dead with ritual and argue in anger that God, if he is a loving God, should not have done this. I hope, however, that it is possible to read the book if you do not share my preoccupation with religion.

Increasingly, I find that someone I like is Graham Greene. And not only for the overt books like *The Power and the Glory*. Once you have listened to what he says, even the thrillers have those little moments when something ticks into place. Some guy stands in front of a shop window and there's a cross in it, and that's all he says. He just moves on. What I see in that is exactly what I think the book of Job says—that there really is no way to prove the existence of a Divine Creator who oversees the world. If you see it, you will see it. If you don't see it, no one can persuade you. It is not an argument in nature or events. It is an overlay that you place on things or don't. Once you place it, you are in an impossible situation for persuading modern people. So I write with that consciousness. My overlay is there, but I have in my books people who do not have that overlay, who do not see it and who will never see it. The ending of this new novel will seem to some to be ambiguous. In the end, the man's child has died, he is in despair, he has just rescued a child from a wreck. The reader is supposed to feel a sense of coming out of that despair. He rides on the way to the hospital to see if she is going to recover; he rides by his mother's house who seems to him a shining Christian who has always been convinced. He does not know that she is in utter despair. So he rides by this dark house, having made this turn in himself, and is convinced that she has just said her prayers for him and gone to sleep. But the reader knows something different. You can have either despair or hope. And the hope is not supported by very much evidence if you're going to approach it with the scientific method.

Q: *That reminds me of many of your characters—Homer Beam at the end of the "Astronomer," not having understood scripture very well. And the wonderful character in "The Very Old Are Beautiful" who has the sort of faith you're calling an overlay. There's so much in your books about faith and about living well. For me one of the most memorable images in* The River to Pickle Beach *is Jack Sellers watching the bird in the birdbath. The bird that comes and everyday, everyday, stops up there and looks and takes a long time before he sticks his foot in the birdbath. And you suggest that's the way a lot of us live our lives. And you have another character who talks about "trickling out our days," just living, as opposed to living well. John 10 stuff. Abundant life. Is that a big concern for you?*
BETTS: Yes. "Life in all its abundance"—that's a biblical quotation I love. That may be one of the differences between my attitude toward fiction and, say, Flannery O'Connor's way. She literally wanted at some moment in her story to have the eternal break through. There is a moment in which the veil goes thin and you see the pines and the sun breaks through as a wound. I guess I am not as confident as she. I also don't see that it breaks through very often. If it does break through for me, it's apt to be in something that some person does. I am more interested in the fact that, with this overlay, the pilgrimage can be now. We can be in route to the kingdom now, though that may be as much as we are expected to be able to do without apparent miracle, without apparent intervention, certainly without an intervention that you can justify to anyone else. I concentrate very much on redeeming the time, *this time*, this time is what we've got.

Q: *And, "Lord I believe, help thou mine unbelief." Isn't there a constant tension that you're very aware of?*
BETTS: Always, always. I don't think most modern people can proceed, if they are honest, without that tension under their feet. It's all about learning to balance that.

Q: *Jonathan Yardley says that you've never gotten the attention you deserve. But you seem, like Emily Dickinson, to enjoy your anonymity. Is there a way in which a writer like yourself, preoccupied with the meaning of things, winds up as the odd one out? I remember your characters saying things like "It's dying that really makes us wonder." Your characters are caught up in that sort of in-trospection. Are there ways in which your work is uncongenial to the publishing industry?*

BETTS: I don't think I'm as entertaining a writer for people who like excite-ment in short bursts, who like MTV, who like action. In fact, I read those books; I'm a great fan of detective stories; I think P. D. James is splendid. She has existentialist ideas herself. But again really good detective stories are stories about good and evil too—that's what intrigues you. But I'm not a flashy writer.

Well, this popularity business; it is a difficult thing. For example, right now most people doing an anthology, when they come to a woman's name, they really are looking for a story that illustrates feminist values. The publishing industry is all about relevance and relevance passes, it seems to me, very quickly. Like fads. I think that has a lot to do with many of the anthologies which focus on short-term issues. I have thought that perhaps this new nov-el, since it does deal with medical ethics, a hot topic to some degree, might plug in. But I'm not much interested in medicine; I'm only interested in the fact that human beings can find the same questions that Peter and John and Mark do.

Q: It seems to me, ironically, that your books are full of the big issues: race, for instance (who can forget Jube in The Scarlet Thread?*), and feminism (so many strong and interesting characters like Nancy in* Heading West*).*

BETTS: I don't know. But it's just as well. I have a busy enough life anyway. I do a lot of public speaking in my small pond here, and I find travel tiresome. I need time to read, and think and teach. That's more important.

Q: You have sold film rights to Heading West, *I think.*

BETTS: Yes. That was the only real money I have ever made. I built a house with the money from it; I am very happy with it. However, I was happier until I found out that long after I had taken my one-time amount, somebody, whose name is a legendary Mafia kind of name so you might as well have the legend, bought the rights and has been collecting a thousand dollars per week ever since without producing it. Don't ask me who is paying the money; it doesn't make any sense to me, except that Hollywood is another strange world. So I have the dubious realization that somebody is making more money off my novel by doing nothing with it than I am making at the University of North Carolina. This strikes me as so funny. Only in America, right?

Q: A film version of your short story, "The Ugliest Pilgrim," won an Academy Award?

BETTS: It was a good film. It sometimes shows up on educational television. It was made by a young woman who picked the story for feminism not religion. She picked it because Violet Karl, my character, is a young woman who takes her life into her own hands; that's what interested her and so the religious issues become stylized and a bit stereotyped. The young man that Violet meets at the Oral Roberts headquarters is extremely good looking, not at all as I had viewed it, and she lets Violet go off and leave her Bible on the desk, which Violet would have never done. That was a mistake. There are little things that bother me. But it's still a good film; I like to watch what film can do that words cannot. There is for example, a moment in there in which they do in one quick picture what took me a page to do. They have Violet looking at the Bible and it's underlined with yellow highlighter, and they have Monty looking at the motorcycle magazine, and he looks over and swaps the Bible for the magazine. He gives her the motorcycle magazine and takes the Bible, but he gets it upside-down at first. I thought at the time, "Yes, I like that."

Q: Another topic I'd love to hear you tackle is education. Your books take an occasional shot at education. In an interview last year with William Walsh, you talked about the secular education of your students. With Farley in The River to Pickle Beach, *you criticize the overspecialization of today's academy. How do you feel about your students and the job we are doing in higher education?*

BETTS: Well, higher education is hurting in so many ways that I don't want to contribute to the hurt. We're hurting financially, of course. Students are not as well read as they used to be maybe, and I don't want to just blame television. It's more the whole culture which has shifted away from reading to visualization. What I have objected to sometimes about higher education is that in an attempt to separate church and state, we have removed from our textbooks the religious impulse which actually caused a great many historical activities, literary works and so forth. I don't think that was the intent in the Supreme Court decision.

I teach a course in recent literature and it seems reasonable to include books that present various views of life, various philosophical answers. I include a religious one, not because that was a way of persuading someone, but to leave it out strikes me as false. I think we do our students a disservice, because often they see nothing about religious faith except the lowest common denominator. They see nothing but TV evangelists and fools and it doesn't occur to them that intelligent people might find this religious business worth living their lives by. We leave them to make up their own faiths and they do try. A touch of Buddhism, a touch of drugs, and the New Age stuff, but they really ought to have clearer options even if they say no. And they are entitled to say no. So that is one of my criticisms about American life. I think becoming so secular that you are anti-religious is not a favor to human beings in a very difficult world.

Q: *We've talked a lot about your taking religion seriously. At the same time there's a kind of suspicion of the church or the institution. I remember Bebe who becomes "an everythingist" and Rosa who can no longer believe in Romans 8:28. And Nancy, who says "nobody gets past age 13 and believes any of this anymore." The sense of the institution as numbing, as mere ritual. Do you feel some of that?*

BETTS: Yes. Yet, if it were all that I felt I wouldn't be in the church myself. I would be on the outside. It seems to me we have a responsibility to continue to make the church more of what it was meant to be. But I don't think my objections are any different from the ones Dostoevsky makes with his Grand Inquisitor. The church is a human institution; its hierarchy is human. We have this treasure in earthen vessels, so there is a great deal that is quite unsatisfactory about the church, and it has very little to do with what God said. Even so I don't know an institution any better. In a cold-blooded sense, as I say to students, who else are you going to get to marry you, to name your child, and to bury you? And why do you want the church to do it? Legalistic institutions do not substitute for our demands at those moments, those important moments, in our lives. We long to be allied with two things: with all the people who came before us—tradition—and also with our hope, so we can transcend life. The church is indeed often a failure, but we don't have anything any better. It isn't fair just to walk away from it.

Q: *We've talked about abundant life and paying attention. Do you mean to suggest that maybe God is making patterns that we're just not noticing?*

BETTS: Exactly. I do believe that. If you see it, you see it. It is biblical, of course. "He who has eyes to see, let him see."

Q: *That life is not just going anywhere but somewhere?*

BETTS: I think so. If it isn't, it's still better to hope for it and to put your energies into that.

Q: In "The Fingerprint of Style" you say, "I have never found life, faith, or art really so neat. I continue to outlive many days surveying this world with the suspicion that Deus has really absconded. With the funds." And many of your stories contain such preoccupations with the personality of God. You've said, for example, that the yearning for religious faith and the difficulty of having one nowadays is what "The Astronomer" is about, and The River to Pickle Beach *certainly has that feel. But all of the interviews I read seemed to avoid such questions. Do any of the critics of your work pick up on this at all?*

BETTS: Not much. A few at least address the question, but they address the question because I mentioned it and so they feel they have to. It seems obvious to me but evidently it is not obvious. What I'm saying to you about overlay pertains to what you read as well. If you expect it to be there, you will see it. But nowadays, if you are not obvious, if you're not writing for the Logos Bookstore, and I'm not so sure I want to get categorized that way, you can have a problem. And I don't think the job of literature is preaching. It's something else, but it is literature's job not to ignore the fundamental questions everybody lives with.

Q: Say a word or two about the new book; is it Souls Raised from the Dead?

BETTS: Yes. In fact I had already written it and chosen that title when I found a poem by Czeslaw Milosz which actually says, "Raise me from the dead." It's a wonderful poem about the death of the poet's mother who was apparently a victim of WWI, and he comes out of European suffering what for us is hearsay. He gives his poems and his faith such a resilience that he doesn't have to mention it; he exudes it. I got the title though from a note that was sent up to me when I was reading at the University in Charlotte. I didn't have a title then, but read a section in which a woman goes to Durham into this seedy neighborhood where they make keys and stuff. A woman sent up this note on the back of a supermarket slip. She suggested the title. She said there used to be a plate-glass window in Atlanta that has now been torn down for urban renewal but it had painted on it "keys made, palms read, souls raised from the dead." I thought—that's a gift—so I took it, and the fact that there was a poem with the same theme and almost the same phrasing was ideal.

Q: Is there a preacher in the novel?

BETTS: There's a preacher and I'm afraid he's a satiric figure—he's deaf, he's deaf.

Q: You're often very tough on preachers. I remember the one in Tall Houses in Winter. *Nasty man. And there's the preacher in "The Ugliest Pilgrim."*

BETTS: This one is bad too but it may not matter. You know what Percy does at the end of *The Second Coming*, with the priest who just says the same old things over and over again but it may not matter. O'Connor does that too and I have a priest who is deaf, but it may not matter.

Q: Like Greene's whiskey priest?
BETTS: Exactly. It may not matter; one may be a channel nonetheless. In the new book, the soul to be raised is the highway patrolman. I've always felt that to work with the big questions, you didn't have to use only archbishops and kings. Surely it can be done with middle-class workers, and farmers, and beauticians. If not, then the Good News is not true, and so he is a highway patrolman whose daddy was a shoe salesman. These are lower middle-class southern people who happen to live in Chapel Hill and don't understand the university at all and find the professors rather puzzling. It is his daughter who dies, and it is his despair we wonder over. Will it lift?

I've done several readings from the manuscript in different places, and it's amazing the people that come up out of the audience. They'll come up terribly upset, because something has been touched there. One is that they have either had or cannot get kidney transplants, one of the issues in the book. The other is that they have lost a child, often through an automobile wreck, and they confirm for me that nothing is worse. If you're ever going to have to forgive the universe for anything, that's the hardest, that you should live on with your child having been ripped away. They all say one thing: "Don't you have it just get better, it never gets better." I believe that and I don't want to be false to that, so I don't have him end up with a miracle because he's going to grieve all of his life. I do, however, believe it can be mitigated, that there is a context for that.

Q: There's lots of Bible in your books isn't there? I mean you talk about being "raised in a snow storm of biblical illusion."
BETTS: Aren't you glad you can read the Bible as literature now? I didn't know it was a gift; I thought it was a nuisance. Turns out to be very useful.

Q: I remember Homer Bean in "Astronomer" and his problems with scripture. And I remember that wondrous woman, Wanda Quincy, in "The Glory of His Nostrils" who memorizes Job.
BETTS: Yes. That's a story about abortion by the way. Look how quickly that got dated; when I wrote the story, abortion was illegal. And Homer's story goes back to a series of sermons I once heard on the book of Hosea.

Q: *I wonder if people notice that?*
BETTS: No. They never have and it doesn't matter to me. Until then I had never been able to read all the way through Hosea; I just didn't really like Old Testament prophets, especially the minor ones.

Q: *You say writing is "a gift the church gave you." Is that what you're referring to? A seriousness, an attitude toward words, taking words seriously?*
BETTS: Yes. Both the seriousness about what the issues were and the beauty of the language. I know I should like the *Good News Bible* but I never will. I will read it and it has its uses, but I will not prefer it. It has been translated by people with tin ears. It may be more accurate but it's not as beautiful.

Q: *You also frequently get into observations on popular culture. You refer somewhere to our culture as "an open wound." That reminded me of a Bobbie Ann Mason image: she labels it "an oil slick." Now you have Wal-Mart and Hardees and K-Mart in the South. Just like the rest of us. Is there some shift here that you mourn?*
BETTS: I do. But then I live far away from it. The farm is not more than two miles outside of Pittsboro, but it's really very far. You can't see the road but the airplanes come over. We have horses and dogs and trees and I find that essential. I don't believe I could live in New York City; I really think that the scale is weighted too much toward the human beings.

Q: *I have to talk about one of my favorite books—*Tall Houses in Winter. *I suspect you don't like it?*
BETTS: Dreadful. I'd like it burned. It's morbid. It's melancholy, and very young.

Q: *But there's something even there about love and how it validates your characters. And other stories like "The Ugliest Pilgrim" and "Astronomer," or even Jack and Bebe in* Pickle Beach. *If someone were to say to me, "What are Doris Betts's books about," I would have to say something about that.*
BETTS: I think that is true, but I would avoid saying that because it seems so sappy. There isn't any way to say that.

Q: *But does that suggest a religious core?*
BETTS: It seems to me it does, because if you don't have it grounded in something larger than touchy-feely California love, it goes sappy very quickly. It

goes sentimental. There's a big difference between sentiment and sentimental-
ity and it seems to me that that's the great risk when you say love conquers all.
It doesn't conquer all, but it is the best thing of all and, at least in Christianity,
it is rooted in the belief that that is the metaphor of the New Testament. God
is love.

Q: I'd almost call that optimism in your books.
BETTS: It is kind of an optimism. It's what I mean by hope. I mean not only
do we survive after this life, which to me is not crucial, but it would be nice
so I have a hope. But there is a hope in Christianity that comes through the
suffering. That does seem to me to be the message of the gospels, that on the
other side of it all, in fact overarching at every moment, there is optimism,
there is love, there is hope. That's the Good News after all. You don't get that,
or I don't get that, when I listen to the TV evangelists, and I don't want to
get it when I listen to the guy in the Glass Cathedral saying God Loves You.
I shrink and wince: I don't want a little brass harp to hang around my wrist.

Q: Yet despite the affirmation, there's sadness too. What is that line in The Scarlet Thread *about the sparrows? "God knows the sparrows fall, but they keep
falling. Ain't creation just one dead bird after another?"*
BETTS: Well, look at Flannery O'Connor. Remember that story where the
boy goes in the river and is baptized and presumably passes through. She
sees that moment of passing out of this life into the next as the achievement,
the promotion. I'm a little less confident; therefore, my inclination is to pull
that boy out of the river and go give him a haircut and something to eat. Live
as well as you can and leave the rest to the Father. Maybe that's a difference
between Catholicism and Protestantism.

Q: I haven't said much about The Scarlet Thread. *There's the "sins of the father"
business and Thomas, the villain, is the one who survives. A Jason Compson sort
inheriting the new world. And the people the reader really like, either die or, like
Esther, take off.*
BETTS: But she still is alive; you know she'll be okay.

*Q: The most remarkable character, I think, is David and that extraordinary rela-
tionship with Bungo. Did you do a lot of research into gravestones and all that?*
BETTS: It's probably the best thing in the book. I did get interested in that.
We were living in Sanford then and there was a lot of sandstone. I actually

tried to carve out some faces. Then I found out how hard stone working is. You sort of need to know where the bruises are to write about it. This goes back to what the Bible teaches. The Bible teaches you, I think, that if you want to talk about the spirit you have to get to it by way of the body and hence Job. If you really want to talk about art, you have to talk about where you mash your finger.

Q: *The book shows a deep incompleteness too. And you are often on that subject. Elizabeth Evans says of your story "Dead Mule" that it's a story where "laughter turns into sardonic grimace."*
BETTS: Isn't that what being grown-up is about?

Q: *Frederick Beuchner talks about the tragedy and the comedy.*
BETTS: That's right and the way that they link. It is what I look for in mature writers. They may never talk about it out loud, but their characters will. It's so often what I miss in contemporary fiction. There's vitality and passion and great sex and all that, but they haven't arrived at that sense of doubleness and cannot be hurried to it. It has to be earned. It cannot be imposed.

Q: *What's a part-time Calvinist?*
BETTS: I do ascribe to much that is called Calvinist, I suppose, but it seems that we're back to balance. We still don't understand sin and failure. It would have been better for the church as an institution if it had plunged right into that and got that digested and stopped being self-righteous.

Q: *So, how do you feel when the Republicans are talking about "family values" and the whole world pushes toward a notion of Christianity that is everything but David and Noah and Lot.*
BETTS: That's right. All those nutty people that God loved. I like all those nutty eccentrics that God chose, even Calvin.

Q: *I'm thinking of Clyde Edgerton's character, Raney, who goes to an Episcopal church for the first time. Do you remember that? She likes it okay, but she says, there's "no spunk." Do you feel that? Given your ARP background, do you sometimes feel a passionlessness? These folks we call fundamentalists, at least they have spunk.*
BETTS: Yes. I guess both extremes are equally bad. I have a woman friend who is a minister, but she really has a mixture of various California religions.

After a while I can't sit through any more about my child within, or about my anima and animus; I can go read anywhere about all that. But that is not what I come to church for. I come to church to learn whether this thing is really true and what difference it really makes to me. I don't come to it with some Kiwanis Club ethics or behavior, so I agree that we have lost something in losing the people who are committed to something. We've tried to be all things to all people so that anybody can come in. Just believe any little ol' thing, you just come right in and smile, have a little sunshine. So we're back to balance, to the risks of spelling it all out very clearly and becoming Pharisees. It's very interesting the paradox that's involved. It's like a dance.

Q: *Where should people start with your work?*
BETTS: They should start with the next one.

Q: *So you're never satisfied?*
BETTS: Never satisfied. It's sort of like saying, if you wanted to get to know me, would you start five years ago? No, you'd start right from now.

Q: *What about labels? I know you dislike "Christian novelist." How about "southern novelist" or "gothic novelist?" Louis Simpson used the term gothic to classify you in his introduction to the anthology that included* Beasts of the Southern Wild. *But I must say that his definition surprised me; it seems that anything concerned with spirituality would be labeled gothic.*
BETTS: Yes. I never thought of myself as gothic writer. That in itself shows the age which we are living in; it's very peculiar. And Simpson's introduction surprises me because it's not typical of his criticism. Repeatedly, you're confronted with some kind of stereotype. Clyde Edgerton now has always played into the stereotypes about southerners more than I do. He'll do the take-off on Senator Flaghorn or somebody and have a good time of it and laugh all the way to the bank. I don't enjoy it. The stereotypes annoy me, so I tend to resist all that. I don't read writers because of such labels. I read them for something else. Right now, for instance, to be a woman writer means to be a writer supporting the radical feminist cause. I think I am a feminist but I don't believe the label would suit me. I write about the South but I'm not really into the mall fiction that people talk about so much. So I resist the label.

Q: *Do you still think that "there's a moment in every day that the Devil can't touch?"*
BETTS: Yes, I guess I do think that though sometimes I don't find it.

Q: There's that romantic sense in some of your books, a sense of that possibility that keeps coming back.

BETTS: That story you've mentioned, "Astronomer," certainly has that. It was written when I'd been reading William Blake and it has that translucent universe. At that moment, I believed it very strongly. It's hard to sustain. There are waves.

Q: Have there been times when your writing has disturbed the peace, gotten you in trouble with some group or another?

BETTS: Yes. In North Carolina some of it has been the straightlaced reaction. Many people feel that you can't be religious and write about sex too, that it's automatically beyond the pale. So I've had some letters like that. If they sign them, which they don't always do, I always try to write back and raise those issues and talk about them. I don't believe you persuade those people, but it would be an act of arrogance not to try. My duty is to continue to speak of such things, because God made the pleasures.

Q: What about your treatment of race? You use the word "nigger" for example.

BETTS: Yes. And now people are down on Twain. I guess the rest of us go with him. Well, I haven't had too much controversy. The one thing you mentioned, "The Sympathetic Visitor," was the only story I was ever sued for. I was a sophomore in college, and we received a letter threatening a suit from Thurgood Marshall, from his law firm. He did view the story as racist and he was acting on behalf of the real black people in Statesville upon whom I had based the story. He was viewing it as an invasion of privacy. It was a shock to me because they were all friends of mine and because we had no money; my husband and I were struggling students. I was eighteen and very stupid. I used one of the person's real names. I never thought about her reading it and being hurt. But she did and she was. So I went to see her and explained that I never meant to hurt her and that the story was meant to make her and her family heroic, not the other way around. We had a personal reconciliation and ultimately the whole business of the suit was dropped. It did teach me about my responsibility as a writer. I would never again invade privacy in that way. I do not have the view that Faulkner had when he said one good poem is worth any number of little old ladies or something like that. I think that's not true. I think there's a number of good poems already, and little old ladies do make a difference.

Q: You're always aware of the depravity business, aren't you? I wonder if Heading West isn't a study of evil. Doesn't Nancy Finch become fascinated with the abomination? Aren't you trying to figure out what makes Dwight Anderson so evil? Or is it finally about Nancy's realizing, as she says at the end, that she is capable of evil herself?

BETTS: When I autograph books for people, I often write something like, "To one Pharisee learning to be a publican," which is what I think happens. There's a moment when Nancy realizes that she didn't kill Dwight purposely but she could have. In that moment, her whole notion of evil is altered and with it her easy judgment of all the people she left behind. She sees them differently when she comes back home. They are not really any better than they were—Faye is just as frivolous, Momma is just as domineering—but her view of them has been altered by the fact that she is not superior. She realizes that she cannot judge them.

Q: That's almost Flannery O'Connor again. Like the grandmother in "A Good Man Is Hard to Find" who realizes the Misfit is one of their own children.

BETTS: That again strikes me as being part of the growing up process. Nobody is more judgmental than adolescents. They know who the good guys and the bad guys are. It's a tiresome attitude.

Q: So you do not begin with some idea to demonstrate, some thesis to prove?

BETTS: Once I've done the first draft and the thing is there, I might go back and sharpen it. I didn't write this new book because I wanted to write something about theodicy. I was driving and I saw this highway patrolman beside the road. Apparently, a chicken truck had run off the road and broken apart. Chickens were running loose, and the way they are raised now you know, they'd never been loose before. So you have a scene of mixed horror and humor, and you have this man trying to bring some order out of this chaos. It was just fabulous. I was both laughing and appalled because there was chicken blood and people were trying to steal chickens. This is a scene Jean Paul Sartre would have gotten something out of; indeed you can get that on a highway in North Carolina just as easy. The whole novel started from that. Later I realized my character's daughter was like the chickens. He had protected her, kept her in a heated and cooled place, but you can't protect like that. But that grew; it wasn't that I started from that. I think that's true with most storytellers. You get an intersection, a moment that for some reason is a spark. You start from there and whoever you are.

Larry Brown ❧ 1991

SUSAN KETCHIN

Larry Brown was born in 1951 and raised in Yocona, Mississippi, a crossroads community near Oxford. After graduating from high school in 1970, he served a two-year stint in the Marines, and in 1973 returned home to marry and raise a family. From 1973 until early 1990, he was a member of the Oxford Fire Department, attaining the rank of captain in 1986. He and his wife, Mary Annie, and three children have made their home outside Oxford on farmland that was Mary Annie's family homeplace.

As a young man, Brown worked variously as a housepainter, carpet cleaner, lumberjack, and carpenter. In 1980, at the age of twenty-nine, he decided, as he puts it, to "do something with my life" and began teaching himself the art and craft of fiction writing. An avid reader since childhood, Brown began reading every kind of fiction he could find, from detective thrillers to Henry James and William Faulkner, studying various styles and "how they did things." He cites writers such as Raymond Carver, Flannery O'Connor, Tobias Wolff, and Stephen King as particularly influential. By 1990, while he was still employed full-time as a firefighter, he had completed manuscripts of five novels, over one hundred short stories and a stage play.

In 1988, Brown published a short-story collection, Facing the Music, *to critical acclaim. His first published novel,* Dirty Work *(1989), was awarded the Mississippi Institute of Arts and Letters Award for fiction. In 1990, Brown left the fire department to write full-time. In that same year, his second collection of short stories,* Big Bad Love, *was published. His second novel,* Joe, *was published in 1991. American Playhouse is currently developing the stage and television production of* Dirty Work *for which Brown has written the screenplay. His work is represented in anthologies, including* Best American Short Stories *(1989, 1992) edited by Shannon Ravenel, and has appeared in such magazines and journals as* Fiction International, Mississippi Quarterly, Paris Review, *and* Southern

Originally published as Susan Ketchin, "An Interview with Larry Brown," Vol. 32, no. 2 (1994), 95–109.

Exposure. *He is currently at work on a nonfiction book,* On Fire, *about his life as a firefighter.*

In his first collection of short fiction, Facing the Music, *Brown introduces us to people who seem to be paralyzed by calamity and who eventually must learn, often with only the slightest glimmer of understanding, how to deal with it—through resignation, denial, or a wan faith. In* Dirty Work, *he creates two distinctive narrative voices—one of Walter James, a white man, and the other Braiden Chaney, a black man, both of Mississippi. Both men have sustained severe, permanent wounds in Vietnam and, lying side by side in a veterans' hospital, they seek deliverance from their suffering from one another. In* Big Bad Love, *Brown examines with bitterness and humor the inexorable death of love in marriage.* Joe *has been acclaimed by critics as the complex and powerful work of a mature writer. The essence of Brown's artistry is summed up by one reviewer, writing in* Booklist: *"The authenticity of Brown's voice and the seamless world he creates are breathtaking. His themes of love and redemption, hope and dignity, weakness and strength are universal, and the telling is mercilessly compelling."*

This interview with Larry Brown took place over the course of three meetings in Tula and Taylor, Mississippi, and Durham, North Carolina. Though we had met before, our talks about religion and fiction began in July 1991 when my family and I came to Mississippi to visit Larry's family on the occasion of his fortieth birthday.

Having rendezvoused with Richard Howorth (to whom Facing the Music *is dedicated) at his Square Books store in Oxford, we traveled in a two-car caravan to Taylor. We were planning to surprise Larry at a catfish place, about ten miles south of Oxford, where Mary Annie and two cousins would be eating supper.*

There were no billboards or road signs or markers to guide us along the twists and turns in the backroads, none that I could see, at any rate, nothing for miles, it seemed, but dark kudzu in the summer twilight. Kudzu rose up sometimes two or three stories high on both sides of the road between Oxford and Taylor.

Taylor Restaurant is situated at a sharp bend in the road; along with the one-room post office, it comprises most of downtown Taylor. Worn, sagging wooden steps lead to its narrow porch. One solid wooden carpenter's bench sits outside the entrance; on the other side of the black, double screen doors is the drink box. People come here from all around to eat catfish and drink beer, especially on Friday nights after work. Huge live oak trees, "must be a hundred years old," someone says, brood over the sandy sideroads and walks.

We waited in the heat in the gravel parking lot (though it was past seven in the evening, it was still over 90 degrees and humid) until we saw Mary Annie and Larry go inside. A moment later, we walked in to find them in a booth in back.

Larry Brown is a slightly built, but strong and wiry-looking fellow, whose face shows years of hard work and pain. He has fine features (long thin nose, sad hazel eyes) and sunburned skin from many years in the Mississippi sun.

We ate fresh fried catfish, French fries, cole slaw, hush puppies and drank beer; we had homemade apple pie (fried) for dessert. We sat on benches at a long wooden table, big enough for the eight people who had gathered to celebrate. The slatted floors creaked as customers walked to and from the combination bathroom/broom closet in back; ropes of exposed wiring crawled up the walls to the pressed tin ceiling and over it like snakes toward two or three overburdened outlets. Stark puddles of light emanated from bare bulbs in the high ceiling.

The waitress brought platters of fried fish, as fast as the owner could fry them, to the tables from the grill that ran the length of one side of the room. Initials and hearts, names and platitudes were carved all over the booth backs and walls. Larry was in a bemused and philosophical (though by no means solemn) mood; he talked readily about the meaning of his fiction, and of the good life, what it takes, who's got it, who doesn't and why. After about the third platter of crisp, salty food and pitchers of beer, we concluded that truth in fiction and truth in friendship, not to mention truth in vino figure prominently in the equation. Our booth was near the jukebox. We played "I Fall to Pieces" and "You Don't Know About Lonely 'Til It's Chiseled in Stone" for Larry—Patsy Cline and Vern Gosdin easing him into his forty-first year.

The next morning, Larry took us out to a ten-acre parcel of land he'd recently purchased. On it are a pond and a small shack Larry is fixing up for writing. It is near the small store and post office on the side of the road in Tula (this store is Tula) that his mother used to run. As we worked clearing under brush and briars around the pond, we talked about his early life, his writing, and, of course, religion.

Later that fall, Larry came to give a reading from his novel Joe at the Regulator Bookshop, an independent bookstore in Durham, North Carolina. He is dressed in his usual Lee jeans, baseball cap, tweed jacket, cowboy boots, and a Flannery O'Connor tee-shirt (he opens his jacket to display the front—large caricature of O'Connor clutching a Bible, with a comical-looking peacock in the background). Larry is smoking Camels and looks a little nervous. "I always hate it on the road," he says. "I don't sleep too good away from home."

People are already drifting in for the reading that will take place an hour and a half later; they visit a moment or two, a few asking him to sign books. The store owner shows us a sun- filled room in back where we can talk for an hour or so before the reading. We drink soft drinks and, as Larry lights a cigarette, we settle in on the sofa to talk. As always, I am struck by Brown's quiet manner—he speaks in a low, soft Mississippi accent, an undertone of sorrow ever-present in it; his hazel eyes seem to look far off and deep within as he talks. When he speaks about ancient myths and the lure and power of storytelling in ancient cultures, it strikes me that he's been there. He is an "old soul."

QUESTION: *Let's talk about "Facing the Music." People not only seem to react very strongly to that story, but there seems to be a remarkable disparity in their reactions. Some decry it as unrealistically bleak; others see it as a story about redemption—or at least that its ending redeems the bleakness by suggesting hope in the midst of loss. What were you thinking as you wrote this story and what is your reaction to it now?*

BROWN: It's true that most of the stuff I write does come from things I've seen, or lived through myself—with the exception of "Facing the Music." It's funny. People think that story is autobiographical. I get letters all the time about that one from people consoling me and my wife about her "mastectomy." But this story is really about pain and loss wherever you find it. I just believe that my fiction, anybody's fiction, is simply supposed to illuminate the human condition, tell us something about ourselves. I did see it as having a hopeful ending.

Q: *Your fiction does seem to reach its fullest power when you are writing about what lies at the heart of human suffering. One of the most powerful scenes in your first novel,* Dirty Work, *occurs when Jesus comes to Braiden in his hospital bed. As Jesus lights a cigarette for him, the paralyzed Braiden asks how long he must continue to suffer. This scene portrays a startlingly human Jesus who suffers along with the world in sorrow and grief.*

BROWN: Some people get upset about that scene. They want to know whether the scene is actually occurring. Is Jesus actually there, or is it a vision, or something in Braiden's mind? To tell you the truth, I don't know. Braiden—he's helpless. He's tired. He wants suicide. But he has no way to do it. He doesn't think it's wrong any more. He believes in it. By that I mean, he believes God is merciful, and that he's suffered enough; he can't stand any more. He longs for death. It's not a sin in his case. I can understand Braiden. But, I believe the Lord don't ever put more on you than you can bear.

Some people just have harder lives than others. I've got an aunt who I figure is probably one of the most devout Christian people that there is in the world. I know a lot of other people who profess to be that but who don't live life—I don't believe they live it—or practice their religion the way that she does, and her mama before her, my grandmother, all my aunts. Some people have such a harder time than other people do, some people have to pay more in life. I don't know why.

Q: *It makes you understand why one might consider giving up, or suicide. Some of your fiction seems to deal with this notion.*
BROWN: For a long time I've been trying to understand suicide, and I do see how it is not a sin for some people, in some cases. The story, "Old Frank and Jesus," is drawn from a man who used to cut my hair. One day, he borrowed a pistol and shot himself through the head. I knew him well—I'd picked cotton with him and things like that. There was no outward indication of any trouble. That was when I began imagining, What is the pressure? What would cause someone to do that? Years later, I learned that he had been losing his land to taxes. He'd lost twenty, thirty acres. Mr. P. in the story was concerned with two things he couldn't understand: How could anybody be so mean to Jesus? How did he let his wife talk him into shooting his old dog? That kind of despair was what I was thinking about in "Samaritans," too. Since then, I've known others who were caught in something like that.

Q: *Does the story end in despair?*
BROWN: I was thinking about despair when I wrote the story. Mr. P. was at the end of his rope. There was no help for him, the pressures were too much. I wanted to show how the loss of love can bring it on, can bring on very strong emotions. Grief can kill you, I mean literally, it can. When Harry Crews talked about his boy drowning, he said you think you are going to die, that you couldn't survive that. Most of the time, you can, but sometimes you can't. When our baby died, in 1977, I didn't think I would survive. It was a very rocky time ... tough. You meet other people who have suffered the same thing ... it comes up in conversation—it's the same each time—you never get over it. But my fiction is about people surviving, about people proceeding out from calamity. I write about loss. These people are aware of their need

for redemption. We all spend our time dealing with some kind of hurt and looking for love. We are all striving for the same thing, for some kind of love. But love is a big word. It covers a lot of territory. I try to tell it in a fresh, new way, to be innovative.

Q: *Several of the titles of your stories refer to biblical images, maybe in an ironic way. Tell me about the origins of the titles, "Old Frank and Jesus" and "Samaritans."*
BROWN: Even though "Samaritans" has a suggestive title, it's not a "message story." I wanted it to say a lot of things, some contradictory. Like, it's about the futility of helping people who do nothing to help themselves, the outcasts of society. But it's also about that it's a good thing to try. That's what Jesus would have done. It's an ironic title.

Q: *Partly because it's in the plural. Only one character in the story actually acts like the Good Samaritan of the parable, yet the title suggests that other people in the story, including the itinerants, could be considered Samaritans. Do you see your stories as growing out of a particular view of God and humankind?*
BROWN: I'm asked about this a lot of times, and I always say I think it's evident in my work, in some of it anyway. I don't take a specific stand about things like that, but it's in there, in certain stories, in certain models. I think a lot about God in the humanity of Jesus, like with the conversation between Braiden and Jesus. It helps me. But most of my stories aren't directly concerned with religion—except for "Roadside Resurrection." Now that is a religious story. It's about a real faith healer, someone who really heals the afflicted. It's all about faith and trust, where they come from. This famous healer has lost his faith, but no one knows it yet. It has humor in it, too. There is an ex-Elvis impersonator who needs healing.

Q: *It is, in fact, a very funny story.*
BROWN: I've always thought being able to write humor is the mark of a superior writer, but it's going to ruin me. People think I'm mocking their beliefs, and I'm not. I have a strong belief in God.

Q: *Tell me more about that. What do you believe are the origins of your beliefs, for instance?*
BROWN: I was raised in the Methodist Church in Memphis. That's where all my cousins, aunts, and uncles went. When we moved, we went to a country

church, Mama's church, for a while. We belong to the Methodist Church here, but I don't go like I should. My faith has gotten deeper over the years. It seems to have developed because of the suffering I see—of mine and of others. I believe suffering is here to make you strong. See what you can endure. Some are weak, some are stronger.

Q: *It is often said that your experiences as a firefighter shaped your vision as a person and as a fiction writer. How about your beliefs?*
BROWN: I write about life-and-death situations in my nonfiction book that I am working on now, *On Fire*. Sometimes things would happen where you'd get put in an utterly helpless position. When it was really bad was when everybody would be looking at me: What we gonna do, Captain Brown? So, when you've got the rank, and you're drawing the pay, it's up to you. Somebody's life can be in your hands, and it's a heavy responsibility.

The bad thing is, you've got fifty or a hundred people standing there watching you, watching every mistake you make, ain't going to miss a thing. They ain't going to walk off and leave. And you got to do something. And you're going to hear all this noise, people second-guessing you afterward. I could hardly stand to do it, sometimes, the situation would be so bad, but I had to kind of detach myself from my feelings about what the person was going through. In most cases, I could not concentrate on their pain. I could only concentrate on the speed and efficiency of my crew in removing the person from the situation, so that they could go to the hospital.

Q: *If you thought about their pain, you wouldn't be able to move them because it would hurt them too much.*
BROWN: That's right. And you know, you sometimes have people there screaming, "Y'all are killing me, you're killing me!" What can you do? You're there to try to help them and remedy the situation. But it's a very nerve-wracking business to be in. But it wasn't the excitement that I left, it was the boredom. The hours sitting there with nothing going on, and I was wishing I was home writing.

Q: *You got caught between two worlds.*
BROWN: Yes. But I didn't back off from anything I ever got sent to. I always preferred to be the first one there, so that I could size it up, and figure out what was going on, whether I had to call in more people, or certain pieces of equipment, or whatever.

Q: Many southerners speak vividly of the time when they were "saved" as being as emotionally intense an experience as they have ever undergone. Have you had such an experience?

BROWN: I've felt I've been saved many, many times. No joke. Once, when I worked as a fireman, my partner, a black guy, and I worked a long time together—for hours, one night, to get someone out of a car that was wrapped around a telephone pole. It was a boy who had this terrible, terrible wreck. Inside the city limits. Normally, you wouldn't have that bad an accident inside the city limits. I can't remember whether this boy was running from the police, or what, but he'd wrapped the car completely around a telephone pole. It was on the right side of the street, headed the wrong way, so the driver's door was up against this pole. His chest was all broken up internally, he was bleeding out the mouth, ears, nose, and everywhere else. This nurse was in the seat with him, trying to clear his airway with a piece of surgical tubing, which was steadily getting clogged with blood. So the boy was in real danger of dying right there, but there wasn't any way for him to come out. His legs were in this door behind him, and his body was lodged over up against the shifter. That's what had him caught. This nurse was screaming at me to do something; I was in charge of the crew. But I couldn't see any way to bring him out. He was going to lay right there and die before we could get him out. Only thing I could see was that he couldn't come out sideways, he'd have to come out straight up. So I said, Okay, we'll chop the windshield out, reach in and bend the shifter off of him, and bring him out.

That's what we did. We covered him up in a blanket and took our fire axes and chopped around the windshield, pulled it out and throwed it out on the street. I climbed up on the hood and reached down for the shifter, but I couldn't bend it. So, Mack was there, the black guy who worked with me. I told him to get up here and help me. I said, "Put your hand on top of mine, let's bend the shifter, that's what's got him hung." He nearly crushed my hand with his, but the thing started moving. We bent it on over. We both fell down into the floor boards, but we got it off of him. Then we put the backboard on the boy, pulled traction on it and brought him on out. They loaded him in the ambulance, took him on down to the hospital. He lived, too. The whole rescue depended on the strength of this one guy's arm pushing the gear shift out of the way.

It's about life and death—the real thing. I had another experience one time like that that I would call a conversion experience. It was a truly religious experience. When my partner, that black guy I was telling you about died, he died while he was rabbit hunting, real quick. Had a stroke. I went to his church for the funeral. And the ladies coming in, and they're starting to sing; they don't have any hymnals in their hands. It was in the summertime, and it was this church, way out in the woods. I mean off this sure enough tiny pig trail. We had to take the fire trucks up there, and it was muddy. It was really bad. And the place he was buried in was a really scrubby little piece of piti-ful land with these stunted trees and weeds and just wasn't a pretty place to be buried. But they all had this faith, and the way it came out was that this preacher stood up and started preaching and then he got to moving and he got to kind of rocking and rolling and people started getting so excited they'd jump up and holler Amen! Yeah brother, tell it! You know, we were just sit-ting there just looking around with our white faces. And it just made me see how strong they were, how much faith they had, and it also made me realize that God ain't got no color. It's something I wouldn't ever forget. One God, no particular color, one God for everybody.

Q: *Your fiction reveals this same intensity of feeling.*
BROWN: All kinds of things have a deep meaning to me. All kinds of ex-periences. They move me. When I write, all I'm doing is trying to tell a story. Above all is the art. Your art must evolve from your experience and it must evolve as art.

Q: *You have told me that some folks have criticized the violence, the alcoholism, the graphic language, and so on in your work. They point to the "brutality" in your work, its sexism and the so-called "anti-religious" nature of it.*
BROWN: I can't be concerned about who's going to think what. I try to make as good a story as I can, and let the chips fall where they may. I can't write to please others; I must please me. I must trust my own judgment, and, above all, I must be honest. Your art must evolve from your honesty, your experience. If they are seeing only negative things in my fiction, then they aren't reading it right, not seeing what's there.

Q: *What do you think impels you to create fiction?*
BROWN: At around age thirty, I realized that I was still being bossed by someone else. I had done about everything I could think of, being a fireman, setting out trees, a carpenter's helper, and so on. I was married and had three kids by then. I realized I must do something else with my life, make some-thing of myself. I had always loved books and reading; it was what I cared

most about. I figured writing was the only thing I could teach myself to do on my own.

I checked out books from the library by the armload—Flannery O'Connor, Raymond Carver, William Faulkner, Harry Crews, Cormac McCarthy. I found out that I wanted to write "literature," the kind of stories that I had read over and over again. At first, I thought it would be simple. It's not. I think everybody who wants to write well has to go through an apprenticeship, with a blind faith that says you can't take no for an answer. In a way it was like the Marine Corps—it's all in your mind. To be successful in boot camp or in writing, you must become an automaton: keep going, keep working, keep believing. And I've always believed in the trash can as a valuable tool. I burned a novel one time.

Q: You did not.
BROWN: Burned it in the back yard. I sure did. I felt like I had to.

Q: How come?
BROWN: Wasn't any good. And there wasn't any saving it. I had finished it and it didn't work. I said I believe it's a kindness to take that into the woods and burn it, lose it forever. I think the main thing was that in destroying it, I knew that I was never going to see it. Once I made that decision, it was irrevocable. That work was up in smoke just like the paper was.

Q: Did burning it free you?
BROWN: Yes. I wrote two more bad ones, wrote five bad ones altogether, before *Facing the Music* was published. Over time I came to love the act of writing, the inventing, the imagining of a character. Now, it's not even work, and when it's going well, it's pure recreation.

Q: Let's talk more about "Roadside Resurrection." It has just recently come out in the Paris Review. *What are some reactions you've gotten to that story?*
BROWN: People seem to be spellbound by it. It's the idiot, I think. In fact, I'm spellbound by it. It's a wild story. The writing of it was a process of discovery, one of those things that just started telling itself. The first draft took a week—it was really cooking, burning to be finished. The rhythm of the words developed a life of its own; it assumed its own way of being told. I revised it at least six times to take out stuff and tighten my control on the language. The story just came—it was as if I were just a transmitter. The main character, a

youthful healer, is ambiguous. He's lost his faith. He is caught up in a dilemma. What is he going to do? Has God turned his face away from him? Flenco, the ex-Elvis impersonator's wife, is on a quest of faith, too, but she doesn't get what she wants. She believes if she can just find him then everything's going to be okay. But the faith healer has no awareness of this woman's looking for him. It's not even a part of his life.

Q: *Tell me about the ending of the story. The crosses on the roadside—what did they suggest to you?*
BROWN: The crosses at the end of the story are a mystery to me. You see them all over the South, along the sides of roads and interstates. I've seen them in Mississippi, Alabama, Georgia. Nobody knows where they come from. Who puts them up? Nobody ever sees them being put up. It's a great deal of trouble—they're huge, like telephone poles.

Q: *It may be stretching it a bit, but just as those crosses might be seen to be imposing a startling image of faith on the consciousness of those who are driving by, do you see your stories as possibly posing startling problems of faith for the reader?*
BROWN: Yes, I do, sure do. I think any literature, if it's going to be any good, has to be about right and wrong, good and bad, good versus evil. Like my novel, *Joe*. Joe must do something bad to get rid of the evil in his world. He must do what he does (he gives his enemies plenty of warning, too), but he must do what he does as a moral imperative. Even though he wasn't directly affected, Joe felt he must take care of the problem. Joe knows that evil is real, not some abstraction. Whatever good is in this world has to have teeth in it if evil is to be dealt with.

Q: *Is there redemption in this suffering, any hope for these characters?*
BROWN: You can't tack a happy ending on tragedy. Braiden in *Dirty Work*, for example, loves his life. It was what he wanted all along. But his problems are too much. He wants release. In his case it is not a sin to seek suicide. The ministers I've talked to about this story agree with me. God wouldn't punish Braiden; God would pity him. Braiden has a strong, unwavering faith in God. He seeks release and peace.

Q: *Why do you think so many southern writers write about religion? Notable southern writers, you, and others such as Robert Penn Warren and William*

*Faulkner have talked very compellingly about the moral imperative of fiction—
that is, that it must deal with these ultimate questions of good and evil, life and
death. Somehow it always seems to come up, whether it's Faulkner's sermon in*
The Sound and the Fury, *or the three crosses and the faith healer in "Roadside
Resurrection," or simply in a title that gets you thinking, like "Samaritans."*
BROWN: Well, I think in my case religion crops up so much because I heard
it all my life. From the earliest times I can remember, I was in the church,
raised in the church, went to Sunday School, Vacation Bible School, church
on Sunday night, church on Sunday morning, all that stuff. And my whole
family was heavily involved in it. I think probably the reason it crops up in
so many other southern writers' works is for the same reason. Because they
were exposed to so much of it at an early age, it makes an impression on them.

*Q: Harry Crews has said that he feels matters of life and death, suffering and
meaning so deeply that he has to write about them in his fiction, sort out these
emotions through his characters. The characters themselves start talking to him
about their struggles.*
BROWN: Yeah, I've seen other writers that are doing it, too. Cormac McCarthy's got a couple of lines—this preacher is traveling around, doing this talking and he says, "A blind feller hollered out one day and said, 'Look at me' (and
he only had one leg). He said, 'Look at me, legless and everything; I reckon
you think I ought to love God.' And the feller said, 'Yeah,' said, 'I reckon you
ought. An old blind mess and legless fool is a flower in the garden of God.'"

Yes, that's what my fiction is about and I guess that's what religion is all
about, too. The basic concept is either to be good or to be bad. And in order
to be good you got to fight the bad. So those are the issues that most of my
characters are struggling with. They are struggling to be good people. They
know the difference between good and bad, and right and wrong. They don't
always do what's right, because they're imperfect, like all of us. Like all people.
And I try to give my characters those human traits that we all recognize and
all have and all feel. I try to make them as real as I can. And therefore, very
simply, a story's about a person who has a problem, and he or she will either
resolve that problem or they will not resolve that problem. The problems may
be many-faceted, especially in the course of a novel. In a good novel there is
always something going on: either they are not satisfied with their life, or they
have some major problem that's disrupting their life. I mean if you go along
happy-go-lucky, one scene to another, nothing ever happens, there's never any

trouble, everybody in the world is nice and treats everybody with kindness, that's not representative of the real world, and it's not representative of a real novel, either. It's got to be a major struggle. More than one, nothing simple.

Q: *And you pile them on, too.*
BROWN: Yes, I pile them on. I think you should sandbag your characters— load 'em up with as much as you can, then see what they do. That's why I make things so tough on them. I want them to have some kind of conflict going on within themselves and with the other characters around them. I think the thing to do is pull the character in early in the first few sentences and keep him. And once you get him by the throat, don't let him go. Don't let him go until you're finished with him—the way I look at a novel, the way I tell a novel's finished, is the point when I think I have done all I can for them, have helped the characters as much as I can, helped them all I can.

Q: *And these characters mostly, well, all of them except Wade in the novel,* Joe, *and that idiot-monster in "Roadside Resurrection," it seems to me, are basically well-meaning people.*
BROWN: I have some bad people in my stories, but they're there as antagonists. They're the ones who are making the problems.

Q: *And even Wade is human.*
BROWN: Yeah, he's human. He doesn't have very many redeeming human qualities about him—

Q: *Can't think of any.*
BROWN: Can't think of a thing.

Q: *He's incorrigible, yet, it doesn't come across as if it's being done for effect. He, unfortunately, is all too human.*
BROWN: He's got some concerns. But, his are mainly selfish, pertaining to himself only.

Q: *Atavistic, primitive concerns. Right now, I am reading in* Joe *where Wade has killed a black guy for his food coupons. Wade laid his hands on something in the grass, picked it up and knocked the man's brains out. Nice guy.*
BROWN: Yeah, Joe and him have difficulties, a hard time.

Q: In the book I'm doing, each chapter title will try to capture what each author's work is about. Reynolds Price, for example, has said that most of his characters might be termed "saintly outlaws," that is, good-hearted people who live and act, nonetheless, outside the norms of society. Harry Crews sees that the sacred role of the writer in the community is to tell stories about who we are; through hearing and telling stories about the individual and community, the writer serves as shaman or healer. How would you describe your characters or your role as writer in this regard?

BROWN: Some of my work is on the other side of reality sometimes. Maybe you would want to describe my work in terms of myths and dreams. *Dirty Work* involves so much myth you're not able to tell what's real and what's not, sometimes.

Q: Myths and dreams . . .

BROWN: Yes, and that's the way I want it to be. I wanted the reader to be uncertain what really was occurring, what was fantasy and what was reality.

When I read the *Iliad* and the *Odyssey* when I was little, on my own, it got me thinking in terms of myths and dreams; I was really into Greek mythology, all the battles and gods, what each one did and what each one was responsible for. They formed the core of my belief about storytelling.

Q: What do you see as the importance of storytelling?

BROWN: I think people depend on storytellers down through history to carry on the stories of things that came before. When Alex Haley went all the way to Africa chasing down his ancestors, he got finally to that village where Kunta Kinte was from and the guy there told the story that many years ago, there was another person in the tribe named Kunta Kinte who went into the woods to get wood for a drum and we never saw him again, and that was the day they kidnapped him and put him on a slave ship and brought him to America. That was the storyteller's job: to keep all the information and relay it—the whole history of not only his tribe but also the individual families and what all had happened before. And once he made that connection, he knew irrevocably that this was his family; he knew where he was from and thus who he was.

Q: Before we go, can you tell me how you think living where you do, in Yocona, Mississippi, has shaped your writing?

BROWN: Well, for one thing, I'm the real native son of Oxford. Faulkner wasn't from around here. He was from Ripley, sixty miles away. Seriously, though, living in the country shapes my whole life and work. My writing is formed by the people, by the lives they lead around here, and the land. In the country, you can swim, fish, ride your bike on dirt roads. I hate cities. I lived for ten years in Memphis, and I was not happy. Things here are peaceful, quiet, no hassles. When I spent some time in Los Angeles, I got downright scared. It's depressing.

That's where my fiction comes from, I think. I use everything: memory, imagination, and what people have told me. Like with "Waiting for the Ladies"—the guy in that story exposed himself at a dumpster. The thing some people don't realize is there was a real guy like that, lived here and I followed him once. He was simply not right in the head.

Donald Harington ∿ 1998–1999

LARRY VONALT

The following interview consists of conversations I had with Donald Harington on two late October Saturday afternoons, one in 1998 and the other in 1999. On both occasions we sat across from each other at the dining table in the great room of the brick house Don and his wife Kim built in 1994 in the eastern part of Fayetteville, Arkansas.

The focal point of the great room is a large fireplace above which are the twenty pencil drawings of Don's that head each of the chapters of The Architecture of the Arkansas Ozarks *(1975). On the other walls in the great room and throughout the house are prints that Don made while he was working on his MFA in printmaking at the University of Arkansas in Fayetteville in the mid-1950s.*

Don's study is off the great room and the kitchen. He designed it to store materials that relate to his writing and to make the act of writing comfortable. Although the room holds a large table and a desk on which his computer sits, it seems dominated by a large overstuffed chair in which Don sits, his computer keyboard in his lap, when he writes his fabulous stories.

QUESTION: *When you seriously began to write, what was your writing habit? Did you, for example, write only in the evening, only in the summer?*
HARINGTON: By "writing seriously" I assume you are referring to the writing of *The Cherry Pit*, my first published novel. At the time I was not teaching. I had given up my teaching job at Bennett College and was living in Vermont. I didn't even have any idea of a writing schedule. I was free to write as soon as I got up in the morning; I was free to keep on writing through the evening. When I wrote the first few chapters of *The Cherry Pit*, I was working all day long. Later on, I got in the habit of working mostly in the morning, and I've

---

Originally published as Larry Vonalt, "An Interview with Donald Harington," Vol. 40, no. 2 (2002), 69–85.

stuck to that habit most of my life. In fact I became superstitious at one point about not being able to write in the evening, so I've done very little writing in the evening.

Q: *What made you superstitious about writing in the evening?*
HARINGTON: I wrote a bad short story in the evening, and I thought that having written it in the evening may have had something to do with it being bad. Maybe it had nothing at all to do with it, but that's the way superstitions get started. You base them on personal experiences.

Q: *When you stop writing for the day do you have an idea of where you want to go the next day?*
HARINGTON: I always make a point of stopping in the middle of a sentence or the middle of a paragraph at least. I never complete anything when I stop for the day. So the next day when I have to complete the sentence or the paragraph from the day before to get started, it just gives me the momentum to keep on going for that day.

Q: *When you started to write did you have a subject in mind—like the Ozarks— that you wanted to make your own?*
HARINGTON: Not when I started writing. I did not discover the Ozarks as a subject until my third novel—when I wrote *Lightning Bug. The Cherry Pit* was just about Little Rock, but I knew that I would have to write about a world that I knew fairly well. So I wrote *The Cherry Pit* about Little Rock but it had characters in it from the Ozarks. The same was true of my unpublished second novel, *A Work of Fiction*, which had several characters in it from the Ozarks even though it wasn't set in the Ozarks.

Q: *But that novel is set in Arkansas, isn't it?*
HARINGTON: Most of it was set either in Little Rock or the Ouachita Mountains.

Q: *You said that you found the subject of the Ozarks when you wrote* Lightning Bug.
HARINGTON: Yes, that's when I discovered the Ozarks as a subject, but remember that I wrote *Lightning Bug* as a swan song to the Ozarks, and had no intention of writing about the Ozarks again.

Q: *What was it in writing your next novel,* Some Other Place. The Right Place, *that brought you back to the Ozarks?*

HARINGTON: I knew that part 4 of *Some Other Place* would be in the Ozarks, but I investigated all kinds of places in the Ozarks as possible settings before I realized that I might as well go ahead and make it Stay More or Stick Around, as I call it to disguise it. But when I started out writing *Some Other Place. The Right Place*, I had no idea that I'd wind up back in Stay More. It wasn't until I was well along in that book when I realized that I was going to have to "Stay More" for the rest of my career in that place.

Q: *But when you finished,* The Architecture of the Arkansas Ozarks, *the novel that you wrote after* Some Other Place, *did you think that perhaps you'd finished writing the story of Stay More in writing the history of Stay More?*

HARINGTON: In other words, did I feel that I had exhausted Stay More?

Q: *Yes.*

HARINGTON: Not really, because I had intended *Architecture* to be volume one in a trilogy. Volume two would to be called *Interiors* and would cover the whole thing again from a different perspective. Volume three would be called *Outbuildings and Others,* or *OO* [He shapes this fingers into two Os], the double hole privy. I was going to make a whole series of stories out of that one story, but I decided that I probably couldn't, so I went on to write *Farther Along.* I knew, though, that I would probably be writing about Stay More for the rest of my life.

Q: *Do you think that there is something about* Farther Along *that from your own perspective has kept it from being published?*

HARINGTON: There were two different editors who rejected it for different reasons, but from my own perspective, it was probably a case of "second-novelitis," but belated "second-novelitis" if you think of *Architecture* where you want to hit it big and you put everything into it, and you don't really have enough left for the second one—that was probably a factor. Another factor is that I was probably drinking too much at the time, and it was making the writing kind of sloppy. I was having personal problems. I had lost my father, my college was collapsing, and my marriage was collapsing—all those problems were happening when I was trying to write *Farther Along.*

I have gone back to *Farther Along.* You know, of course, that originally *Farther Along* was in four different versions before I settled on one version that I thought might be acceptable. I've gone back to that version a couple of times and tried to write some more. Kim certainly wants me to finish it, but I really don't have the heart for it. It was a story of Clifford Stone, the narrator and main character of *The Cherry Pit*, having left Boston and come back to Stay More, taken existence as a hermit living up in the same magical glen of the waterfall that occurs in so many other of my books and is about to become crucial in *Falling Off the Mountain*. He lives in that glen of the waterfall and has some medical problems that were very closely parallel to mine such as pancreatitis, which almost killed him. I was probably making Clifford too autobiographical, but I was also discovering that Clifford Stone of *Cherry Pit* just could not fit into that scheme that I had in mind for him. I was forcing him into a situation that he would not fit. I'm just not happy with the whole results. I thought, too, that if I did finish it then I would have to incorporate Clifford into the novels that I have done since then, particularly *Falling Off the Mountain*. I do not see any possible place for him in *Falling Off the Mountain*. Supposedly he uses his skills as a restorationist to help Ekaterina restore Jacob Ingledew's house, but, if he did, I've never mentioned him by name.

Q: *while we're talking about an unpublished novel of yours, do you have any plans for publishing* A Work of Fiction, *the novel you wrote between* The Cherry Pit *and* Lightning Bug.
HARINGTON: I think that since *A Work of Fiction* is outside the mainstream of Stay More—it just has an indirect reference to it in that Alfred Arrington apparently was born up the creek a ways from Stay More—that it is the ideal kind of posthumous novel. It's published after the author's death—if he has an established reputation—as something that he did earlier. Let's look at Hemingway. They keep finding new books by Hemingway. *A Work of Fiction* will probably be like one of those. I don't think *Farther Along* will. In fact, I wouldn't want *Farther Along* to be published in its current condition, but I have no objection to the publication of *A Work of Fiction* as it is.

Q: *Talking about some of your other novels, do you think, for example, that you'll ever come back to writing about the characters in that wonderful book of yours,* The Cockroaches of Stay More?
HARINGTON: [He chuckles] No, I don't think I'll do that. That was a one-time-only experiment. I think it's reasonable to assume, however, that since Ekaterina took over Holy House and fixed it up that she probably had exterminators brought in who fumigated it and got rid of all the cockroaches.

Sharon and Larry Bract are living in the house that was store/post office of Latha Bourne. Did I call that "Parthenon" in *The Cockroaches of Stay More*?

Q: Yes.
HARINGTON: It was Sharon who picked the hero and heroine up out of a toilet and rescued them. She probably tolerates any surviving cockroaches left over from that novel. Larry probably still shoots them!

Q: You've said before that you wrote part of The Cherry Pit *at William Styron's house.*
HARINGTON: I finished it there. I actually wrote the first fifteen pages of it in Little Rock when we had gone home for Christmas vacation in '63. Then I came back to Vermont from that Christmas vacation and worked on it constantly all that spring. In the summer of '64 I went back to Little Rock and wrote more of it. It was later in that same summer of '64 that I finished it at Styron's house.

Q: When was it that you lived in Cavendish, Vermont?
HARINGTON: When I gave up teaching at Bennett College, we bought this rundown house in Cavendish, and I spent all of one summer and into the autumn trying to fix it up, unsuccessfully. When winter came in, two sweet old ladies who managed the parsonage for the Congregational Church in Weathersfield Center let us move into the parsonage for the winter. And it was in that parsonage where I wrote most of *The Cherry Pit*.

Q: Was it when you lived in Cavendish that you became aware of Five Corners, the Vermont ghost town so important to Some Other Place?
HARINGTON: Nita, my first wife, and I used to camp out a lot, and Five Corners is very close to Plymouth State Park, and I think it was while we were camping out at Plymouth State Park that we heard about Five Corners and went over and explored it. We had discovered Vermont just about this time in the fall of 1958 or maybe '59, that would make it forty years ago this week that we left our place in Boston and drove up on a glorious autumn day and saw Vermont and fell in love with it. We went back every chance that we got.

Q: You left Arkansas and went to Boston in 1957?
HARINGTON: No, '58. I got my MFA degree from here and went to Boston in the fall of '58.

Q: And you began teaching at Bennett College in 1960?

HARINGTON: My oldest daughter, Jennifer, was born at Millbrook when we were at Bennett College. She spent the first fifteen months of her life there before I decided to quit Bennett College and move off to Vermont. By the weirdest of coincidences, Jennifer is now working in Millbrook, the same place she was born.

Q: What's she doing?

HARINGTON: She's working as an editor for a newspaper supplement, and one of the things her newspaper put out was this brochure called "Come to Millbrook." She asked me as a favor for her if I would write an article about Bennett College to include in the supplement so I did this "Halcyon Days" piece on Bennett College.

Q: [Looking at the article] My God, this building!

HARINGTON: That was Bennett College. It's been abandoned for fifteen or twenty years. I refer to it in the article as—how did I put it?—"like a cicada's molted shell."

Q: What was the house at Cavendish like?

HARINGTON: The house we'd bought was in no condition to live in during cold weather. I had disassembled the fireplace to start to rebuild it. There was no heat. Well, there was one cast iron stove. But with a young baby it was just no place to contemplate spending the winter, so these benevolent ladies who managed the parsonage heard about our plight and invited us to live in the parsonage. I had nothing more to do with the house. I just let it stay there until a couple years later I sold it. I sold it to some guy from New York who wanted to put money into it, converting it into a summer home. But he just let it disintegrate and it's not there anymore.

Q: Speaking of young babies, what were some of the difficulties of being a husband and father when you were trying to write?

HARINGTON: I wasn't really aware that I was having any difficulties, not any more than any man does when he has to be a husband and a father. I was never accused of slighting my daughter or my wife. I didn't mistreat them except, perhaps, I didn't provide well for them in the sense that I subjected them to that horrible situation in that old house in Cavendish. But I did get them into the parsonage and they were comfortable there. Every writer who has a family has the problem that while he writes he cannot be distracted by his family, so he just has to learn to accommodate himself to spending so many hours a day writing without any distractions and then paying attention to his family. That's what I tried to do.

I remember when we moved to Ludlow after we had left Weathersfield Center—I had rented a nice house in Ludlow. That's where my second daughter, Calico, was born—that whenever I went to the grocery store about a block away I'd take Jennifer with me and hold her hand. We'd walk down this path between shrubbery. I can remember her, at a very early age, saying, "Daddy, we in the woods."

On one of those trips, when we got to the grocery store we found everybody in the store all excited. They were jabbering and talking excitedly, and I didn't know what was going on. But I bought my loaf of bread, bananas, milk, whatever. On the way home, I said, "Jennifer, what was all that excitement in there about?" And she said, "Somebody shot the President." So, of course, I couldn't wait to get home and turn the TV on and I discovered that Kennedy had been shot.

In Ludlow, I did most of the writing on *Cherry Pit*, then we went to Little Rock for the summer where I finished *The Cherry Pit*. It was while we were in Little Rock that I got a letter from the new president of Windham College inviting us to come to Putney. No, wait a minute. I'm sorry. Back up. We left Little Rock in June because I had been invited by William Styron to have his guest house for the summer because every summer they go to Martha's Vineyard, and he wanted someone to live in his guest house and keep an eye on the place, and we spent the whole summer in Roxbury, Connecticut, at William Styron's guest house. Calico was just a baby and Jennifer was three.

It was in August, while we were in the guest house, that I received the letter, forwarded from Little Rock, from the new president of Windham College inviting me to come to Windham to be interviewed for the job. So we didn't have very far to go from Roxbury up to Putney. They hired me on the spot. Two or three weeks later, we packed up and moved from Roxbury to Putney, where we spent the next sixteen years.

Q: Did you move immediately into the house that you lived in in Putney?
HARINGTON: Not at first. When we first went to Putney, we rented. I think the business manager had a cottage that he let us use for a few weeks, and then we heard about a mansion owned by some guy who goes to Florida every winter. He let us come out and see it and let us rent it for practically a song

through the first year. It was on a really big estate, 200 acres, big, old two-story colonial house with twelve or thirteen rooms, a separate guest house that I used for my study. I didn't get any writing done there because I was waiting for *Cherry Pit* to come out. I think it was in March of that year that we heard from Florida that the owner had been hit by a train and was killed. His widow wanted to come back and put the house on the market. We would have loved to have bought it, but back then it was selling for the ungodly sum of forty-five thousand dollars. If I had been able to scrape up or borrow forty-five thousand dollars that house today would be worth a half million at least. But we couldn't buy it, so we started looking for a place and we found that house that we finally did move into in April. We got it for sixteen and a half, which was more our price range.

Q: Is the description of the house that "G" in Some Other Place. The Right Place, *lives in pretty much that house?*
HARINGTON: That's the house. That's where I wrote *A Work of Fiction, Lightning Bug, Some Other Place. The Right Place, The Architecture of the Arkansas Ozarks,* and *Farther Along.*

Q: What was your study in that house like?
HARINGTON: Very tiny. It was about six feet wide, maybe eight feet deep. Just room for me, my desk, my filing cabinet, and my phonograph. That's about all I had room for. I covered the walls with topographic maps of Arkansas and, of course, the poster of Vanessa Redgrave as she appeared in *Blow Up* that inspired me for the writing of *Lightning Bug.* It was a very tiny study, but it was cozy. Right after getting the house, I had a fluorescent light put in the ceiling so it had good lighting. I had a space heater so I was never cold in that room.

Q: Isn't it in the "Acknowledgments" in The Architecture of the Arkansas Ozarks *that you write about looking out the window of that study?*
HARINGTON: At the sycamore tree that's exactly like the sycamore tree that Noah Ingledew built his tree house in as being an inspiration for the—

Q: You spoke of the poster of Vanessa Redgrave as being an inspiration for the writing of Lightning Bug. *I wonder if there was a visual inspiration for* Some Other Place. The Right Place.
HARINGTON: Not one picture but several pictures. One of the first things I

did when I started on that book was to drive to Dudleytown and take a whole bunch of snapshots of cellar holes and Dark Entry Road and just whatever was left of Dudleytown. I had a stack of photographs—none of them on the wall—but spread out. I can't really remember putting anything on the wall for *Some Other Place. The Right Place.*

Q: *You used the image of Vanessa Redgrave for the image of Latha Bourne in* Lightning Bug. *Did you have a similar image for Diana in* Some Other Place?
HARINGTON: Just the mental image of Diana. I never used any one picture, which is unusual.

Q: *Do you now use pictures for your characters? For example, do you have a picture of Ekaterina?*
HARINGTON: In *Falling Off the Mountain* I form my characters from actual people. For the Indian maiden I use a nice photo of Joy Harjo, the great contemporary Indian poet. She's a beautiful woman too. I use her as the model for the Indian heroine of part 2 of *Falling Off the Mountain.* I've never had any image of what Vernon Ingledew looks like, but one of the newspaper columnists in the book describes him as a cross between Hugh Grant and Robert Redford, if you can imagine looking like that. He's a younger Robert Redford. So I have sort of pictured Vernon very handsome, which is one of the big things he has in his favor in running for the governorship of Arkansas. Women just fall in love with him at first sight. He has the women voters of Arkansas in his back pocket or his jock strap.

Q: *Be careful. How does the Ingledew men's shyness toward women affect Vernon?*
HARINGTON: You had reminded me of that some time ago. I had written all of Part I of the book and that had slipped my mind. You reminded me of that and I had to go back and rewrite all of Part 1.

Q: *Oh, no.*
HARINGTON: Ever since you reminded me of that, everything I have done in Part 2 takes clearer awareness of the fact that he's not able to look at women if they are strangers. The only reason he could look at and talk with Jelena is that she is his first cousin. She's an Ingledew herself. In going back, I'm going to have to make it clear that he has great difficulty. I mean, when he goes out on the campaign trail he can shake men's hands and slap them on the back, but if any woman approaches him, he's really petrified.

Q: *The poor guy!*
HARINGTON: It makes for some comic situations.

Q: *I am curious about your decision to set* When Angels Rest *during World War II rather than, say, Vietnam.*
HARINGTON: Well, it's one of the loose ends in the saga of Stay More that remained to be filled in. At the end of *Lightning Bug* it says that in the high school at Jasper there is a plaque to the memory of Gerald Coe who died a hero at Iwo Jima. That's all it says about him. So for all these years I've known that I would probably someday have to tell Gerald Coe's story just as I had to tell the story of Doc Swain who had appeared in other stories before I wrote his story in *Butterfly Weed.*

I wouldn't say that *When Angels Rest* is Gerald Coe's story, though he is one of the dominant figures in it. It begins and ends with him, but I'm simply picking World War II because that's a time in the history of Stay More that I needed to write about. I mean *Lightning Bug* ended in 1939. *Architecture of the Arkansas Ozarks* simply has a few paragraphs referring to how John Henry "Hank" Ingledew served in the Pacific and came home to impregnate Sonora and have all of his children. Also in that book are Jelena and Doris, the twin sisters of Ella Jean, whose suicides are mentioned in that book. So those loose ends just sort of formed a background for this particular period in the history of Stay More.

Q: *Even though Stay More is a small town, how do you keep all the lives of the people in your mind when you're writing the story? Why, for example, isn't "Tull" Ingledew in the story?*
HARINGTON: There are many people in *Lightning Bug* and my other novels such as Nail Chism and Viridis Monday who are in Stay More at this time but aren't in *When Angels Rest.* This is not their story. I have to focus on whose story it is and on what is happening in the town at the same time. Presumably, Tull and Nail and all the other people who weren't mentioned in the novel were subscribers to Dawny's newspaper. They are included when he says that he went around to people's houses and asked them if they have any news. They are presumably included in that crowd, but they had nothing to do with the story. That's why Daniel Lyam Montross is not even identified except that he's called Dan. Unless you know better, you don't know that he's the same guy who was the narrator of *Ekaterina* and whose story *Some Other Place. The Right Place* is.

Q: Your mentioning of Daniel Lyam Montross and those two novels reminds me that When Angels Rest *might be paired with* Lightning Bug.

HARINGTON: A parenthesis. Montross had narrated the fourth part of *Some Other Place*, so he narrated the first part of *Ekaterina*. He picked up where he'd left off. Dawny was the narrator of all of *Lightning Bug*, so he continues as the narrator of all of *When Angels Rest*. Even though the question still has not been settled: Was Dawny lost at the end of *Lightning Bug*? That's still an important consideration that should not be neglected—that Dawny was lost at the end of *Lightning Bug* so he could not possibly have participated in any of this activity in World War II.

Q: One of the curious things about Dawny is that, though he narrates both Lightning Bug *and* When Angels Rest, *so little seems to be known about him. We don't know, for example, who his parents are; we don't know what his last name is.*

HARINGTON: We know everything that is important to him. We know he lives with Aunt Murrison—speaking of characters that don't get mentioned, where the hell is Frank Murrison? Frank Murrison was a real villain, a real sonofabitch, and he doesn't even get mentioned in this book. Why not? Dawny doesn't want to mention him! Why doesn't Dawny say who his parents are? He doesn't want to. He doesn't consider it important; it's not relevant. All that matters is what he does mention. In one place in the book he says that the less said about his aunt the better.

Q: When does Dawny tell this story? Is it when he is an adult?

HARINGTON: Obviously, he's telling it as a grown man who's sixty-three years old. He wants to identify with the self he was back then at the time. So, to tell the story he needs to pretend that he has regressed, gone back to the time that the story was taking place, and he's telling it as first person, eye-witnessed narrative at the time it was taking place, but obviously an eleven year-old kid could not use that language. Just as he had to pretend to tell the story of Mare Coe on Iwo Jima. He could not have told that story of Mare Coe on Iwo Jima. He wasn't there. He needs the reader's help. He needs Ernie Pyle's help to make up that story.

I think that one of the hardest things I had to do was to be able to choose a tone and a language which would convince the reader that this really is an eleven year-old boy doing this, but somehow he's using awfully big words and good words and good prose. That's part of the suspension of disbelief. The reader wants to suspend disbelief that Dawny could actually be telling the story in 1945, which he could not have.

Q: *One of the things* When Angels Rest *suggests to me, especially in chapter 24 when Dawny discovers the dead Ella Jean, is that imagination can take us only so far and then we have to deal with loss.*
HARINGTON: Well, keep in mind that in that particular spot Dawny is in a terrible state because he has just discovered Ella Jean's murder, and he's just lashing out in search of help from Gentle Reader or anyone. When you as reader get to that point, you realize, sadly, that there is nothing you can do even if you wanted to. The reader knows that the author has been using him or her throughout the book to do things for him, but if you wanted to, you couldn't bring Ella Jean back to life.

Q: *Both* When Angels Rest *and* Butterfly Weed, *have huge losses in them. Both Dawny and Doc Swain lose a beloved. Yet, both novels also seem to be suggesting ways of coping with such loss. But* Butterfly Weed *seems more comic than* When Angels Rest.
HARINGTON: You can't be too funny about war, and also an eleven-year-old boy doesn't have the rich sense of humor that Doc Swain and Vance Randolph have.

Q: *And a lot less sex than in* Butterfly Weed.
HARINGTON: There's no sex at all in *When Angels Rest.*

Q: *Even the sex between Mare Coe and Gypsy is only alluded to and not shown.*
HARINGTON: We never see anyone making love in *When Angels Rest.*

Q: *I think one of the reasons there's so much sexual activity in* Butterfly Weed *is because of the allusions that novel makes to classical mythology.*
HARINGTON: The Greek gods and goddesses did lots of screwing! There's no mythology at all in *When Angels Rest.* You know that scene in the outhouse between Dawny and Gypsy? I wrote it originally so that they stay out there in the outhouse for what seems forever, and she eventually takes his virginity. But I realized after writing the whole scene of Dawny and Gypsy making love in the outhouse that, for many reasons, it was just not going to work. I wanted Dawny to still be a virgin when the book was over.

Q: Why did you want him to be a virgin?
HARINGTON: Because it implies that although he has lost his innocence in the sense of being exposed to the effects of war, being exposed to the murder of his girlfriend, being exposed to cruelty in the form of Sog Allen and the beating of old Jarhead—all of these things that are making Dawny grow up—he still has one big step to go to reach manhood, and that's not going to happen in the book.

Q: Some of your novels have strong relationships with other works of literature. Cockroaches of Stay More, *for example, with its connection to Thomas Hardy's* Tess of the D'Urbervilles. *Does* When Angels Rest *have a connection with another author's war novel?*
HARINGTON: Not that I know of. I haven't read very many war novels myself. There are models for all my books but there isn't one for *When Angels Rest.* There are at least three things I consciously did with this book in an effort to break the jinx of obscurity. I did not use heavy Ozark dialect because I felt that might turn off the reader. I wanted to make the story more universal; this story could take place in Ireland or Maine or Europe for that matter. It's a departure from my other books also in the sense that you can't say, well, that's just a kind of variation. Of course I'm just guessing. I don't know why critics or the public—the public more than critics—I don't know why the public has just refused to buy my work. It's a big mystery to me. I think it could be a matter of the fact that it's regionalism, and I wanted to get away from that regionalism. It could be the fact that maybe the reader feels that I have heard this story before—wasn't this *Tess of the D'Urbervilles* in a different form? I don't know. I'm just making wild guesses, but when I wrote this book I did deliberately set out to do something that would break that jinx. Apparently it did not work, so it must be some other reason.

Q: Let's talk about how you start your novels. What's the seed, for example, of Butterfly Weed?
HARINGTON: I started that novel with Dawny grown up and sobered up talking to Vance Randolph on his death bed. That actually happened and it is the seed for that story. *When Angels Rest* starts with Dawny getting his arm broken. Well, in fact, originally chapter 1 was that chapter about Mare Coe getting killed in Iwo Jima. I decided that before I could do that I would have to give some background information and get my chronology straightened out and so forth. But the seed for this novel was trying to tell the story of how

Mare Coe, who was posthumously awarded the congressional Medal of Honor, how did he win that medal? I had no idea, so I had to make all of that up. And that was the seed for this story.

Q: *Now the story of Mare Coe's death appears as chapter 7. Do you usually do much revision when you write your novels?*
HARINGTON: I usually do very little revision. In the case of *When Angels Rest*, I simply moved chapter 1 to chapter 7 and started writing six chapters before it. In terms of rewriting passage, I didn't do that much, though maybe more than in *Butterfly Weed*. I don't like to revise.

Q: *Do you see Dawny as being a version of you as say "G" is in* Some Other Place?
HARINGTON: "I" in *Ekaterina*, "Harrigan" in *Let Us Build Us a City*. I mean I have a persona in every one of my books. You could perhaps make a strong argument that all these personae are the same Person under different names. But I think there are enough differences that a sharp critic could discover that Dawny who calls himself "G" and meets Daniel Lyam Montross in the end of *Some Other Place. The Right Place*, could not possibly be the same Dawny that's in *When Angels Rest* because there are too many discrepancies. The point is that none of them is me, because nothing that happened to any of them ever happened to me except that I ran a neighborhood newspaper in Little Rock when I was eleven years old. I had a hectograph and printed out my neighborhood newspaper. That's the only thing that happened to me and to this Dawny.

Q: *This Dawny, unlike the one in* Lightning Bug *never goes to Little Rock. He lives all the time in Stay More.*
HARINGTON: You just reminded me of something that I had forgotten: that in *Lightning Bug* Dawny does mention that one thing he has in common with Sonora is that they both came from Little Rock and were just spending the summer in Stay More. This Dawny in *When Angels Rest* never mentions Little Rock.

Q: *The Dawny in* Lightning Bug *was lost and we don't know if he was found, so, as you said earlier, we don't know if this is the same Dawny as the earlier one.*
HARINGTON: Except that his relationship with Latha is the same; and he does have an Aunt Murrison. Is she ever called Aunt Murrison in *When Angels Rest*?

Q: What's the difference between history and story?
HARINGTON: Oh, you mean in history that all of this would fit together and it would be consistent?

Q: Yes.
HARINGTON: I'm not sure about that, because Stay More's history is not history so much as it is just story. It's historical in the sense that it has a chronology to it, but it's not history in the sense of facts. Even the history in *Let Us Build Us a City* is not necessarily history. All of that stuff that Harrigan supposedly found with Kim in as the history of these those various towns—all of that was made up and presented towns of Arkansas, things like the sinking of the sultana, when the steamboat sinks in the Mississippi and this guy tries to rescue the girl and he eventually finds his way to dry land and winds up over in Sulphur City, Arkansas. His entire story is just fiction!

Q: Because the Stay More novels are set in the same locale and often are concerned with the same characters, readers often tend to see them as being a kind of history as well as story.
HARINGTON: Are you asking if there are any inconsistencies in any of the characters? Don't you think it's the same Doc Swain that speaks up in *When Angels Rest* as the Doc Swain who speaks up in *Butterfly Weed* and in *Lightning Bug*?

Q: How does McPherson know about Sull Jerram being assassinated on the way to the waterfall glen in 1914?
HARINGTON: He must have read *The Choiring of the Trees*.

Q: [Laughs]
HARINGTON: No. He couldn't have read *Choiring of the Trees* in 1945. It must be part of magic realism. For that matter, how did McPherson know that the bluff dweller Indians inhabited the glen of the waterfall for generations? Has Dawny told him that he was lost there at the age of six? I mean there's no way McPherson would have known any of that except that McPherson himself had hid out in the glen of the waterfall.

Q: Why is When Angels Rest *divided into two parts?*
HARINGTON: It's divided into before and after the war comes to Stay More.

Q: *In* Butterfly Weed *and* When Angels Rest *there seems to be more concern with grief for the loss of the beloved than in your other novels.*
HARINGTON: I never like sad stories. Where I part company with Cormac McCarthy is that all of his books are unremittingly tragic. I don't like the tragic. I'm not denying tragedy, but I want my stories to be happy stories for the most part. Despite the profound sadness of Ella Jean's death, I don't think that *When Angels Rest* is that much concerned with grief.

Q: *How would you characterize a Harington novel?*
HARINGTON: I don't think that any of my novels are alike.

Q: *Do you think that the fact that none of your novels is alike has cost you some popularity in that many readers want to read novels that are essentially the same?*
HARINGTON: You think I'd have more readers if I was more consistently doing the same kind of novel?

Q: *Yes. None of your novels has that quality of sameness that a lot of readers expect. But there are some qualities that I do think characterize a Harington novel, such as a sense of humor.*
HARINGTON: Oh, you can talk in broad terms: a love of the language, a sense of humor, a hatred for endings. If there's any one thing that runs consistently through my novels is the fact that they all begin in the past tense, they shift into the present tense, and they ultimately shift into the future tense. Every one of them does that, so there's a consistency of forms which reflects my hatred of endings and my desire to keep any book from ending. You could say that's a characteristic of a Harington novel.

But regardless of how famous I might become, there will never be parody contests the way there are for Faulkner and Hemingway. You know, every year they give a prize to the person who writes the best imitation Faulkner, the best imitation Hemingway. No one can ever write the best imitation of Harington because there's not enough to hang your hat on.

Q: *Would you say that in terms of your prose style that it isn't as excessive as the styles of Faulkner and Hemingway?*
HARINGTON: My prose style has no style. I am very aware of the language but I am not consciously working on a particular style. I think that

Hemingway constantly told himself when he was writing, "I'd better keep this sentence short," and Faulkner constantly told himself when he was writing, "I can't have any periods in here, I've got to have commas, semi-colons; I can't stop." I think they were both consciously aware of their styles. When I write I am never aware of a style. I'm never telling myself that I'd better slow it down here, speed it up there. I don't ever think about the mechanics of writing. Certainly not to the extent of conforming to any style or stylistic formula.

Q: I think some readers tend to see your novels as being set in the past rather than dealing with contemporary events.
HARINGTON: Just as I am opposed to style, I am opposed to date. I don't think of any of my books as belonging to a period. I do not do period pieces. Wherever possible I avoid mentioning actual dates. The story of *The Choiring of the Trees* was set way back in 1907 to 1914. I don't think of it as belonging to that period. I think most of people who read it and enjoy it think that it could happen right now. Or they just become indifferent to the fact that it is set way back then. Then some of my novels, such as *Ekaterina*, are set in the present. *Falling Off the Mountain* is set in the present; in fact, *Falling Off the Mountain* is set in the future. It happens in the year 2000. Almost all novels are set at a time before you're writing about them, but I don't think you can say that my work is about the past.

Q: You say that Falling Off the Mountain *is set in the year 2000 and deals with contemporary politics?*
HARINGTON: Although it is set in the year 2000, I never identified the year. There are enough references, however, that any one who buys the novel next year and reads it—assuming it gets published—next year will know that it is the year 2000. For example, it's the last year of Bill Clinton being in office. I would hope that thirty or forty years from now when readers read the book that they don't necessarily remember that 2000 was the year Clinton left office. The actual date is irrelevant, but it is a book about contemporary politics.

Q: Is the Osage woman in Falling Off the Mountain *modeled perhaps on the Indian woman in* A Work of Fiction?
HARINGTON: The woman in that book was a Creek woman named Sugar Creek whom Albert Pike was keeping as a mistress and Arrington, the narrator of the book, fell in love with, so she might have been the remote inspiration for my Osage woman. But I think that when I wrote about Sugar Creek I

still had this noble savage concept that I think I have now outgrown. My character—her name is Julianna—is a thoroughly modern woman who happens to be not only of Indian ancestry but she is also a direct descendent of Jacob Ingledew. Jacob Ingledew had sex with Fanshaw's wife and the offspring was eventually Julianna, which makes her one more cousin of Vernon's. So he's not only been living in sin for thirty years with his first cousin Jelena but now he gets involved with his twelfth cousin fifteen times removed or whatever.

Q: Are you concerned with the Osage from a political angle?
HARINGTON: The Osage were the settlers of the Ozarks and, just coincidentally, they happened to be the tribe that became filthy rich when oil was discovered on their reservation in Oklahoma. So Julianna is quite rich. I am sure that some critics are going to call attention to the fact that there are so many rich people in the book. There's Ekaterina who made a fortune off her novels, there's Vernon who made a fortune from selling his Ingledew hams— that's the money he's using to run the campaign with. Diana is fabulously wealthy from her inheritance from her grandfather who founded an insurance company in Little Rock. She has money coming out of her ears, and now here is Julianna, who has God knows how many millions of dollars. The place is just overrun with money. Somebody's going to ask me at some future date "Why did you feel the need to have so much money in your book?" And I'll probably say, "well, because I never had much of it myself."

Q: Vernon's relationship with his "cousins" makes me wonder about the question of incest in your book?
HARINGTON: Julianna is such a remote "cousin" to Vernon. This sort of relationship between "cousins" is commonplace in the Ozarks. If you go out in Newton County, Madison County, Arkansas, you'll find that everybody is related to everybody, so that if you are going to get married, you have to marry somebody who is a distant cousin or even a close cousin.

Q: No, not a close cousin.
HARINGTON: Lots of people marry their own cousins. It happens all the time. But this sort of "incest" is not like that with Daniel Lyam Montross in *Some Other Place.*

Q: Do you think that the incest with Daniel Lyam Montross is related to the theme of solipsism in Some Other Place?

HARINGTON: It could have some relation. I haven't thought about it that much. Incest is usually sensational and it makes for good plot excitement and that's probably why I used it in *Some Other Place*. It isn't a theme that appears in my other books.

Q: That's true. It is most strongly associated with Dan Montross.
HARINGTON: Maybe he was just the bringer of incest to the Ozarks. I've never really thought about that.

Q: Well, you don't have to think about it. You've mentioned before that in 1973 you were working on Architecture, *in 1983 you were working on* Let Us Build Us a City *and some on* Cockroaches, *in 1993 you were working on* Butterfly Weed, *and I wonder if you can say what you will be working on in 2003?*
HARINGTON: It's a retelling of *Green Mansions* by W. H. Hudson, about a man in South America who discovers the bird girl named Rima who has this magnificent voice and is just a child of nature. Did you ever see the movie *Nell* with Jodi Foster? My novel won't be like *Nell* and not really *Green Mansions*, but those are the only two works—a novel and a movie—that I can think of that are remotely similar. It's a story about a Chism girl—I haven't given it enough thought at this point, but she could be directly descended from Viridis Monday and Nail Chism. Maybe not. Maybe just part of the same family. But because of circumstances, she has grown up in the Ozarks without any contact with the outside world, in almost total seclusion. What happens to her when she is forced to come into contact with the outside world. It will be a romance involving her and the man who discovers her. I haven't plotted it out because I am still so busy with *Falling Off the Mountain*. That story is what I will probably be doing in 2003.

Josephine Humphreys ～ 1992

ALPHONSE VINH

In one of her essays, Josephine Humphreys writes, "To tell the truth the South is once again in ruins." There is much truth in her comment. That enigmatic American region, more written about than any other part of the United States, a country within a country, has had its rises and falls. The new ruins are to be found in the constant destruction and reconstruction of the southern landscape by the developers of the New South, frequent objects of satirical attack by Josephine Humphreys. But more than simply speaking of a new reconstructed South, a South of glittering skyscrapers and tourist booms, Humphreys speaks of the ruins of the traditional southern family, of traditions held on to and lost. In her three highly original novels, Dreams of Sleep (1984), Rich in Love (1987), and Fireman's Fair (1991), she chronicles the lives of families in her native city, mod-ern-day Charleston, South Carolina. When we enter the lives of the Charleston men and women in her novels, we meet them at critical turning points in their existence, when the old bonds are disintegrating and new bonds are sought. Love lost must be regained, albeit in different ways not yet imagined. In the complicated lives of her characters, Humphreys mirrors the South's protean abil-ity to remain ever itself and yet constantly changing. To read Humphreys is to encounter a creative imagination richly humorous and yet fully aware of the aching sadness of daily life, especially the sadness of women.

Josephine Humphreys was born 2 February 1945 in Charleston, South Caro-lina. She was reared in Charleston and has lived most of her life there. Her family belongs to Old Charleston society, and among her ancestors was the Con-federacy's last treasury secretary. Educated at Duke University (BA) where she learned the craft of writing from Reynolds Price (who has remained a lifelong friend), Humphreys went on to do graduate work at Yale University and the University of Texas. She married Thomas Hutcheson, an attorney, whom she

Originally published as Alphonse Vinh, "Talking with Josephine Humphreys," Vol. 32, no. 4 (1994), 131–40.

met as an undergraduate at Duke. The couple returned to Charleston in 1970 and have lived there ever since. Both of their sons are now at Harvard. (When I last visited Josephine Humphreys at her family's weekend home on Johns Island back in March 1994, she told me her sons resolutely refused to attend Duke because their parents had gone there.)

In 1985 her novel Dreams of Sleep *won the PEN/Ernest Hemingway Prize for the best American first novel. She has also secured a Guggenheim Fellowship and a Lyndhurst Fellowship. Recently the Fellowship of Southern Writers awarded her their annual prize for best novel by a southern author.*

The following interview was done with Josephine Humphreys in April 1992 at Spartanburg, South Carolina. I had the pleasure of visiting her in Charleston in April 1994. At that time she was inducted into the South Carolina Academy of Authors. Currently she is working on a new novel, which will be a great departure for her. Her previous three novels were set in contemporary Charleston; the current work, however, takes place in the Charleston of the 1890s.

QUESTION: *You were brought up in Charleston. Did you have any sense of a literary community growing up there, did your family know about this community, and how did you get stimulated by literature?*
HUMPHREYS: I knew of writers. Charleston had writers and this was a part of its heritage—but I knew of it only through rumor. I didn't know any of the writers. I never even read any of their books. They were minor writers, but good writers. Josephine Pinckney was one and the South Carolina Poetry Society was a very active group, but by the time I was a teenager the thing had dwindled down to old ladies writing poetry. So there was a sense of a literary tradition, but it wasn't anything that seemed alive to me. It wasn't really there; it was just a ghost of a tradition that was there. Writers in the nineteenth century and early twentieth century were not really read; nobody ever read them.

Q: *Nobody ever read them: William Gilmore Simms or Julia Peterkin?*
HUMPHREYS: Right. I never even heard of Julia Peterkin until I was in my twenties—which is really amazing! Her book won the Pulitzer Prize, *Scarlet Sister Mary.* I would say that it was not a literary community in Charleston. It was more of a community that liked to think it was literary than actually being literary; but my family was a reading family and we had a lot of books. My parents never bought any books. We didn't have any money, but they had books left over from their parents and so I had a big library to read around in our house, and my parents were great public library-goers. My mother took

us to a public library every week and we loaded up on the maximum number of books and we read all the time. My mother is a great reader and that was her main pastime. My father has never understood the purpose of reading fiction. It totally eludes him. And he'll say, "What can you learn from a novel? It's made up, it's not true. You can't really acquire any information," so he reads things about how to make wine and how to grow trees, but not fiction.

Q: Do you think there is anything remaining from the old southern tradition? I came from such a gentry family where the idea of a man, for example, writing poetry professionally was unheard of.
HUMPHREYS: Right. I always did have encouragement in writing. From just the earliest stage my mother and grandmother told me that I was a good writer and they would ask me to write little stories and little poems. This was before I was in school and then in school my teachers all the way through school encouraged me. By the time I got to high school, I was in an all-girls' school which had a very active and truly inspiring writing program. They had a literary magazine that they published four or five times a year and we met once a week and read each other's work. We had a teacher who made writing seem like the most important thing that you could do, and it never was presented as a sort of girl's hobby. The teachers really thought it was important, and a lot of people who were with me at school in that same society wanted to write. Later on writing for us became something that we wanted to do with our lives.

Q: Southern writers have emphasized the importance of place and community in the lives of their people. In Firemen's Fair *you can see the exodus of the Charleston families from the city into the suburbs and exurbs. Tell me, what do you think people's sense of place and community is now? Is it vanishing? It seems to be from your book.*
HUMPHREYS: I think it's vanishing quickly in some places more than in others and I think it's vanishing very fast in the coastal regions including Charleston because those are the places where the big money has come in and really changed the community. But if you travel to other parts of the South I find the sense of community still as strong, and, in fact, I like to travel now to other southern towns because it reminds me of what my town used to be like, where there is still a sense of community, a real love for the land. It's hard to love the land in Charleston now because it's hard to find it. The suburbs have so small a wilderness that it's very difficult to find the wilderness.

Q: In your first novel, Dreams of Sleep, *your character, Will, has a strong streak of conservatism in him. He does not want his mother, who is the epitome of the New South realtor/developer, to sell the family home, property, and furniture. I have seen that streak in other characters of yours—Lucille, for instance, with her antiques. In them it's a sense of trying to preserve the heritage.*

HUMPHREYS: Trying to hold onto things, but it's impossible and you really can't expect even the most honorable people to preserve their land because so much money is at stake. I had friends who owned a whole coastal island and they wanted it to stay that way, but they were offered—I think it was eleven million dollars by an Arab investment group back in the seventies. You can't, I mean no one would have asked them to turn that money down. It's something that we couldn't do anything about.

Q: You were saying in one of your novels that your characters are always trying to escape. Alice Reese says, "I want to go to sleep, I want to be lost in dreams." Or else your characters want to go AWOL, hiding out at a friend's farm, for instance. Tell me about that. What is this escape business?

HUMPHREYS: Well, I don't know. I suppose it was always an idea in my head from the earliest times. I mean, Charleston was a place that demanded your loyalty and I don't know if other cities put that kind of pressure on their people. For example, there was a tradition in Charleston that when a young woman married a man from elsewhere, she would bring him back there to live. That was what was expected of her; it was always sort of a joke when people said, "Oh, you are marrying a man from Chicago, you are going to bring him back here to live," and I said, "No, of course not," but I did do it!

Q: Well, didn't it say somewhere that you did not intend to go back to Charleston?

HUMPHREYS: No, I didn't want to, but Tom really liked it and so he said, "Let's try it." The reason I didn't want to live there was that I didn't want to raise my children there. I wanted my children to grow up with more encouragement to be different and with less pressure on them to do the right thing, to follow the rules of the town. What happened was that both had changed; I had changed and the town had changed in my absence during my school years. It turned out to be a very good place to raise children and they turned out pretty much as I wanted them to. So I'm glad that it worked out and we went back.

Q: Vladimir Nabokov said one time that his characters were galley slaves. How do you feel toward your characters? Do they just come up in your mind?

HUMPHREYS: Yes, they do. They appear out of personal metaphors. To talk about how it works is hard because writers don't really know. I think it's a very mysterious and interesting thing. Writing sometimes reminds me of dreaming in that the source seems to come to you from somewhere else. But it's not coming from somewhere else, it's coming from you. In a dream you are not really aware of its process and how it gets to you. The characters remind me of accounts I've read and radio programs I've heard about the psychotic disorder of multiple personalities. The persona, the human psyche has the ability to fragment like that, and if it's out of control, you become a multiple personality and you are not really suited for real life. Novelists are a lot like that. I am anyway, and when I am writing a novel it is as if my own persona splits into these five or six different characters and so each one is sort of me in different ways.

Q: *Tolstoy's great novel,* Anna Karenina, *begins with this sentence: "All happy families are alike, all unhappy families are unhappy each in their own way." True?*
HUMPHREYS: Yes, I think Tolstoy was right. Happiness in families, I think, depends on a few important things. But unhappiness can come from a thousand different directions, so I think there are just more possibilities for variation in kinds of unhappiness.

Q: *The psychological term for it today would be "dysfunctional" families. As your Billie Poe said, she doesn't know any normal families.*
HUMPHREYS: The family I grew up in—my mother, father, two sisters, and I were a happy family, but we had an inheritance of unhappiness in my mother's family which was a terrifically unhappy family and one that totally fell apart, and we were aware of that. My sisters and I were aware from an early age of this having happened and it was so horrible! Even when my mother did talk about it, she would often burst into tears at the dinner table. So to a child something like that seems the worst thing that could possibly happen. In my mother's case her father left the family, abandoned the family, and then tried to have his wife committed to a mental institution in order to divorce her because divorce was difficult to get on any other ground. My mother had told me that before it happened she thought they had a happy family. She didn't know that this was going to happen. She had no suspicion at all, and so I always thought, well, gosh, I didn't consciously think this, but I was aware that even a family that looks okay, that looks secure, can really fall apart overnight. So I think it was something that I was very afraid of when I was little.

Q: *Along with the struggles in families, your novels seem to focus on them at the point when they disintegrate. Loneliness is a recurring companion for your characters. You mentioned the dangerous loneliness of Billie Poe that Rob could sense when he touched her.*

HUMPHREYS: Loneliness has always been my closest companion. I don't know why. I mean I think these things are just part of us from the beginning, but I have always been very shy, as a child very shy, very withdrawn and dependent on myself for company. I never had a lot of friends. As a reader and writer, loneliness is really compounded because it is not a social activity; it is not a job in which you meet a lot of people. What you do is sit by yourself for a couple of years and then you get to go out and see other people!

Q: *That reminds me of Lucille talking about how her family cannot be touched by the pain and problems of other families. She wanted a hermit family that was able to be cut off in their own solitude.*

HUMPHREYS: Their own solitude which is impossible and that idea gets families into trouble because they think they can be self-sufficient and I think that's very dangerous for a family to overstate what we now call family values. We need much more than family values. Family values often means the dominance of someone who then tries to control and keep intact the rest of the family which is designed to break up; that's what it's supposed to do. If it's a successful family, the children move away. You know I hope that mine don't live far away, but they must move out, they must make their own families.

Q: *What do you think happens to the relationship between Iris Moon and Fay at the end of* Dreams of Sleep, *speaking of families?*

HUMPHREYS: I think those two have moved onto a functional level together which they were not on before when Iris was taking care of Ben. I think Fay, the mother, has grown up. She has finally grown up and realized that Owen is not going to come back. She's now facing reality and dealing with things on a much more adult level than she has before which allows her child to be an adult as well.

Q: *Why do you think your characters often have the desire to keep everything they have, all the relationships they have. They don't want any changes. Will Reese clinging onto his love triangle in* Dreams of Sleep, *or Lucille Odom and her family, in* Rich in Love, *where her parents break up and she wants everybody back to the way things were.*

HUMPHREYS: I think people are often afraid of change. It's a natural fear because, you know it's just a fear of the unknown. But people are afraid if something like that changes, that they will lose what they have. They don't know what the alternatives are, they don't know what will happen. In that book, *Dreams of Sleep*, Alice is actually afraid of the possibility that her husband is going to lose his lover. That frightens her because it would be a change; it will take her forward into something else that she doesn't know how to deal with, so that was an odd sort of thing that she would be afraid of that—but she was.

Q: That's one thing I've noticed in your writings, the presence of fear. I think you once mentioned in an interview that fear is the worst influence in people's lives. Fear, for example, caused Will Reese in Dreams of Sleep *to gravitate towards financial success and stasis, thus risking the loss of Alice, his wife.*
HUMPHREYS: My parents were both rather fearful. They were afraid—I think their main fear was poverty and the Civil War and its legacy had something to do with that. Moreover, I think the Depression in the South during the thirties changed my father forever. He was always afraid of not having enough money; secondly, my parents were afraid and I think a good many southerners were afraid of foreigners and by that I mean somebody from anywhere else, including people of other religions, other races. I've never understood where that fear came from except that if you have nothing, if you are very poor, if you have suffered enormous defeats in war and your region is considered evil and the worst in the world, which is what the southern image was from 1865 to 1965, all you then have is your community. You tighten it up and you don't let anybody else in; you exaggerate the importance of ancestors who were wealthy and honorable and you hang onto those things because of the things you don't have and you sort of shift values. I think that's what happened in Charleston and maybe in other parts of the South. We were raised to believe that money wasn't important. Well, it's a good thing because we didn't have any and the important things were your history and your family and these were over-stressed.

Q: Growing up in the South, you may have heard the phrase, "You were not half the man your daddy was." A Virginian friend of mine said that southern men have to live with the legacy of the South's failure and defeat. I'm thinking especially of Walker Percy's characters like Will Barrett and your own like Will Reese and Rob Wyatt.

HUMPHREYS: I wish I could talk more authoritatively about southern men. I like men, I like southern men and to think that they have a love affair with honor and defeat—that's probably right. The best ones do because there were a real lot of men who never consider or even learn these two things. The thought never crosses their minds, but the best ones do have that sense of honor. I think that is what makes southern men interesting and good to the extent that they question themselves. Surely the military loss in the Civil War must have had an effect on men in that way. It was a defeat and women don't usually think of that when we think about the defeat of the South in the Civil War. We never think of it in the way that men must have back then—the idea that they were beaten, it was a loss of honor for them because they were beaten. We women don't think of it in that way at all—I don't anyway! I never have!

Q: *The first time I read* Dreams of Sleep *I was so struck by a kind of spiritual kinship you seem to have with Walker Percy.*
HUMPHREYS: I will never, never be able to write a single sentence as good as any of Walker Percy's. When I first read *The Last Gentleman*, which I read in 1966 or '67, it really just overwhelmed me! It was the first southern novel I had ever read that seemed real, that seemed about my South. Flannery O'Connor I loved and Eudora Welty I loved, but they were writing about a rural South. While I had some connection to it, it was not really mine; but Percy was writing about the urban South and it was so exciting and I thought it was so funny! It was so exciting to me—I like his style, I liked the humor in his book and the main characters, too. The narrators were all the kinds of men that I liked and hoped to find some day.

Q: *You were telling me at lunchtime that you have a great story about Percy.*
HUMPHREYS: Yes, this was at the Chattanooga Conference on Southern Literature about two years ago, and it was at a dinner. I was sitting between Walker Percy and Shelby Foote who evidently went to high school together in the same town in Mississippi—Greenville or Greenburg or something like that.

Q: *Greenville.*
HUMPHREYS: Right. They were talking about their English class, their teacher, and they were reminiscing about all the bad poetry she made them memorize. She also made them write a sonnet and Walker Percy said, "Shelby,

I remember the sonnet you wrote," and then he proceeded to quote it, to re-
cite the sonnet that Shelby wrote as a high school senior in Greenville, Mississippi, which I thought was absolutely amazing that he could. I know they
were friends and sort of rivals if they were together like that, and to imagine
that Percy remembered the whole sonnet that his friend had written was outstanding. Shelby said, "Well, that's a terrific feat of memory." He then said,
"I remember a sonnet you wrote," and then he recited Walker Percy's sonnet. They both had remembered each other's fourteen-line poem from I don't
know how many years ago. What would it have been, fifty, sixty years before
that?

Q: *I wonder if there is some kind of subconscious Percy influence in, for example, the name and personality of your character Will Reese?*
HUMPHREYS: Probably. Then my father's name is Will and my son's name
is Will.

Q: *It seems that your characters often seek after signs and portents; that's another Percy thing, looking for the signs in the world. Alice in* Dreams of Sleep
trying to find in mathematics personal symbols in order to combat chaos.
HUMPHREYS: I think that's probable. I don't know why they do that, but
many of Percy's characters are religious in the traditional sense, in what you
call the Christian South. None of my characters are churchgoing members
and yet they all have a religious—what I think of as a religious longing for
meaning and they don't know where to look for that. They really don't know
how to find it. They have no road map to turn to, so they turn to things that
are, I think, unreliable, like the weather and little signs like that because it is
the only thing they've got.

Q: *Do you feel a commonality with the sadness of your women characters?*
HUMPHREYS: Sure. When I started writing I was really sad, that was the
huge emotion in my life. At the time I was thirty-three and I had this thing
that I wanted to do. I wanted to write, it was a big dream of mine and I hadn't
done it and I felt that I had wasted so much time and that I was absolutely
worthless. When I sat down to write that first novel, I just had a terminal case
of melancholy and it just came out especially into Alice. The poor thing, she
just got too much of it and as I continued on writing, I think there is less of
it. I think it is overpowering in *Dreams of Sleep*; but I think there is a great
deal of sadness in women's lives that really has no outlet and it is both an

unknown factor and an unknown quantity. People don't really realize how much sadness there is and it doesn't always have a good reason, but I know that it is there, not from my parents, but from women that I see now, when I am away, when I am traveling, when I am speaking and reading. There is an enormous sadness among women and it may be this which is driving them to attend writers' conferences. I feel that there is this need somehow for them to do something with their lives that will, in a sense, give them significance, a significance within themselves that they don't feel in their regular lives. It is sort of a cliché by now in the women's movement and it has been talked about a lot. There's this person who's a wife and mother essentially getting her sense of self as a helper to others and I think many people can do this. They can live this sort of life successfully for a long time, but the sadness of it accumulates and builds up. I know that it did for me and I think it's very important for women to have some kind of life of their own separate from their families.

Q: One last question for you. Where do you envision Lucille Odom twenty years from now?
HUMPHREYS: Twenty years from now at age forty? No, thirty-seven? Thirty-nine? Well, I think she'll be what I'd like to call a crazy lady, that is someone who is like me, who appears to live a normal life, who goes to the grocery store, who takes care of her children, who does all the apparently correct things, but who also does some odd things, who has her own thing, whatever it is. My children sometimes call me crazy and they know that I like being called that. They know that I take it as a compliment and I think that Lucille would do that.

Q: Well, thank you very much for your time.
HUMPHREYS: You're welcome!

Mary Lee Settle ～ 1994

JENNIFER HOWARD

Mary Lee Settle has made her name writing novels, including the much-praised Beulah quintet—O Beulah Land *(1956),* Know Nothing *(1961),* Prisons *(1973),* The Scapegoat *(1980), and* The Killing Ground *(1982)—and* Blood Tie, *which won her the National Book Award in 1978. Though she's famous for it, the form is a late love for Settle, who began her literary career as a journalist and writer of plays—six of them, all but two ("The Enormous Purple" and "Juana La Loco," which can be found among her papers at Boston University) now lost. Born in Charleston, West Virginia, in 1918, Settle set her sights on an acting career long before she discovered writing. "I thought that my life would be over if I didn't go into the theater," she says. Most of Settle's plays were written between 1948 and 1954, when she was living in England. Her earliest pieces touched on classical themes: Helen and Paris ten years later; a little-known episode from Roman history in which the Empire is auctioned off to the highest bidder (even Robert Graves thought she was making up the story, and stopped by her house in London one morning to apologize after finding the passage in Gibbon). Two plays metamorphosed into novels: "Strike Night" into* The Scapegoat, *"Deed" into* The Kiss of Kin. *Settle's last play (and the only one ever produced) was "Juana La Loco," commissioned by the American Place Theater and performed off-Broadway by the troupe in 1965. Interviewed on May 31, 1994, at the house outside Charlottesville, Virginia, that she shares with her husband, writer William Tazewell, Settle talked about her youthful thespian ambition and how the actress became the playwright became the novelist.*

QUESTION: *I read somewhere that you wrote a number of plays before you ever tried a novel.*
SETTLE: I did. I wrote one when I was twenty-nine and I stayed up all night to finish something before I was thirty—something, anything! I can't even

---

Originally published as Jennifer Howard, "Interview with Mary Lee Settle," Vol. 33, nos. 2–3 (1995), 79–83.

remember what it was called, but it was very mythic. Then the second one I wrote was called "The Enormous Purple," and it was about the auctioning off of the Roman Empire. It was auctioned off after the death of one of the emperors. I still love that play. The third was, oh, let me see—I think it was called "Where Helen Lies," and that one I liked a lot too. It was about Helen and Paris ten years later. The fifth one was called "Strike Night," a title that I used abortively later, and that was about an accident where somebody got killed in the coalfields. Then I made a play called "Deed," about a family reading a will, and by that time I was so tired of actors and producers taking me to dinner and telling me how wonderful I was and then not doing the play, that I thought, "All right, I'll make it into an ideal play. I'll be the actors and the director and the props and everything, put it all down on paper." And that's what everybody called a novel. I turned it into a novel.

Q: Why were you drawn to historical subjects early on?

SETTLE: I was trained as a Shakespearian actress, and so I had very little sense of the past as such, as something remote. From the time I was ten, when I was sent to a teacher—used to be called elocution, now it's called something-therapy or some damn thing, I don't know! I had two impediments in my speech: I couldn't say "l," and I couldn't say "r." I still can't very well. So I went to Mr. Drew, Maurice Drew of the great Drew family, who had been cast ashore in Charleston, West Virginia, and was teaching a bunch of brats how to speak. And he found a kindred soul in me. So I was doing Shakespearian monologues when I was about eleven. And it was wonderful. So all I had to offer, when I went to New York and was going to be an actress, was a pretty well complete knowledge of Shakespearian heroines. Nobody seemed to want Shakespearian heroines at the time!

Q: So what did you do?

SETTLE: I modeled for John Morris and Harry Conover, who were the two top modeling agencies in New York. And then there was a war, so I went to that. Do you know what the Barter Theater is? Well, it's a Virginia institution, a very famous summer stock company. What had happened was my mother decided between my sophomore and my junior year at Sweet Briar that I should go and be an apprentice, because she thought I was interested in the theater. And also it was a bore having me home all summer, hanging around the country club. I've always been grateful to her for making that decision. I didn't go back to Sweet Briar, I went up to New York. It was the summer of

1938, and a scout for Selznick was going around summer theaters looking for people, and I was taken to New York to read for Scarlett O'Hara. We didn't quite realize that it was a big publicity [stunt]—they really had a hard time finding a Scarlett, and I was of course completely wrong for it, too tall and the whole thing, but they seemed to have a passion for getting as many [of] what they thought were southern ladies there as possible to all twirl around. I was offered a stock contract and I didn't go. My instinct was wrong about it.

Q: *What would a stock contract have involved?*
SETTLE: Being stuck with Selznick for eight years or something in small parts. I was very snobbish, I thought I wasn't interested in film, I was interested in Shakespearian drama.

Q: *Life would have been very different if you had gone to Hollywood.*
SETTLE: I don't think I would have been much of a success in Hollywood.

Q: *It might have been very hard to write there. Did you think at that point that you would be writing?*
SETTLE: Nope. That was all before I wrote anything. I can't think of anything—I keep saying this—I can't think of anything that's more useful [training for a writer]. For a long time I thought, "Oh, I wasted several years," but I didn't. I've used them ever since. I did earn my living as an actress for a long time, and I think it's probably the best training that a writer of fiction could possibly have, in that it forces you to—not identify, 'cause that's loony—empathize with your characters and realize they're not all you. I think anybody who's doing one of these workshop writing things should join a theater group. It's very, very good for them. It teaches them about spoken words, about directness, gets them out of themselves so that they have to observe and be somebody else for a little bit.

Q: *Why do you especially like "The Enormous Purple" and "Where Helen Lies"?*
SETTLE: Because they're magic.

Q: *Are they subjects you would try in fiction?*
SETTLE: I don't think so. I'm just trying to think if I have tried them. I was reading in the British Museum, and I came on an emperor, Claudidius Julianus, who bought the Roman Empire in an auction sale. The emperor Severus had refused to pay the bribe, the donative, to the Praetorian Guard, so they

killed him. And they all got drunk and one of them, the head of the Praeto-rian Guard, climbed up on the wall of the Praetorian camp and said, "The world's for sale to the highest bidder!" There was a rich businessman, Clau-didius Julianus, and he bid on it and won, gambling that there was money in the Imperial Treasury. There wasn't. I thought this was a wonderful idea.

Q: *Is it tragedy, comedy, somewhere in between?*
SETTLE: There are some funny bits, but everybody gets killed. I'm just trying to think as I talk—you know, I have written it in completely other forms. I've always been fascinated with where history has a turning point, and that turn-ing point is very seldom recognized. It's that turning point in *O Beulah Land*, the point that ended in revolution; it's the turning point in *Know Nothing*, which ended in the American Civil War. And that's why both *Beulah Land* and *Know Nothing* have been taught in history departments. Everybody talks about the wars, but that movement toward it, where it becomes inevitable, people tend to neglect, and I've always been fascinated with it. ["The Enor-mous Purple"] really was a play about that turning point.

Q: *You've said that "Juana La Loco" was written as a political play. How is it political?*
SETTLE: It was written at a time in American politics when to call some-body "communist" was as pejorative and as killing as to call somebody a Protestant in Spain, so in a way it was a hidden political play. Juana was the second daughter—there may be others I can't remember now—of Ferdinand and Isabella. And Ferdinand and Isabella were just like on-the-make Ameri-can parents. They wanted their daughters to marry well. Juana La Loco—means "Joanna the Mad"—was married to Philip the Fair of Burgundy, so she went from having Torquemada for her tutor to one of the most open courts in Europe. As far as Philip was concerned, it was an imperial marriage and that was that, but she took it a bit too seriously and fell in love with him and was very jealous and so forth. Well, at the same time she was exposed to as liberal an atmosphere as there was in Europe at the time. When Isabella died, Juana and Philip the Fair came back to Spain and broke the Inquisition. There was no way to stop her except terrible stories of her being mad. Philip died of plague and in order to keep his body from being stolen she kept it with her . . . so her enemies, including the Inquisition, started the story that she kissed him every night and so forth . . . Anyway, she was jailed for forty years. Forty years! At one point she was let out in a kind of palace revolution,

but by that time it was too late. She was extremely intelligent, but she'd been in jail too long, and she waffled and waffled.

Q: Had you been reading a lot of history then? How did you come across the story?
SETTLE: I found it by accident in the British Museum. I picked up a volume of state papers and found the story of Juana, because at one point she and Philip came to England. It was years later that I wrote the thing. But I'm slow witted, because I read about Mother Jones—several speeches of Mother Jones and about a strike in West Virginia in 1912 in the *Congressional Record*, and it was thirty years before I used it to write *The Scapegoat*, which as I say partly harks back to one of the plays ["Strike Night"].

Q: By the time you wrote "Juana" in the 1960s, you had gone on to write several books. Was it strange to go back to the play form?
SETTLE: No, it was happy. The experience was absolutely wonderful, because I called the director at the beginning and said, "Now what is my role in this?" And he said, "Your role is to act the playwright, and what you do is watch very carefully and see how little dialogue is needed." It was a great lesson, because an actor—a good actor makes a gesture and the whole paragraph of dialogue goes. It's not needed. So—this is marvelous training.

You know, it's so hard for me to try and revive an ambition that was, in Shakespearian terms, "a vaunting ambition which o'erlept itself." I thought that my life would be over if I didn't go into the theater, and this was true from the time I was eleven until I was in my twenties. I was never out of a play. That was my life. And then, after the war, it just disappeared. I found out—I didn't do it consciously, you don't find things out consciously, you grow toward things—I grew toward the realization that it was too confining: somebody else's words, somebody else's direction and finally not enough to pour one's life into—for me, anyway. I always wanted to be up on the stage far more than I ever wanted to write. I think anybody who "wants to write" is a fool who works too hard. You either just do or you don't.

Elizabeth Spencer ✎ 1994

DAVID HAMMOND

EDWARD . . . Who's Edward Glenn to be worth a second thought? He comes and goes too much. Still has a place in the old law firm, can get his old twice-a-week teaching job back at the junior college school of business administration, legal branch. Does a little fishing, kills a duck or two in the winter, has a drink or two every time you see him, marriage broken up. And what's all this about Mexico? ALINE I wondered that, too. What is all this about Mexico?

—*From* For Lease or Sale
Act II, Scene I

She leaned forward and laid her head on his knee. Close and warm, his hand moved on her hair.

He said: "Today, down in the village, I saw this Mexican, an older guy, riding a bicycle in a muddy street, holding this kid, a little girl, before him on the seat. She had grabbed onto the handle bars, close to the middle. They were both laughing. I never saw two people so happy. I guess it was his granddaughter—it would have to be. I think I'll remember it forever. There in a muddy street of a dirt poor town on a half-broke old bicycle—pure happiness. You don't see it often."

"You didn't kill your wife," she said.

—*From* The Runaways

Looking up at the house, mysterious in the westering light that slanted before us, I marvelled at how weightless its presence before us seemed. I could suddenly not imagine being anywhere else. 'I kissed a strange man in the library,' I almost said, almost adding, 'I live here.' I had found in the thought a different meaning for that simple phrase, I live here. I turned it in my mind, just as in an exercise I had often had my students do. Here, I live.

—*From* Shongalo

Originally published as David Hammond, "'Parts of a Novel That Will Probably Never Get Written': An Interview with Elizabeth Spencer," Vol. 33, nos. 2–3 (1995), 85–106.

I first met Elizabeth Spencer in 1987, when she brought the manuscript of her play, For Lease or Sale *to PlayMakers Repertory Company, the resident theater at the University of North Carolina at Chapel Hill, where she had recently joined the faculty. Over the next year and a half we worked on revising the manuscript, and I directed the play's premiere in early 1989. It was warmly received and was subsequently published by the University Press of Mississippi in Volume IV of* Mississippi Writers: Reflections of Childhood and Youth. *During the months spent preparing the play, Elizabeth and her husband, John Rusher became my good friends.*

For Lease or Sale *centers on Edward Glenn, a lawyer in his late thirties, who has recently returned from a stay in Mexico to a small Mississippi town to assist his mother in the sale of the family home. Other characters include Edward's mother Jeannie; his niece, Patsy; his embittered ex-wife, Aline; and Claire, a woman in her twenties who has begun a flirtation with Edward.*

About a year ago Elizabeth mentioned to me in a telephone conversation that she had completed a short story I might enjoy. She sent me a copy of The Runaways, *in which Edward Glenn, at an isolated resort in Mexico, finds some moments of tenderness and compassion with a dying woman named Joclyn.*

Another Edward story Shongalo, *came in January of 1994. "Shongalo" is the name of the Stratton family's house, to which Milly Weldon, the high-school teacher who narrates the story, is invited for a summer weekend by an adoring pupil. The Strattons are distant cousins of the Glenn family, who originally owned Shongalo among other family properties. On a hot afternoon when family members are napping, Milly finds Edward searching through a desk in the house.*

Intrigued by the recurring appearances of the Edward Glenn character, I talked with Elizabeth at her home in Chapel Hill on two afternoons in January and March of 1994. The text of the interview that follows has been edited from those conversations, and some sections have been transposed for continuity.

QUESTION: There are now two Edward stories.
SPENCER: And the play.

Q: And the play.
SPENCER: I think I've seen the last of him.

Q: Reading the stories, I was fascinated by the idea of Edward as a character outside the main structure of people's lives who, nonetheless, has a very powerful effect on them.
SPENCER: Uh huh, uh huh.

Q: *I felt the two stories went together very well in a wonderfully disjointed kind of way.*
SPENCER: I think they do, too, but why they do, I don't know. I just—wandering character at this point; he might show up anywhere.

Q: *But you said you thought this was the last of him.*
SPENCER: I don't know. People wander in and out, you know. But what it seems to me is that these are disjointed parts of a novel that will probably never get written. What turned me on to doing the first of those stories, *The Runaways*, was the fact that he had been in Mexico, according to the context of the play, and there were passages in the play about Mexico that I never got to use, but they had been lying around in my consciousness, so I constructed the first story out of those leftovers—a meal out of leftovers, so to speak.

Q: *It's five years now since we did the play. Obviously, something about Edward Glenn has stuck with you for a very long time.*
SPENCER: I know. Isn't that funny?

Q: *He keeps coming back.*
SPENCER: I don't know why that is.

Q: *Is that a creative experience that you've had before—that something pops up in one work and returns in another work in a new form?*
SPENCER: Yes. That happened between my first novel and the second one. I thought of using one of the characters that was in the earlier work. It's when people start a story about themselves that isn't finished. Then I think, "Well, I know the rest of that story, it just didn't fit into what I was writing." So the story will hang around in my mind. I always experience the characters I write about as though they were alive—I mean, they're real, living people, even though I made them all up, which is a bit crazy. I know Elizabeth Bowen, the Irish novelist, actually fell in love with one of her characters, and she used to think she saw him everywhere and expected to hear from him some time. It must be pretty frustrating to fall in love with a character, wouldn't you think, because you could never hope to meet him.

Q: *I don't know—you could write great romantic adventures—*
SPENCER: But you wouldn't be able to see them, touch them, or be with them! Anyway—I think the reason Edward preys on my mind is that he's

the kind of southern man that's rather elusive and probably doesn't exist, but . . . he's sort of put together, stuck together from a lot of impressions I've had through the years about southern men. And maybe I'm creating more of an ideal of a type rather than an actual person—but I don't know how to explain all that—except I always had a feeling about maybe actually finding somebody like that. It is kind of a lingering thing throughout a lot of my life.

Q: *The charming, intelligent—*
SPENCER: —charming and witty and intelligent—

Q:—*borderline alcoholic*
SPENCER: —maybe an alcoholic and maybe no good. Something like that goes around in my mind. But the underlying intelligence, I think, is what intrigues me. And also the sense of somebody that is, in a way, caustic, also being very vulnerable is intriguing, I think. The person doesn't exist, but many qualities from other people have come to exist in him . . . maybe he's sort of like the guy Elizabeth Bowen fell in love with. Maybe he's really my long lost love or something, and I can't ever find him. But, at any rate—no, I think, basically, I always felt—well, I'm married to an Englishman, obviously there's bound to be some kind of basis for departure. I always felt a kind of disappointment with southern men, and I don't guess it's their fault. I guess I build up too high an ideal for them, and nobody could really reach to that . . . Or maybe it's an unresolved part of my psyche.

Q: *But you like Edward.*
SPENCER: I like him, yes. But I said when we were doing the play, I'd rather write about him than know him. Because he's mean, you know.

Q: *He can be.*
SPENCER: I think what attracts me, though, is the same thing that attracted me to write about those young men in a story of mine you like, *The Cousins.* He's a type of southerner that isn't written about much. He's intellectual. Southerners when they are brilliant, the way I've always experienced it, are very, very bright indeed. And this is a phenomenon. I remember just the tail end of this conversation. I recall that somebody in Italy who knew the country awfully well was talking about Sicily one day, and I said it was kind of like the Mississippi of Italy. I meant in a far-South, hot, undeveloped sense. She said, "Don't underrate the Sicilians, there are very, very brilliant people down

there, you know. They're probably the most intelligent people in Italy." There have been some brilliant talents from Sicily, like Pirandello. And so, this quality attracts me because I don't think it's been done enough in literature about the South.

Q: I looked this week at the interviews done at the time of the production, and you always said, when someone asked "Why is this a play?," "I started to write, and I saw a man and a young girl on a space that I knew was a stage." When you saw the man and the girl on the stage, did you know that the man was Edward? I mean, did Edward come to you first, or did simply a dialogue between a middle-aged man and a younger girl come to you?
SPENCER: Well, the whole idea that he was bantering with her in a personal way—I've had that happen to me all my life, that older relatives would start out in a kind of teasing way, and I felt sure of my ground there, because I knew how she would feel in that circumstance, though, of course, I wasn't drawing on any particular scene in my own personal history. But then, of course, that led immediately to the idea of who and what the guy was that was doing this and what relationship there was. And it was kind of exploring outward from that that gave me the story of the play, because I often have this experience with characters that I imagine, whether it's fiction or, in this case, the play, that they're just suddenly—they're full-grown, complicated people, and then there's really something to explore. But where they come from I have no idea.

Q: You've said where the impulse for starting to write For Lease or Sale *came from, but why did you bother to do it as a play? What attracted you to writing for the theater?*
SPENCER: Oh, I think all novelists want to write for the theater! I think, if you look, I bet you won't find any novelist anywhere that doesn't have a play they've always wanted to write or have actually written and maybe never had produced. When Toni Morrison was here, we were sitting at dinner, and somebody said, "Elizabeth has also written a play," and I said, "I bet Toni Morrison has, too." She said, "Oh yes I did, and it was produced" somewhere, I don't know. She wasn't terribly proud of it, but just the same, she had. And I—well, it's the instinct toward character, and I thought that would be fulfilled and would stop when *Light in the Piazza* was made into a movie and I could actually see my characters. But the living experience of the stage to

me is more exciting than movies, it always has been and remains so. Just to see the—it was a wonderful experience for me that you were able to teach me how to work on that script, for one thing. And then when we began to embody the things we had exchanged and talked about and got the dialogue certain. When they became flesh, as it were, to use religious terms, and there they all were—that was very exciting to me. I know it's old hat to you, but I think you still get excitement each time that happens.

Q: *When it works.*
SPENCER: It was like they were coming to life, you know, in a real—there's more of a creative feeling in that experience than just having turned out your own work and seeing it on the page. I get something of the same thrill when people actually read the things I've done, and I see them come alive in somebody else's terms. But if you're just hooked up with your own work and playing it back to yourself, that's not—that's not real communication. I want to see it out there being read and affecting other people.

I've been trying to start another play from time to time. I had a play in my head about a brother and sister relationship through the years, and I've written a few scenes, but it doesn't seem to catch fire like this, because I'm not so intrigued by the characters as I was by this. This must have touched something very basic in my own experience in a way that flowed into the characters in a similar way.

Q: *It was wonderfully easy to act.*
SPENCER: I hope so.

Q: *As soon as the cast spoke the dialogue, it was very clear that it was theatrically active dialogue.*
SPENCER: A lot of that was due to you, because you were able to trim out a lot of the dead wood. But the main thing that somewhat got out of hand about the play was that—and I guess it was in the dialogue or she wouldn't have been able to do that—the mother's role got a little bit—

Q: *Dominating.*
SPENCER: Domineering. And I think that was because there were too many lines given to her. She's supposed to be more of an archetypal frame for the play, which really belonged to Edward, and after him, I suppose to Patsy, I

would think. In another way, Claire was the romantic attachment an audience expects. That frames the story, too.

Q: *She's a bit like Milly in* Shongalo, *but seen from another point of view.*
SPENCER: Yeah, maybe so, maybe so.

Q: *Do you think that way when you write stories? Do you see a structure as clearly as what you just described?*
SPENCER: I saw that between the mother and son in that play very clearly because I thought, well, I've got to have her, in a sense she's the spirit of the house speaking, you know, and the house is very important. So, when so many lines made it possible for the actress to, in a way, take over the play, I thought that jarred in the production. We worked on that, and we never quite got it out.

Q: *In the published version you shifted the focus.*
SPENCER: After we revised it, yes, she's shortened. She was supposed to be more of a murmurous background.

Q: *The vision of Mrs. Glenn as the voice of the house—did that emerge as you were partway through writing the play, or did you know as soon as she joined the plot that that's what she was?*
SPENCER: I—I wrote the whole first thing that you said needed weeding out so long a time ago, and I've forgotten what I thought. But I thought of him as central and her—sort of spinning, not spinning around, but as in "spinning a web"—weaving the whole thing of the past, and the past carrying into the future, and finally reaching a place where it couldn't carry any further. And then, you know, he's got to become something, and so—that was the point, it seemed to me, that he must find himself. His identity emerged out of that.

Q: *Do you think if you were writing it as a story or novella Mrs. Glenn would be less present?*
SPENCER: Oh, goodness, I don't know. I never thought of writing it as a story. You think I should? My trouble in adapting anything I've written to the stage, or—people have asked me to do TV scripts and different things like that—is that after I've written it I'm through with it so I wouldn't be exploring anything anymore.

Q: *But this keeps coming back. You keep writing Edward stories.*
SPENCER: Well, the characters do. But the specific form of this and their exchange and their dramatic confrontations, I feel I've got them down and that's enough. So I don't cherish the idea of writing it any other way. Do you think I should? Maybe if somebody gave me a push in the right direction I could. I'm not sure that I want to.

Q: *I just know I'm fascinated every time there's another Edward story.*
SPENCER: Really?

Q: *Yes.*
SPENCER: Well, maybe I'll go on writing them, then. Maybe it will all be a collection of well, you know, those stories I wrote around that character Marilee, they kept coming one after another, and I still have two or three in my mind that I never have written. She's more a voice than anything else. I don't know what he is, he's a physical presence, an attractive male presence. But I feel that she's more a voice talking to me. So I think of the things she has to say. But, about Edward—I don't know, maybe I'll finally write something that will be a new appearance—I think he's a wandering planet.

Q: *In the newest story,* Shongalo, *he's a tangential presence that has a profound effect on the young teacher.*
SPENCER: Well, it was just that moment that was very highly charged sexually. Do you remember—I just thought of this, I hadn't thought of it before— *Last Tango in Paris,* where those two people are alone in an empty apartment, you know, and it winds up in an overt love scene?

Q: *Mmm hmm.*
SPENCER: But this was, you know, it was a little more romantic and sort of dreamy, not so physical.

Q: *But it really could be the same story without having it be Edward Glenn that Milly has the experience with.*
SPENCER: No!

Q: *It just needs to be the attractive male.*
SPENCER: The attractive male.

Q: But for you—
SPENCER: But for me—

Q:—it was Edward Glenn.
SPENCER: It was Edward. That's the way I looked on him myself. Somebody to find someday.

Q: When you told me over the telephone there was another Edward story, I could hardly wait for it to arrive.
SPENCER: Really?

Q: And it came in the mail, and I started to read it, and said—
SPENCER: "Where *is* he?"

Q: Exactly. And then, ah! There he is, driving a Jaguar.
SPENCER: There he is. But you know, really, the heart of the story is that girl with the crush on her teacher, and it's as if those two forces—I often think of fiction like a play in terms of forces—you know, those two forces get completely overturned when he comes in. It's the idea of the—well, you have the wheel within the wheel sort of thing. A girl getting over her first crush and stuff like that. It's a common enough story. But then, what breaks the circuit is what the story was—yes, it could have been any man, except the whole thing of that house, also, is another—that's the real estate mentioned, because the Glenns must have been diminished at the time of the play, must have been very prominent property owning people, because they had an interest in that property, see.

Q: Yeah.
SPENCER: And then it's gone over to the Strattons, and Mr. Stratton is not in any mood to truck with them anymore. And they refer to Edward's mother, Jeannie, as not wanting to hold on to it. And so that—that's what I said, it's like fragments of a novel, because somehow if you had a multiple generation novel, then you would have different episodes like that coming out. The shadow novel has never emerged. Now, someday, there may be other pieces that relate to that family, not necessarily Edward or anything, but then you could sort of make a whole work, like the fragmented pieces of a total work, light coming through in fragments. And then the reader would have to construct the novel that isn't there. See what I mean?

Q: *Sounds wonderful.*
SPENCER: Maybe someday I'll do it that way.

Q: *Do you know, when you start writing something, that it's going to be a no-vella or a short story or a novel?*
SPENCER: Well, I've deliberately—I did some novels drawn out of shorter things. But when I start doing a novel I deliberately try to map out where it's going to go—sometimes it doesn't work out that way—because I think a novel is such a long trip that you've got to have some idea of the road ahead. But shorter things, I just sort of let them—like a fish struggling on your hook, you let it play where it will and try to land it.

I think *The Light in the Piazza* fooled me because I thought it was going to be about thirty pages, and it suddenly seemed to catch fire and spread out to a larger form. And then, there are things that you encounter that you want to explore that you couldn't ever get to in a short piece, but you really need to explore fully in a novel. I didn't foresee in *The Night Travellers* that I would want to explore that girl Mary Kerr's family situation as much as I did, but since she was a southerner, and I was a southerner, I believed that was very important to her. After I moved here, I began to think once again in terms of place and family and everything. I thought I needed that frame of reference for more fullness. Maybe I was wrong, something about that didn't quite sit right with me. I changed locales in writing the book, and I thought maybe it didn't merge together well.

Q: *Because you physically moved from Montreal to North Carolina?*
SPENCER: Yes. Don't you think that might just get hold of your nerve ends in such a way?

Q: *It might, but I thought the book had a really exciting shape.*
SPENCER: Yes, you thought it flowed very well, and that was very encouraging to me, because I thought it might have seemed strained and—you know, like it didn't mesh together.

Q: *You said to me once that you have become somewhat bored with strict nov-elistic development, that Henry James had more or less finished it off, and that, in* The Night Travellers, *you played with the format—that there was a change from a more structured approach at the beginning of the novel, when the char-acters' lives are more structured, into a more chaotic, almost cinematographic*

approach as their individual worlds disintegrated. Did this use of form emerge from the content by impulse as you worked? Or did you know you were going to do something unusual with the structure when you first conceived the book?
SPENCER: I thought it was full of experimentation . . . well, that came out of a strategy for showing them as far apart, you know. There are devices that are necessary to keep them in touch even though they're separated. And so I worked at that, how best to do that. I could not foresee the events in the dictated form, because I could not perceive those characters' lives in nonconnected blocks of, you know, interrelated action. It was the jazzy nature of the whole thing, the skip, the hit-and-miss, the way people came and went, the way you never knew where anybody was. The way they were frightened by surveillance from the States, which everybody denied, but which was going on, actually. It was revealed that there were people that they got to cooperate through the FBI, the CIA, the Justice Department, all over Canada who were spying. And so this entered the consciousness of people there, so . . . you couldn't use traditional form to get hold of that, I don't think. It would be very hard.

Q: At this stage of your work is experimenting with form of more interest to you than it was previously?
SPENCER: I only realize later that I've experimented with form, because then I look back, and when I'm writing it I—the strategy is "how do I get from here to here?" And that may result in some innovation that I hadn't thought of as innovation until I looked back on it and realized it.

I always remember something Robert Penn Warren said, or wrote somewhere, and I used to have my students say it. "The moment of vision is the moment of revision." That's when you really see what you've done.

Q: I would guess that this is different for every writer, and it may be different for every work that you do, but—what starts you? a character? an event? a mood? what?
SPENCER: Well, different things for different times. In writing *The Night Travellers* I remember that the first thing I thought about was here's an opportunity for me to write about the Canadian scene, and bring in an era that was rather mysterious to people in the States. And I thought about, well—the first title of the novel in my head was *The Lost Children*, but then I thought, that's so discouraging and pathetic! Who would want to read a book called *The Lost Children*? But they did seem to me a bit lost in a lot of ways, in a strange

kind of way, and I thought first of this girl, she was always the major one in my mind who had somehow gotten abandoned by a lover or a husband, or somebody who had died, or in some way was not there. And that her mother came and took the child away, and that she had to kidnap her own child back. That was the original idea. I don't know if I ever heard of such a thing happening or not. I may have, but, on the whole, I thought I thought of it. So that central episode—to me that's very central to the book, when she sneaks down there with that Jewish man she met. You remember that scene? I wrote that first. And then I began to think about—it was very vivid to me—that whole landscape down there in Vermont, and Vermont in the summer and how innocent and pastoral it looks, and then those sort of convoluted family things happening. I thought it would be a short novel, and then I began to ask myself questions. "Why does she want the baby back from the mother?" "Who is this guy with the mother who's not her father, what's he like?" And then "Why is the husband or lover or whatever absent?" Well, I knew that the Vietnam background was what I was getting at all along, because that was a separating force in American life, don't you think? I think it was the most separating force since the Civil War.

Q: *Changed my life.*
SPENCER: Did it? I was the World War II generation more than that one, but I can very well see how it would have changed people's lives all up and down the line. Well, the more I began to ask questions about where this boy was—he suddenly had a way of showing up in my thoughts, and very vividly, as an image. And then I began to think back, because I'd had a couple of short chapters written in about her life in North Carolina. And then at about that time I moved—

Q: *—to Chapel Hill—*
SPENCER:—and then you and I got involved in the play. So, by the time I came back to the novel, I'd absorbed a lot back into myself of that southern living and mores and ways of looking at things and voices. So in order to place the two characters in their milieu it became a longer novel. But I thought in a way it was strengthened, because I see them both as very southern, Jeff and Mary Kerr, and I saw the whole thing grew out of a locale.

Q: *You're describing what sounds like a discovery process that you began with the episode in Vermont with Mary Kerr and the child.*

SPENCER: It grows out of that. You know, you accumulate a huge mess of a manuscript, and then suddenly you realize, well, this is a novel, I'm going to see whether it shapes itself well enough to be a novel.

Q: It shapes itself? Or do you—
SPENCER: Yes . . . well, I think, by this time, goodness, I've written nine novels. The first novel I wrote I was very timid about all that, and I tried to lay out a plot, you know, like a dress pattern. Did you ever cut a dress pattern? No.

Q: No, I never did.
SPENCER: My mother tried in vain to teach me to sew; I think I made two or three dresses. But, at any rate, what I knew about novel form I learned from people like Thomas Hardy and Henry James, and other people—but I began to see that I would have to have some kind of formal structure to put the content of that first book into. So I went about it very carefully.

Q: This is Fire in the Morning.
SPENCER: Yes, that first little book. And, then, later on, when I came to write, say, *The Voice at the Back Door*, I was still very much in the traditional southern pattern, don't you think? It had its roots in the past, but it . . .

Q: I think it's very original.
SPENCER: You do? Well, I hope so. People said so at the time. Critics come along and say these things. But you did have a certain balance of character there; you had the four main characters sort of balancing against one another, weren't they? That's a typical Jamesian approach. I don't know . . . I think of a novel now differently from what I thought of it at first. I think of it as a kind of an expansion from within. An exploration from a central point is the way I did *The Night Travellers* and the way I did—what was the one before that? *The Salt Line*. It seemed to me it was expanded out of—the funny thing about *The Salt Line* was that I never wanted that character Lex Graham, you know, that hateful person, in it. He just wouldn't stay out! And I hated him so, and I thought, well, if he's in here, he's got to get some devilment done, so finally I made use of him, I thought, but I really didn't like him.

Q: Where did you start on The Salt Line?
SPENCER: Where? I started with chapter 1 in that one.

Q: Really? With Arnie shopping?
SPENCER: Yeah, Arnie was shopping and he saw Lex. I was trying—I don't know, Lex just appeared, but I wanted to show a glimpse of the devastation on the coast, and I was trying to send Arnie on his way to meet that girl, Mavis, for the first time, but there had to be something that was kind of upsetting him, some challenge to him. I was going to throw Lex away after that, he was just going to be a motive for recalling the past. But then he just kept coming back.

Q: Let's just take a few more examples. How did you begin work on The Voice at the Back Door?
SPENCER: I'd been thinking about that a long time, and I wrote bits and pieces of it in Mississippi. It was a bunch of disconnected scenes, and I don't even know what they were, because I had sort of a crack-up, a health break-down about that time. I had applied for a Guggenheim, and I got it, but I was too ill to take it, and I had to postpone it for six months and do a little time in the hospital. And when I got out I think I weighed about ninety-eight pounds, but I insisted on taking the Guggenheim and going to Italy. My family were horrified. Thought I wouldn't survive. But I did it anyway. And then I took all these bits and pieces—but, doing it in Italy, I really took a new start. I had my characters in mind, but I don't think I paid any attention to that old manuscript.

Q: Okay, what about a short story—like First Dark. *Can you remember what made you want to tell it?*
SPENCER: The ghost, the ghost, the ghost! I wanted to write about the ghost. I thought about two people being drawn together, a frankly kind of romantic story. What might bring them together better than seeing a ghost? So, that was how it started, and then it just kind of developed.

Q: And the Edward stories?
SPENCER: Actually, *Shongalo* stretched out—it came out of a dream I had about a house like that and a sunken garden and being out there with it. And then I found that I had heard the name, but I don't know where that house was. If my mother ever took me there as a child, I don't remember. But there was an old town named Shongalo, a small town near home, and it was ab-sorbed into a larger town. I drove through there on the way back from my

hometown to Jackson and found there's still a Shongalo Church on the outskirts of that town. I was going in the courthouse to ask for the records, but
the name was all the verification I really was seeking for. But sometime when
I have more time, I'm going to see if there's a house named that, too, because
that would be kind of neat, you know—if I really was dreaming an absolute
recollection of a recalled thing, or whether it just came out of nowhere. But
the name's the same. It's an Indian name, undoubtedly. "Shongalo." It's pretty.

Q: *In* The Runaways Edward *is staying at a small resort in Mexico. In the play,*
For Lease or Sale, *he refers to a visit to Mexico following a disastrous encoun-*
ter with his ex-wife. Is the story about that same visit?
SPENCER: Well, I got to wondering, since he has some recollections . . .
I actually saw that thing in a Mexican village of a man riding around on
a bicycle with his little granddaughter, and I thought they looked like the
two happiest people I'd ever seen in my life. I told John it was like a vision
of paradise to see those two people. And, somehow, that crept into the play
as something he recalled about Mexico. And then it got into the story, too,
so maybe I was being drawn to try to put down something that I had felt
about Mexico.

Q: *So when you mentioned in the play that Edward had spent some time in*
Mexico, was the episode with Joclyn already in your mind? In other words, did
you know the story of The Runaways *and chose to omit it from the play?*
SPENCER: No, it wasn't specific to me. But after that encounter with—I've
forgotten what her name was, the ex-wife.

Q: *Aline.*
SPENCER: Yes. After his encounter, that disastrous encounter after the divorce—he ran into her on the beach, and all this kind of almost terrifying
sexual passion they had for each other suddenly came about again, and it was
devastating to him, and he went off to Mexico. Now, what happened during
that encounter I hesitate to say. I'm sure there was a lot of sex, but there must
have been a lot of anger mixed up in it, too. And he just—he felt torn by that,
as if everything that he'd been trying to get out of had come back again. When
people get dragged back into relationships that are over—I'm sure we've all
had that experience—that are really finished, but you get dragged back . . . it's
really terrifying in a way, isn't it?

I just—I could, in a little way, identify with that. But, at any rate, he took off for parts unknown, and for him it was Mexico. And then I just filled in a gap when I wrote that story, *The Runaways*. I had the story in mind as a romantic encounter between him and a California woman, but the more I looked at her, the more I saw that it wasn't going to be a romance at all, it was going to be compassion and empathy, and real—you know, taking away the mask that each of them wore, but it was going to be more tenderness and feeling than it was going to be anything romantic.

Q: You see in that story very clearly how shattered he is and how much healing he has to do.
SPENCER: But a lot of times you heal by healing other people, too, you know. So . . . you said once that I resembled Edward, and I—

Q: I did?
SPENCER: Yeah, you said—

Q: You probably slapped me.
SPENCER: No, maybe mentally I did, but then I began to ponder on it, the way anyone would if you—maybe I didn't hear you right, but I began to think, "Lord, how am I like him, he's so mean sometimes." But I think the meanness streams out of a sense of frustration at trying to express the wholeness of himself. You know, I think this marriage business was a terrible declivity he fell into.

Q: Mmm, hmm.
SPENCER: Do you feel that about him? That came out in the Mexico story, didn't it?

Q: I think his ex-wife's a horror.
SPENCER: I do, too, I think she's awful. But several people told me they thought, oh, she was trying to convince him to do the right thing. It became a kind of watershed question with people. I would say, "What did you think of her?" and the people who thought she was right and he was just being stubborn, I thought, "Well, I never liked you much anyway!" I probably shouldn't say that in an interview.

Q: Are any of your characters ever—forgive me if this is a stupid question—
SPENCER: That's all right.

Q: —but do you ever write a character consciously based on yourself?
SPENCER: No. I can see parts of my own nature in a good many of them. I mean, for instance, you take a character like Marilee—people asked me that so much when those stories first started coming out in the *New Yorker* I said, "Well, call her an alter-ego"—that I might have been like that if I'd stayed at home. But I really don't know. I can't be sure . . .

Q: What about Theresa Stubblefield in The White Azalea, *who buries the letter from home in the azalea pot?*
SPENCER: Oh, heavens, no! I could never think why anybody thought that could be me, because she was about twice my age when I wrote that! And then I grew up to being that old, but I don't think I was remotely like her.

Q: What seems to me to be you in it is that she has a wonderful sense of proportion about the dilemma and a great sense of humor about it.
SPENCER: Well, I thought she was a rather depressed and put down and defeated individual.

Q: But when she's reasoning about what's going to happen with the letter—
SPENCER: Oh, that! That was funny!

Q: That definitely sounds like your humor.
SPENCER: Yeah, well . . .

Q: Surely the seed for that story came from something personal?
SPENCER: Well, I don't know . . . I don't think so. I just—I just thought of people being . . . well, I had an aunt who—the greatest thing that ever happened—she went abroad. I saw so many people at home—that I escaped from that trap early on—constrained to be part of the family all their lives, and if by some circumstance they didn't marry and have a home of their own, they were considered idle—they didn't have anything to do. You know, a your-life-is-ours-to-command sort of thing. I wouldn't give in to that for a minute, but I know a lot of people that got trapped. That girl in *First Dark* almost—you know, that's the threat in that story, that she won't decide to live. That she'll be a ghost. And so, I think that's what the fear . . .

Q: So it's really working from a situation that you emotionally understand.
SPENCER: But if I can't emotionally understand it, I can't—

Q: *The impulse comes from something that you understand because of your own experience, but it's not necessarily taking a piece of your experience and fictionalizing it.*
SPENCER: Oh, no! I see what you're getting at. No, I find the character, and then I try to see if I can empathize and become sort of at one with that person's experience, really, rather than my experience. I'm not trying to tell about myself.

Q: *It's an empathy.*
SPENCER: Yes. I think that's . . . I mean, if people can't . . . they can't communicate, if you can't cross that bridge between what's you and what's me, we would just be two isolated planets! And so . . . this thread is what holds people together, I think. It just gets stronger in fiction. The person isn't there and alive, but you have to have that sense of knowing somebody. I think that's a fine thing about life, don't you? Except that, I must say this though—there's always part of a character or person that remains mysterious. And I very much object to fiction that pretends to be telling me about everything, you know?

Q: *Because you can't know that about anybody?*
SPENCER: No. It's not life, you know. I just really don't buy that kind of fiction. It's pretense.

Q: *You have a very specific relationship, in your writing, always, to food, and drink, and flowers, and—*
SPENCER: —sex

Q: *—and touching—*
SPENCER: —and trees, and—

Q: *—combing hair, the feel of clothing. Physical sensation and sensory stimuli.*
SPENCER: Yeah, I guess so. It's a sensual world, you're right about that . . . that's why I take so to Italy, I guess. Because it's a very sensual country.

Q: *When we were working on the play I said in an interview that I was fascinated by the sensory awareness in your novels and short stories, that you had this wonderful way of finding the psychology in sensory experience and therefore conveying awful lot about people through what they touched and smelt and felt, and that, deprived of the ability to put in description, you still managed to put that*

quality into the play. The characters' experiencing of the physical world is imbued with meaning. We feel what they're feeling, and it adds to our understanding.
SPENCER: Well, I hope so. But I didn't know I could communicate that in a play script . . . I felt it, so maybe it got in.

Q: There's a passage in The Voice at the Back Door *about some children. Their mother brushes their hair with a wet brush—they're lying on her bed—and she reflects for a moment about how adorable rambunctious children can be made to look, how neat and clean, with just a wet brush. And that passage captures a very complex interaction with the entire environment, which contains all the circumstances of her life, and a few simple actions in that environment embody her handling of her family and her children, and, therefore, her needs and herself. It's rather like the way an actor might work on a role. When you write a passage like this, do you physically feel things as you write? Do your senses lead you?*
SPENCER: Well, I do feel all that sensory . . . I can identify with the senses. I think most people—yes. Well, if I hear—I write from the voice I hear in my head, you know. Hear the rhythms of speech and how the rhythms vary between, say, Patsy and Mrs. Glenn and so on. And just hearing those rhythms also creates what they're feeling. And what they're feeling derives from what they're experiencing. So it's just all a linked-together chain, isn't it? So you can't lose the link out of it without losing the whole thing, in a way . . .

Q: I think that sense of the "linked-together chain" is what made the dialogue work so well in For Lease or Sale.
SPENCER: Well, I hope so, because I can't write anything unless my feelings are totally involved in it. I was working on a short novel when I was down at St. Simon's. I told you I went down there. It's a beautiful place.

Q: Yes. I didn't know you were working on a novel.
SPENCER: I've written several new manuscripts that could be short novels. What I want to do now is maybe one or two short novels. And I did some more short stories last year, as you know. And so I have a lot of manuscripts, but the peculiar intense drive at the center of them is not coming very easily, and I was trying to get to that more and more in these two short novels. And I hope I'm getting to it in the one I took down there to work on, because I'm not quite sure. But one would feel so—feel strongly about any central character, as I should, so I have to keep on and on writing about them in order to generate the feeling that I need to have to do the book. Because, well, let's say

for granted in the first place my characters are so seldom drawn from life as you just rule that out completely. They aren't taken from life. I wouldn't dream of writing a story about you, for instance. But something about you might get into a character I was imagining. Maybe it will someday.

Q: *Are you warning me?*
SPENCER: No, but it could happen!

Q: *So you go to St. Simon's—*
SPENCER: Well, I did this time. I have been—one year I went over to Savannah, another time I went to Beaufort. When I was working on *The Night Travellers* I went up to XXX [*sic*] and spent a miserable ten days at the term break. I don't like XXX very much, but—I know you're not supposed to say so—but that was the Kingsbury in the novel. And then people that I knew there that I talked to contributed even more to the kind of impression I had. They're very money-conscious and very—oh, I don't know, somebody said about XXX it was trying to be a little Atlanta.

Q: *If I keep this in, I'll leave out the name of the town.*
SPENCER: Well, that was the kind of society environment that I tried to build up in the first part of the novel, and it seemed real to me. Because I couldn't believe in any central character I would write about as really being in sympathy with it.

Q: *So, do you pick these places consciously? Places where you go to write?*
SPENCER: Well, XXX I picked because it fitted in what I was writing about.

Q: *Right. And does St. Simon's fit—*
SPENCER: No. I'm very attracted to the sea. I love the coast. And I feel much more alive around it. I just need it. I need to be close to water sometimes, I don't know what that means or doesn't mean.

Q: *That's a recurring reference in your work.*
SPENCER: Yeah, it really is. The tide. I've written so many stories centered around the Gulf.

Q: *There are other recurring references in your writing. Weather, for example.*
SPENCER: Oh, yeah, I am very sensitive to weather.

Q: Especially thunderstorms.
SPENCER: I know ... well, we lived in a town that was—our house was on a hill, and there weren't many other people there, and you could see storms coming a long way off. And then there were trees around, there was this—a kind of moaning. We knew a lot of times that tornadoes did strike, you know, they were very, very dangerous. You've observed here some of the effects, at least. You haven't ever been in one. Well, I've never been in one either, but there used always to be this fear, and the thunderstorms and lightning, they don't have them around here like they did. And so this was a source of real anxiety and sort of fear, I guess, that built up circumstances ... but I once brought this out, just briefly, to a psychiatrist I saw at one time, and my father was a man of great rages and thunderous temper—and the psychiatrist said, "Well, there was a storm within and a storm without," you know? So maybe the two things contributed to this sense of fear. A lot of people have remarked this—these things about storms.

Q: Sunlight, heat.
SPENCER: Oh, yeah. I love hot weather and sun. I'm very fond of all those effects. My mother was very sensitive to all that. She used to remark on it.

Q: Well, it's very interesting, because you'll do it as description, and yet it invariably reflects both the physical sensations and the psychology of the characters.
SPENCER: Mmm hmm. The mood of the individual.

Q: Yeah.
SPENCER: If you do that too consciously, it doesn't work.

Q: Well, that's sort of where I'm leading. Is it conscious, or do you sort of feel-think your way?
SPENCER: I feel-think my way! That's good—that's funny!

Q: It leads the reader through a sensory process that results in emotion because the reader is also stimulated physically.
SPENCER: Well, I hope so. I hope to communicate that well.

Q: Two more questions.
SPENCER: What?

Q: *Do you think of your novels and short stories, novellas and plays as separate entities, or as parts of an ongoing whole? In other words, do you feel that your work is an ongoing process, or is it a series of completed units?*

SPENCER: Oh, no, I think it's kind of like a river. It's all part of one stream of effort and feeling. It comes out of me. But something John Cheever said, he said that all literature was a river, and that all of us were little tributaries flowing into it. So . . . I feel like it's all a stream.

Q: *Final question.*

SPENCER: Yes, sir.

Q: *Do you think in words, or do you think in images or pictures?*

SPENCER: Oh, I think in pictures, I really do. I had a big argument like that in this class in college once where the professor just said, "Of course, everyone thinks in words." And I said, "I don't, I think in images." And he said, "Oh no, you don't, you just think you do." But I do. I see things.

Q: *Many linguistic scientists say that people think in images.*

SPENCER: Really? I didn't know that.

Q: *Since language is acquired, there has to be something other than language that is the basis of thought.*

SPENCER: Uh huh. Yeah, sure. But I didn't know. I thought maybe thought had got transferred into language.

Q: *When you say pictures, do you mean pictures, or all your senses?*

SPENCER: Oh! I don't know. To examine yourself thinking is something else, isn't it? But an image always gives rise to some articulation on my part. That's why my conversation is often very disjointed. If you've ever noticed, I change the subject a lot, or seem to, because there's another image fading on the image.

Q: *That makes it fun to interview you. Because where you get to is so much more interesting than where the interviewer planned to take you.*

SPENCER: Okay.

Q: *Alright.*

William Styron ❧ 1995

VIRGINIA GUNN FICK

In 1968, in the heat of the civil rights struggle, William Styron was awarded a Pulitzer Prize for The Confessions of Nat Turner, *a work of fiction based on an actual slave uprising in Southampton County Virginia, in 1831. Weighing against the prize and the popular success of the book was fierce criticism from blacks and whites alike, who charged Styron with distorting the truth and, worse, being a racist.*

Styron himself called the book a "meditation on history" and said he had written, not as a sociologist or historian but as a novelist, trying to understand the master-slave relationship from the point of view of the slave, trying to probe to the bottom of racial animosity. Since grammar school, he said, he had been haunted by the figure of Nat Turner, briefly described, in a textbook on Virginia history.

Years after the firestorm brought on by The Confessions of Nat Turner, *I was curious to know if racial issues still engage Styron's mind and what he thinks about the South today. In the spring of 1995, we spent several hours in conversation on my back porch in High Point, North Carolina, forty-nine years after we had been classmates at Duke University, where I was editor of* The Archive, *a student literary magazine, and he was a regular contributor.*

QUESTION: *When you return to the South, do you get any impressions that are surprising?*
STYRON: Certainly it was surprising to return to the College of William and Mary in Williamsburg, Virginia, to receive an honorary degree and to find that the other two recipients were Douglas Wilder, the first black governor of Virginia, and Bill Cosby, the black entertainer and philanthropist. That would not have happened in the Virginia I grew up in. Had someone told me in 1940 that Virginia would have a black governor, I would have thought that person crazy.

Originally published as Virginia Gunn Fick, "William Styron: An Interview," Vol. 37, no. 2 (1999), 158–162.

Obviously in the South things have changed. Integration has changed things, and there is also a certain kind of fluidity of the community. I don't sense that same remoteness from the rest of the country that once existed. There is less isolation. More homogeneous connection with the rest of the country. I think it's an interesting change. You don't sense the regionalism of the South like it used to be. You don't sense that this is a walled off part of the world. When you can fly from here to New York in a little over an hour, that is likely to change the view of things. The South is being absorbed to some degree by the common American culture. Or vice versa. The two are intersecting each other.

Q: Is this a change for the better?
STYRON: It's a change for the better and for worse, I think. The two are parallel. The black middle class has made enormous strides. But in the black ghettos kids are still slaughtering each other with guns.

Q: Many blacks seem to think that whatever the change is, it's not for the better.
STYRON: I know. In general, there's a great amount of pessimism.

Q: One example I can point to is the push of black students for a separate student center at the University of North Carolina at Chapel Hill. I'm sure you know about that. I think that's not a very good sign that we've made progress toward integrating our society. I understand that they value their heritage and they should celebrate it, but do they have to withdraw to do that?
STYRON: I think a lot of black people feel the way these students apparently do. They claim, with some justification, that they don't feel comfortable with white people. Just as we don't always feel comfortable with blacks. I think that's a central fact of American life. Despite the intersections, when blacks get together with white people on a friendly and interacting basis, those occasions don't happen very often. I wrote many years ago that racial animosity is not grounded on fiction and propinquity, as many believe, but on an almost complete lack of contact. Unhappily, that situation still exists today.

Q: Do those intersections happen only at a certain socioeconomic level?
STYRON: I'm not sure. I don't see many black people on a day-to-day basis, but I probably see more than most whites do. In a certain sense I'm lucky that way, since for many months of the year I live on Martha's Vineyard where there has been a decade's long tradition of mingling between whites and

blacks. Ever since the nineteenth century the Vineyard has been a summer resort center for middle-class and professional black people, and the sense of a mutual acceptance—often more than that, I mean mutual affection—is quite strong. It's a place that should set an example for race relations in America, but I have to observe that it is rather special. So to answer your question: clearly there is much less association between blacks and whites in communities that are not as well off economically, especially in big cities.

Q: *Is that because they are competing for the same turf?*
STYRON: I think it's largely that. I'm afraid that in this country there is a traditional resentment between blacks and whites, try as we might to disavow it. Although racism exists on all levels of society it tends to get more virulent at the bottom where the tensions and stresses are greater. However, I still know quite a few allegedly liberal white middle-class people who are uncomfortable around blacks—uncomfortable being an understatement.

Q: *One black voice I admire is that of William Raspberry. Do you read him?*
STYRON: I occasionally do. He seems very sound. For me the most vital black voice in America is that of Henry Louis Gates Jr., who was at Duke for a time. He now is the director of the W. E. B. Du Bois Institute at Harvard. I've gotten to know him personally, and I think his is the most compelling black voice of its kind since James Baldwin, whom I knew well, too. Baldwin's friendship was invaluable to me as I tried to understand the character of Nat Turner. Baldwin was an elegant polemicist—he wrote some of the best essays on race ever put to paper—whereas Skip Gates is an all-purpose journalist and scholar. But they both have served the same function of illuminating the black experience for white America, and in a sense acting as intermediaries between the races.

Q: *Do you know how the black community regards Gates?*
STYRON: I think they regard him very highly, though I'm sure he's got his critics and adversaries like any forceful intellect. I'm certain he's aware that the violent, fulminating phase of the black revolution is past and that in this period of constraint it is much more important to establish and continue a dialogue between blacks and whites than to prolong the apartheid. And by apartheid I mean the injustice of both hidden and obvious economic sanctions imposed upon blacks by the white establishment—a continuing

scandal—or the agitation of black students at Chapel Hill for a separate student center. Or, I might add, the distinguished black playwright August Wilson announcing that black dramatists should deal only with black themes.
The black power movement of the sixties gave critical impetus to the rear-
rangement of economic and political progress in this country. But that kind
of activism is not going to work any longer simply because to all drama is
played out. Skip Gates's rational response to all this is to reject confrontation
and urge conversation, and his method is proving effective.

*Q: But the black segment of our population is only one component of the multi-
cultural society we have today. Where is this headed? It seems to me that we're
splintering dangerously.*
STYRON: I think this is true, and it has been brilliantly anatomized by Arthur Schlesinger Jr., in his book, *The Disuniting of America*. But there's no
doubt about it. We're headed in a strange direction unforeseen even a few
decades ago.

*Q: We thought we had successfully become a melting pot, but now we find there
never was such a thing.*
STYRON: It seems clear that most ethnic and religious groups have kept
apart and unto themselves, generally speaking. It's equally clear that there has
been considerable intermarriage between Jews and Christians, and to that
extent the American melting pot has been successful. But by and large we
remain a conglomerate of uneasily cohabiting groups.

*Q: What I know of immigrant families of an earlier period indicates they
worked hard at assimilating into American society. They wanted above all to be
American. Those who are coming from elsewhere today seem to want to be here,
but they want also to be what they were somewhere else.*
STYRON: That's quite true. It's natural to identify one's self with one's own
immediate culture, yet still long for ancestral symbols and connections. That's
why so many blacks had a need to embrace a work like *Roots*. My own father
was a passionate genealogist and traced our family back to the great Scottish
rebel William Wallace. At the very worst this was a harmless exercise that
satisfied his need for a sense of continuity, and I respected him for that. Likewise, I can see why black people might wish to surmount the pain of slavery
by establishing a connection with an African chieftain. The success of Jews

in our society may be due at least in part to their apprehension of long ages of religious tradition, which even secular Jews feel. They are extraordinary achievers at every level of our society, amazingly so given the tiny minority they represent in the population.

Q: *Where does that come from?*
STYRON: Back in the late 1950s I read a statement by the distinguished British novelist C. P. Snow, a writer not much read anymore although celebrated at the time for his ability to write from both a literary and a scientific viewpoint. Asked why so many Jews were intellectually superior, he replied that he believed that they shared in an "ethnic gene pool" in which high mental achievement was, generally speaking, foreordained. This struck me as both provocative and—though he didn't mean it to be—potentially inflammatory. If not dangerous. Because, of course, there is a corollary to this theory: other, less intellectually gifted races may share in an inferior "gene pool," making them by definition inferior.

Controversy has raged around this hypothesis for the past decades, especially in the form of disputes over Charles Murray's "Bell Curve," and the work of such scholars as Hernstein and Jensen. All of these researchers claim that statistically, and consistently, blacks score in scholastic testing a significant number of points lower than white students. Even if their methodology were not highly suspect, they cannot convincingly demonstrate the reason for this. They have almost always failed to factor into the genetic equation the dire influence of grinding poverty, near absence of a firm family structure—especially a father—linguistic inadequacy, and other deformed aspects of the childhood nurturing process that encourage failure. This havoc is almost always an indirect consequence of the legacy of slavery. What is striking is that despite these awful deficiencies—two strikes against them at the onset—black men and women have achieved such wondrous things. Becoming a Colin Powell. Becoming an André Watts. A Rita Dove. A Jacob Lawrence. A Bessie Smith. A Ralph Ellison. A Duke Ellington.

Jews, by contrast, whatever their own sufferings and handicaps, have never been saddled with this particular burden of misery. Their passionate need for learning, so often fostered within the family, has helped speed them on their way to success in America.

Having said this, I must add that the racial problem is as critical in this country at the end of our century as it was at the beginning of the 1900s when W. E. B. Du Bois prophesied our tragedy.

Q: By racial you mean more than just black and white?

STYRON: I would have to include other minorities, yes. The Native Americans (except for those running casinos) are in a terrible plight on some of those wretched reservations. Hispanics, too, remain low on the ladder of achievement. But I think the black situation is always going to be the chief thorn in the side of the body politic. In the late l970s, when Senator Daniel Patrick Moynihan was President Jimmy Carter's assistant secretary of labor, he issued a report, that showed that much of black people's seeming inability to succeed in our society was due to the fragmented family, where a father was so often nonexistent and day-to-day life was squalid and chaotic.

Moynihan was reviled and attacked throughout the length and breadth of black America, called a racist and worse. I sympathized with Moynihan because I'd been similarly pummeled for writing *Nat Turner*. But the interesting thing is that fifteen years later Pat Moynihan was vindicated when a report, written by scholars that included a large black contingent, fully affirmed his view that the unstable black family was largely responsible for so much disorder and failure of achievement. It's still at the heart of the ongoing crisis and it interests me that most enlightened black intellectuals now accept this truth, realizing that to deny the ugly reality only hinders progress in the direction of improvement—or even fulfillment.

Q: Have you other reflections?

STYRON: A word about *Nat Turner* might be enlightening, since the novel has become a kind of touchstone for racial attitudes in this country. A year or so after its publication the book was placed at the top of list of works that blacks were told not to read. It stayed there for thirty years. It was difficult for me not to be distressed to see this novel, which I'd intended to be an honest and sympathetic description of the horrors of slavery, mentioned in the same breath as *Mandingo*—which was indisputably a racist novel—as a white man's apology for the slave system. But time works its wonders, everything that goes around comes around, and in America we are accustomed to absolute reversals of opinions and beliefs. Quietly and stealthily *Nat Turner* has become accepted by black academics—Skip Gates is not the only one—and is now required reading in the same black studies programs where it was once anathema. This to me is a marvel. Aside from it for me, I feel that it is an encouraging sign about black attitudes toward their history. It seems to mean that blacks are no longer walled in emotionally and intellectually, unable to accept variant readings of their past by artists because of the color of *their*

skin. I can't help thinking that this is a step forward for blacks and a vindica-
tion for a novel that dwelt for years under a cloud it didn't deserve. Maybe
we'll someday come to understand each other after all. And, oh, I almost forgot to add that fact that a movie is going to be made of *Nat Turner*, directed
by—guess who—*Spike Lee.*

PART IV

2000s

Ernest J. Gaines ❧ 2006

ANNE GRAY BROWN

He's your favorite uncle.

You know, the one who takes you by the hand and lets you buy anything you want at the candy counter despite the "rules about sweets." He's the one who introduces you to his personal motley crew, a rag-tag bunch, drinking "shooters," slapping the table in a serious game of bid-whist being played under the shade tree on a simmering August afternoon and who says, with great pride and a thousand-watt smile, "This is my niece!" He's the one who slips you a few dollars at the family gathering when no one's watching and gives you a nanosecond wink along with a sly grin, silently swearing you to secrecy. And he's the one who always has a gigantic tale that always begins, amid groans and room-exits from relatives and friends, "You know, I knew this fellow one time that . . . ," and you know instinctively that when he finishes the story, everyone will be doubled over in laughter, tears streaming down cheeks, stomachs tightly held, begging him to stop the madness. Or at least take it down a notch. Or two. Saved for the next gathering of the folks.

You claimed him against all others, knowing that you were safe in his company, that no harm would come your way, that with him as chief protector of your youthful exuberance, everything would be all right. He was your human comfort zone, and you embraced the aura of his warmth with carefree abandon.

Meeting Ernest J. Gaines was like re-connecting, after a very long absence, with your favorite uncle, the one who you'd often hear tales about at family gatherings, the one who was ever-present and elusive at the same time. The one who would walk into the room beneath the imaginary halo. You simply couldn't wait to embrace him. But you restrained yourself. After all, you knew that in due time, you'd make that connection.

To be in the presence of Ernest J. Gaines is to be in the presence of your favorite uncle. Only this uncle is a literary icon, a master of the art of storytelling. You

---

Originally published as Anne Gray Brown, "The Scribe of River Lake Plantation: A Conversation with Ernest J. Gaines," Vol. 44, no. 1 (2006), 9–31.

know that you're in the sphere of a man of incredible imagination, bravery, and determination. This gentle giant of a man, soft-spoken, kind, and generous to a fault, gives you much reason to believe that with all the work that he's penned over the years, his work still holds a special place in the hearts of his readers, that his characters are not simply fictional constructs but are, in a sense, real people that we have all come to know, love, and respect.

It is no secret that much of Ernest J. Gaines's strength and fortitude are ancestral. He says so and gives homage to the people who came before him. He claims little credit for himself but offers an abundance of authority to his people. "I am what I am because of them," says Gaines. To say that he learned much from his people is an understatement. Over the years, he has mastered much, but he is quick to say that he is "still learning" the craft of writing. This writer accepts that argument. It's not kosher to disagree with an icon about the business of his craft.

He grew up on the Point Coupee Plantation in Oscar, Louisiana, where he and his wife, Dianne, currently reside, and it's where he derives his power to tell the riveting narratives that readers have all come to enjoy: the stories of Miss Jane, Jefferson, Reverend Phillip Martin, Chippo Simon, Madam Toussaint, Catherine Carmier, and a host of other characters from his eight works of fiction. While the names of the characters may be the author's invention, their tales are quite frequently reality-based, for we have all encountered a Snookum, a Mary Louise, a Copper Lautent, a Tante Lou, a Miss Merle, and a Reverend Ambrose.

If we've elected to forget that such people exist in our lives, it's because we sometimes don't wish to be reminded of where we come from, how we got there, or what took the bus so long to get to the next station. Gaines does none of this conscientious, deliberate forgetting. He embraces his ancestry proudly, wearing it like a banner across his heart. His letter "A" is prominent, representing the pride and strength of his ancestry, not an ancestry of shame, derision, and despair. Whenever he speaks of the kinfolk on the plantation and of his youthful days spent there, a look of respectful remembrance comes to bear. You can rest assured you're hearing the truth be told.

His canon of work includes the classic novel, The Autobiography of Miss Jane Pittman *(1971), and the best-selling novel,* A Lesson Before Dying *(1993). Even though at this stage of his life, the author is enjoying the fruits of his labor, he is still involved in literary endeavors, recently speaking at the Rural Life Museum in Baton Rouge as well as writing an essay for* National Geographic. *"The Turtles," Gaines's first published short story, now enjoys a place of historical significance in the canon of his work. The story about a young boy on the threshold of manhood is fifty years old. It was first published in* Transfer *magazine [San Francisco State College] in 1956. Last year's release of* Mozart and Leadbelly *(2005), a collection of essays and short stories, speaks to the author's continued dedication to the craft of writing and storytelling.*

Over the course of his distinguished career, in addition to being a former professor and writer-in-residence at the University of Louisiana at Lafayette for nearly twenty years, he has racked up an abundance of honors and awards, most notably the (Louisiana) Governor's Arts Awards Lifetime Achievement Award; the National Humanities Medal Award; the (Paris) Chevalier of the Order of Arts and Letters; the MacArthur Foundation Fellow Award; the National Book Critics Circle Award; the Louisiana Humanist of the Year Award; Honorary Doctor of Letters from Brown University, Louisiana State University, Bard College, and Denison College; the Honorary Doctor of Humane Letters from Whittier College; a Guggenheim Fellowship; a National Endowment for the Arts Award; the National Governors Association Award for Lifetime Achievement to the Arts, and the Southern Book Award for Fiction. He's also a member of the American Academy of Arts and Letters. A Lesson Before Dying *was nominated for a Pulitzer Prize in Literature.*

Ernest J. Gaines is a national treasure. When we met, I called him such. A very modest gentleman, he quickly brushed aside the comment, saying, with quiet laughter, "Oh, I don't know about that." To that very demure response, I must add that not only is he a national treasure, he is also a kind and gentle man with a soulful countenance, one who continues to share his gift of imaginative brilliance with us after all these years. We thank him kindly for his presence of words. That, and, of course, always being the favorite uncle who keeps giving us the tall tales at the gathering of the people.

QUESTION: *Writing is a process of discovery. As a writer, what are you still discovering about yourself?*
GAINES: I'm still discovering myself. I'm still finding out who I am, I'm still finding out my weakness, my prejudice, my strength. Through my characters, I'm finding myself. I try to create characters *with* character to better understand my own character and maybe help the character of the people who might read me. So I'm still trying to find out more about myself. I think that's what writing is all about, finding out things about oneself. At the same time, of course, you're writing to make money, if you can make money by writing. You're writing to entertain, whether you're writing a short story or mystery story or crime story, whatever you're writing, you're writing to entertain. All

the time, however, you're creating characters and creating situations, and if you're sincere with your creation you are searching in ways to understand yourself better.

Q: Is it safe to say that from your humble beginnings as the unofficial scribe on the False River Plantation your career as a writer began? How did the people on the plantation come to know you as the go-to person to write their letters? Can you talk about your "appointment" to this coveted position?

GAINES: My aunt raised me. She was crippled, she never did walk. She crawled across the floor all her life, and because she couldn't visit others, the people used to visit our house and they'd sit there and talk and talk and talk all the time. None of these people had ever gone to any school. No education at all. It was my aunt who told me that I should write their letters for them and read their letters for them when they received mail, which I did.

They would come over there, and I'd sit on the floor by their chair. Sometimes, if it was a man that I was writing a letter for, he'd sit on the floor or on the porch, or I'd be sitting on the steps, and I'd have my little yellow pencil and write on a tablet this wide, and I'd write their letters. They would know how to *begin* the letter, but they wouldn't know how to proceed. They'd say, for instance, "Hey, Sarah, how are you? I am well. I'm hoping you are the same." And you'd sit there minutes after minutes, and they don't know what to talk about. And they'd say, "Say something about the garden," or "Say something about the field." So, I'd just say, "OK."

So you just try and put it down, and then you read it back, and then, well, they'd say, "Uh-uh, that ain' right!" [Laughter]. So I had those little pencils with those little pink erasers on top, and then you'd put it down again. But they would always call on me. They wouldn't call on my brother. I was the "chosen one" to do those kinds of things. Well, I'm the eldest of my siblings, and of course, I had to take care of my aunt who could not walk. So I started writing like that.

Q: Long before the published stories and novels, you were the writer then.

GAINES: I realize *now* that I was writing then, but I didn't know that at the time. I was just doing what I was supposed to do. I was just putting these things down for these people. I was asked recently what is the easiest way for me to write my stories, and I said, "I write from the 'I' point-of-view," and I also said, "You know, I think I'm still writing those letters for those people." There's an "I" there. I'm still trying to write the letters for the old people. I think so. Because I can't think of anything else to write about, sometimes I go back there in that cemetery and just sit there and look at some of the graves and those tombs, and I think, "If it were not for them, I wouldn't be the writer I am." Well, I know I would not be a writer. They're the ones who started me off when I was very young.

Q: *How does background shape the writer's art?*
GAINES: You don't write in a void. I need and must have "place" to write about. I can't write about a place I don't know anything about. I can't write about northern Louisiana. I don't care about northern Louisiana. I can't write about New Orleans, although I've written an essay for *National Geographic* [August 2006]. But I've not written anything fictitious about New Orleans, because I don't know New Orleans that well. So my background is that I need to know the indigenous things, the fields, the water, the trees, the vegetation, the people, the clothes they wear, what they eat, songs they sing, that sort of thing. For the infinity of the story you need that kind of background. Well, I do. I can't write about any other place. I can't write about Texas or New York or Hollywood. I need that background. There's so much involved in it until it becomes part of me.

Q: *What is it that younger writers can learn from mature writers in terms of structure, character development, style, and technique?*
GAINES: They can learn all that you have just mentioned! [Laughter] It's something that I learned from reading the great classic writers. By reading, say, the Faulkners, by reading the Hemingways, reading the Tolstoys, reading the Chekovs, reading Turgenev, reading Joyce. You know, reading those writers. You learn those things, because much of what you think you might know to do this work, you soon find out. Writing is much harder than just reading. When you read something, and it comes out very easy you can bet that the writer has spent hours, a long time getting that stuff together to get that sentence right.

Q: *I know that you were influenced by Faulkner's writing. Why were you attracted to his work?*
GAINES: I don't know that I've been much more influenced by Faulkner any more than, say, a writer like Hemingway or Ivan Turgenev. Well, I should take that back. Faulkner has an edge over these writers, but it was not totally Faulkner's influence over me for my style of writing. Of course, we write

about the South, the Mississippi borders, Louisiana, some of the same kind of characters you'd find in Faulkner's small towns, hanging around the store-fronts, working in the fields. You'd find the same sort of characters in Louisiana. Faulkner made me concentrate more on my characters.

He showed me how similar they were, white or black characters in a field. I definitely don't go along with Faulkner's philosophy, his description of the characters, yes. He's a master at capturing that southern dialogue, whether it's white or black. But it was a certain level of dialogue that Faulkner was interested in. He could get the most illiterate of black dialogue, but he was never interested in writing middle class black or upper class black dialogue or middle or upper class characters.

When it came down to writing about peasant life, life in the fields, or life in a small town among the very poor people, yes, Faulkner had that kind of influence over me. He showed me how to describe the country stores, how people stay around on the porches. I knew that, but I didn't know how to do it on paper until I saw what he had done. Another thing he did was show me how to concentrate in a single area. Well, he'd already gotten that from people like [James] Joyce. So it's [the influence] come down through the years from Joyce to Faulkner to others to myself, this concentrating on one general area. I definitely learned that from Faulkner as well as from Joyce. So these are some of the things that influence me.

When it came to philosophy and when it came to my characters reacting, it was my judgment as to how my characters would react, not Faulkner's, be-cause I don't know that Faulkner could have created a Marcus in *Of Love and Dust* (1967) and a Louise. I don't know that he could have created Miss Jane Pittman. He could have created Dilsey [*The Sound and the Fury* (1929)] but not Miss Jane Pittman. Miss Jane, he would not have created her, because he never would have walked her by that white man at the very end of the story. So there are certain things, as I've told others, that Faulkner told Dilsey's story from his kitchen, Miss Jane Pittman told her story from her own kitchen, and they were two different stories, two different interpretations, told in two different ways. There were a lot of similarities, but when you get down to the nitty-gritty, there were some differences there.

I remember talking to someone who told me about the interviewing of the ex-slaves for the WPA [Works Progress Administration] back in the early '30s, when writers needed work, and a white writer could go up to an old person who'd been enslaved and ask questions, and that person would give a certain kind of answer.

When a black person would go to an ex-slave, someone with whom they could understand and communicate, they'd give a different kind of answer. It was a subtle kind of thing that Miss Jane was different from Dilsey. Faulkner gets Dilsey's story. I get Miss Jane's story. Faulkner got Dilsey's story in his kitchen. I get Miss Jane's story in her kitchen. Dilsey would probably have told me a different story, but I did not create Dilsey. Faulkner created Dilsey. I created Miss Jane Pittman.

Q: Many of today's writers of color, male and female, do not write the kinds of narratives that speak to the culture of community, the importance of the land, and the integrity of its people. That's why your work is so important. Can you talk about your affection for the land, this region, and growing up here on the Plantation?
GAINES: I've always had a love for this place. I left here when I was fifteen years old. I had to go because I couldn't attend high school here, I could not go to a library here, and I didn't have any people in a nearby town with whom I could live and go to school. So my folks brought me to California when I was fifteen, but I left an aunt here who had raised me and I also left other family members here, so I left a part of me here. I've told others that the body went to California, but the soul remained here in Louisiana. I left but I didn't leave. Something kept holding me back, holding me back here.

I could not write about anything except Louisiana, even though I spent most of my time in California. I could not write about anything except the land, the bayous, the rivers, the swamps. I had no interest in anything else. I could only write about the things that my people had experienced, my ancestors had experienced. See, we've lived on this particular plantation here for five generations, and I met some people when I was doing research for *A Gathering of Old Men* (1983) who knew my grandparents' grandparents on this same place. So something about it just kept me here. Although I studied creative writing at San Francisco [State College, now University] and at Stanford, and I knew the bohemian life in San Francisco, I'd been in the Army, so I knew the Army life. When it came down to writing I tried to write stories about those places, but nothing was successful.

The only success was here and I knew that the reason why, the only thing that I could write about, truly and deeply, and put all my soul into was this subject here, and I knew that it was because I still felt connected to everything here. When I started teaching at UL [University of Louisiana at Lafayette] in 1981, I was near this place, and I was always coming back, always coming back here and talking to the old people, and when my wife and I had a chance to buy a part of this plantation, of course we jumped at the chance and built a house here. Because I feel that I am still close to the people, my ancestors. They're buried about three-quarters of a mile in the cemetery back here.

Now, this is False River here, the fields of False River. I picked cotton right here, on this place, where we're sitting, right here. My mother and father chopped sugar cane here, and my uncles all pulled corn around this area. This is farmland, nothing but farmland. When we bought the place, it was a field. The church school of Grant's [*A Lesson Before Dying*] is modeled after my church school. It was my church school, y' know, six years in it. We moved the church onto this property before we built the house, during the same time. The church was moved here before the house was built. We started building on the house when we moved the church over here. It was in the quarters.

Q: Now, in terms of the proximity to your present house, where did you live?
GAINES: I lived about three hundred yards from where we are now. The Big House from where my grandmother worked for so many years is just up the road here about two hundred yards, so this is where we lived, right here. Maybe Dianne can take you back there to the church and you can see some of the pictures back there on the wall. But anyway, we moved the church. The church was falling apart and we asked permission, from the people who owned it on the other side of the plantation, if we could have the church and they said, "Yes," and so we moved it over here and renovated it. All of that keeps me connected to the place and to the people and to my past. When we get together, my friends now, we talk about the times when we lived here.

Q: Describe your days here as a youngster on the plantation.
GAINES: There were many hard days, many mean days. You know, that's why we had about five months of school, y' know, because we couldn't go to school when we were needed in the field. In the spring you picked potatoes and pulled onions and whatever else, and in the fall and winter you had to go into the cotton field. We were about seven or eight years old. We were very small children. So those were some terrible, terrible times for us.

There was racism and, of course, everything was segregated at that time. There's still racism, but everything was segregated at that time. I couldn't go to a place and have a decent drink of water or a sandwich or anything like that. At the same time, it seemed like the black people were much closer together. They were constantly helping each other, because they knew you couldn't get help out there, so they would help you on the place. So all of that kind of stuff kept me intact with the place, not with the state of Louisiana, but with this general area, because that's where my folks had come from.

I saw some miserable days. My people suffered. Let me put it this way: I am what I am today because of them, and I cannot ever forget that. They suffered but they endured, and I survived. From their endurance, I survived. That's why I can write it in books today as I did for them, the older people, writing letters for them when I was a teenager, well, before I was a teenager, ten or twelve years old. Because of those letters, I suppose, that's why I can write books. So there's that contact, that connection. I've never tried to disconnect myself from my folks or this general area.

I've never tried to disconnect myself from my folks or this general area. I'm not saying the South. I'm not saying all of Louisiana. I'm saying this general area here. This place. And this kind of thing I learned from Faulkner. Write truly enough about a single place. But you cannot, of course, truly tell all the stories.

Q: If we could shift gears a bit here, let's talk about some of your novels. There is, in many of your works, the presence of some form of (or reference to) music. For instance, Jefferson, in A Lesson Before Dying, *is slightly transformed by the gift of a transistor radio given to him by Grant; there's the great fight scene in the club in* Of Love and Dust; *there's the slow-dance scene in the club with Grant and Vivian in* A Lesson Before Dying, *and there's Reverend Phillip Martin daughter's piano-playing in* In My Father's House. *Why does music have such a prominent place in your work?*

GAINES: I've always enjoyed music. I play music all the time. Usually in the morning there's a radio station here that plays three hours of classical music beginning at ten and ending at one. My wife and I both listen to it. Then, the station plays something else. But music's around all the time. Music has always been around me, both in the country as well as when I lived in San Francisco. So it just naturally comes into my writing. I think I've been influenced by African American music much more than by African American literature, because I never studied a variety of fiction writing or any other writing by African American writers.

During the time I was in high school and college the American white writers or the European white writers were the writers that I studied; their work is what I was taught. But the music was always there at home. Gospel music or blues music or jazz music was always there. Even when I was a small child, music was always around me, so music has just naturally come into the work. Formal music is represented by Mozart, but the music that I grew up listening to, the music that my folks have all listened to is the music of Leadbelly, Bessie Smith, and these people, and there's the jazz music of Count Basie, Louis Armstrong, and others. No, I could not live without music. I love music.

Q: *You mention that you were influenced much more by African American music than you were by African American literature. Now, in terms of your lack of an active physical presence in the civil rights protests in California during the '60s, you were greatly criticized for not being more visible and for not being a protest writer. I believe that your work speaks to the same issues that the more vocal members of the community were visibly protesting: racism, poverty, class, and gender issues. How did you handle the criticism, and did you ever attempt to write a novel, aside from* The Autobiography of Miss Jane Pittman, *that spoke directly to the issues I've mentioned?*

GAINES: I could not write the novels of Baldwin or Richard Wright, although I came from the South. When I left the South, I didn't go to that mean world that Wright ended up in. I went to a small town in Vallejo, California. I went to an integrated neighborhood. My junior high school, high school, and junior college were all totally integrated. As I said earlier, I left a place I loved very much. I have protest in my stories.

If you look at the very first story that I published internationally, "The Sky Is Gray," where those people have to walk up and down the cold street in the town, if that is not protest, I don't know what protest is. Those people are cold, those people are hungry. This child is in pain, the mother is in pain. Isn't that protest? Isn't that protest? What am I supposed to do? Get thrown out of a restaurant or start a demonstration in front of the courthouse or something like that? The struggle was showing the only way I know how to work to better my conditions.

Q: *I suppose those who criticized your physical absence in the civil rights protests wanted all of the protest writers to be Stokley Carmichaels* on paper, *or H. Rap Browns* on paper, *or Huey P. Newtons* on paper, *and when you protested in a different forum, well, I presume that your writings were seen as short stories that did not mean much, because there could be no verbal chanting of the Carmichael/Brown/Newton nature.*

GAINES: Take for instance the short story, "Just Like a Tree" [*Bloodline* (1968)]. "Just Like a Tree" is a protest story. Here's this woman from the North coming to get her aunt because of the violence that's going on down there, and the young man coming to tell her, "I know the bombing is going on, and I know they want me to stop, but I cannot stop. I must continue to protest." I was writing those stories back in the '60s. "The Sky Is Gray" was written in '62; it was published in *Negro Digest* in '63.

Q: I remember Negro Digest *and, as I recall, the publication was a "protest" kind of publication.*
GAINES: Yes! And Hoyt Fuller [publishers] at that time was selling that story as a protest story. I remember when *The Autobiography of Miss Jane Pittman* first came out, one person who reviewed the book for a Chicago paper, one of these "Chicago intellectuals," said she couldn't see anything in that story until she got to the very last book of the story, the last part of the story where this little fellow, Jimmy, goes out in the protest. But she didn't see how Miss Jane had survived all those years and years and years to come to the point where she could teach this young man to go out and do those kinds of things.

This person who reviewed the book had never seen anything like it. Miss Jane was not protesting enough. I said, "Well, how do you deal with those people like that?" You know, I just continue to write. I write as well as I possibly can write. I don't care what other people think. I've never felt that I had to answer any letters or anything when they wrote criticisms of or critical things about my work. I had other things to do. But I think many of them are coming around and seeing now what I have done. At the time, no, they could not accept it. I was not "black" enough.

Q: Yes. Yes. Look at where your work is and how it's viewed, and the canon of your work and all that. Look at the longevity of your work. You have to listen to your heart.
GAINES: Yes. I think *The Autobiography of Miss Jane Pittman* has proven me right for continuing to write other stories. But I used to tell people that every time I'd heard what Bull Connor [a former police chief of Birmingham, Alabama] had done with his prongs and his dogs and with his hoses, I'd try and write a better paragraph that day. I'd say that I was going to write "a better, stronger page today. I'm going to beat him, and this is my protest."

Q: Even as a teenager, when I initially read The Autobiography of Miss Jane Pittman, *I thought the story was protest writing. I didn't know at the time that there was a term, so to speak, for this kind of writing, but I remember calling it*

"*6ostrong story telling." I'd always been a reader and had, as a teen, started read-ing Wright, Baldwin, Cleaver, and others, but when I read* The Autobiography of Miss Jane Pittman, *I felt that the storytelling format would make for its persever-ance. When I was ten years old, I read Ethel Waters's autobiography* His Eye Is on the Sparrow, *in a couple days. Even at that young age my reading interests had started to shift, and I'd started paying more attention to the writers and the writing that seemed to speak to me. Waters's autobiography was about survival.*
GAINES: Yes, yes. What's so great about *The Autobiography of Miss Jane Pitt-man* is that if anybody can survive in this mad, crazy, racist, segregated world to be one hundred ten years old and still appreciate ice-cream, that is what I consider heroic. Those are the heroes that I admire, because those were the ones that would help me up here, to help me get to the shoulders so that I can be able to talk to you. Not many of us can survive, not many of us are willing to survive for our children to the point that we can live to be one hundred years old.

Q: Let's talk briefly about your thematic treatment of father and son separations. The theme governs many of your short stories, from "The Sky Is Gray" to the title story in Bloodline *(1968), to your signature novel of father and son separation,* In My Father's House. *Why is so much of your work devoted to the theme of absent fathers?*
GAINES: Fathers and sons were brought here in chains and then separated on the auction block in slave-holding places. I don't think that they've made a connection since. Too often our fathers cannot help the sons. African Ameri-can fathers do not send us to war. They're very seldom our judges when we're standing at trial. They're not often our doctors. They don't represent us when we're in the courtroom. We often blame him without realizing that he's never been given that opportunity to defend us. We've fought in every war that this country has ever had, beginning with the War of Independence, and yet, when it comes to defending our families, our children, our wives, some way or an-other the white man makes all of those decisions, and that separates father and son. You know, "I can't depend on my father to save me, and I need you to save me."

Q: Can you discuss the thematic parallels of the closing lines in "The Turtles" and "The Sky Is Gray," where each parent tells their young son that he, the child, is a man?

GAINES: You get the same thing with *A Lesson Before Dying*. Tante Lou wants Jefferson to stand up like a man. In *A Gathering of Old Men* when Charlie runs away, and he comes back and tells them all, "I'm a man now. You call me 'Mister.' It's not your old 'Charlie' anymore. I'm a man, and you'll treat me like I'm a man."

In reading so much about why young black men are in prison today, so many are fighting over their manhood in the black community, they're fighting over their woman: "You're not treating me as a man," or they're knocking this woman around because she's not treating him like a man. So much of it is our psyche: "I've got to be a man, I've got to be a man, I've got to be a man." And of course, our mothers, when we're born, it's "my little man." And we want him to be a better person than his father: "You're the man. You're the man. You're the man of the house."

In *In My Father's House*, Robert X does not kill the guy, and his younger brother kills the guy who rapes his sister. And he's "the man." He's the man of the house now. Robert X turns against his father, because he feels that his father should have been there, but it's his own guilt that causes him to blame the father for not being there to protect them. So the "man" stuff is always around. I think I try and put it in my writing as much as I possibly can.

Q: *Can you talk briefly about your relationship with Dorothy "Stinker" Oppenheimer, your literary agent? How critical and brutal was she in terms of the work that you submitted to her?*

GAINES: I don't think she intended to be brutal, I just think that she was trying to make me a better writer. She would comment on incomplete stuff, well, it could be incomplete, but if she thought that I could do much better, then she was sure going to use that little red pencil! [laughter] But she was my confidante; she was everything to me. We had an association for thirty-one years, from 1956 to 1987. She died in 1987. The first story that she read was "The Turtles."

It was published in a little literary magazine at San Francisco State, and she was just beginning her agency in San Francisco at the time. She got in touch with one of my teachers, and my teacher said to me, "There's a literary agent, a little old lady who's looking for writers. She'd like to meet you and talk to you." And she saw "The Turtles," and she said that she loved that story. She told me, "Whenever you write another story or anything like that, always send it to me." And that was the beginning.

She went to San Francisco when she was a teenager, and she'd gone to one of the better schools back east. I think it was either Vassar or Radcliffe. She was extremely well-educated and she loved music. She made me aware of classical music, because I used to go to her place all the time. She lived in Pacific Heights there in San Francisco. There was this big radio, this giant radio, and she'd always play this classical music, because we had all those radio stations there in San Francisco that played music all the time. I was always surrounded by music. When I'd go back home, I would play jazz or something else. But the music was there in her place, and we'd sit around and talk.

But when it came down to writing, she'd say, "E, listen, this is not up to par yet. I know you can write, because I read 'The Turtles.'" Someone once told me that "The Turtles" was the best thing that I had ever written and after that was *The Autobiography of Miss Jane Pittman*. I said, "Come on! 'The Turtles' don't come close!" But they said, "Oh, yes! It's the best thing that you've ever done!" [laughter].

Q: Why was In My Father's House *your most difficult story to write? Were you satisfied with the ending, or were you simply exhausted, after seven years, of telling Phillip's story of redemption, assuming, in fact, that he did indeed redeem himself. Where were you trying to take Rev. Phillip Martin?*
GAINES: I write better in the first-person point of view, but I couldn't tell this story in the first person, because I couldn't have Robert X tell his own story. I had to have someone else talk about Robert X. I had to have someone else talk about Phillip Martin. So I had to tell the story either by third person or totally from the omniscient point of view. I tried several points of view to tell the story, but none of them were successful. I finally ended up with the omniscient. I feel that it [*In My Father's House*] is not up to par with my other works, because I have some difficulty with the omniscient point of view.

But that was not the only problem. The problem was how to have Phillip Martin redeem himself or what would Robert X end up doing: going back or making an attempt to kill his father or [figuring out] exactly what was going to happen, and I had all kinds of problems with that book. It was a book that I had to get right, after I'd finished *The Autobiography of Miss Jane Pittman*. I wanted to go further, but it seemed like this book kept getting in the way.

As I've said in interviews, as I may have said in the story, the father and son were separated during the time of slavery and still, to this date, they have not really reconnected and there's that difficulty there, and I was trying to resolve that. In the conflict between Phillip Martin and Robert X, there's a conflict that I'm not satisfied that I resolved. I don't know if it's possible to resolve or to be resolved. So it was a problem. I was never absolutely satisfied at all with what I did with the book, whether I'm working with the omniscient point of view or with the plot of the story. I wasn't very satisfied. After seven years, I just thought, well, I'd done as well as I could possibly ever do with this.

I'd tried rewriting it from so many different points of view. I tried writing it from Chippo Simon's point of view I tried writing it from multiple points of view, but nothing was coming for me, so I just said, "ok," I'm going with the omniscient point of view, and I'll go as far as I can with that and then, after seven years of it I just said that I'd had enough of it.

Q: *Near the end of* A Lesson Before Dying, *in "Jefferson's Diary," you make an immediate shift from standard, conventional English to a phonetic rendering. To me, that transition and that chapter are the most powerful part of the novel. Can you discuss the significance of this inclusion and the importance of Jefferson's voice?*

GAINES: Well, before the chapter we don't know too much about him. We are getting some information through Grant, but we don't know enough about him and I didn't want him trying to explain himself just before he was going to be executed. No final words. I didn't want that sort of stuff. So what I thought, what you give, is an entire chapter devoted to his thinking. The question was how do you do that. I said, well, just let him tell it; let him tell the story. Let him tell it, and let him tell it in his own way, and so that's why the notebook comes into the story. I needed him to talk. I wanted him to do it in the only way that was possible for him to do it.

Jefferson has limited education and a limited vocabulary. Everything about him was limited. At one time I thought, well, this was after I'd written the diary, I thought maybe I should have written it in a different handwriting, perhaps in a cursive handwriting. We hear about how everyone feels about Jefferson. We hear how Aunt Emma feels, we hear how Tante Lou feels, we hear how the sheriff feels, we hear how Grant feels, and we even hear how the children feel. But we never hear how Jefferson feels.

We never hear Jefferson's voice. It ["Jefferson's Diary"] is the uplift of everything. Someone has said that "Jefferson's Diary" is such a sad story. I said, "No! Once you read 'Jefferson's Diary,' it's uplifted your heart, if you had a heart." He's uplifted you, and he tells you how he feels. That is the turning point, that little "light" that Joyce speaks of, that epiphany. That brings light to the entire story.

You know, I've been asked if it was difficult to write that particular chapter, and I've said, "No. Once I decided how I was going to do it, it wasn't difficult at all to write it, to use the language that he would use, to write with no punctuation or capitalization." It wasn't difficult because he probably would not have known how to do that. By the time I came to writing this chapter, I'd been with him for about five years, because it took me over a period of seven years to write the book, but I was only writing half that time a year. The rest of the time I was not writing. I was teaching over at UL, and when I was not teaching over at UL at Lafayette, I was in San Francisco writing the book. So I knew his language, because I'd been around him for about five years in that jail cell, and if you live around someone in a jail cell for about five years you'll learn something about them. So it was no problem writing it.

I was concerned, though, when I'd finished writing it, when I sent it to New York. I asked my editor, Ash Green, if he had a problem reading it, and he said, "No." I said, "Thank God," because I was worried that the way it was written, that people would say that they couldn't understand it, that they would say that they couldn't understand this dialect that they didn't care for dialect, but that ["Jefferson's Dairy"] was the great uplift of the book. One critic said that the rest of the book is "typical Gaines," but this particular chapter is vintage. From this chapter onward, it just goes over and over and over.

Well, after that chapter, that's when the preparation for the execution takes place. But that chapter should uplift you to the rest of that book. Many people have said how they wept and wept and wept. Yes, well, I've wept there, too, at the play. I've seen the play about a dozen times in different parts of the country. It's very powerful at the very end.

Q: Now, the opening line in A Lesson Before Dying *is such a profound statement: "I was not there, yet I was there." Did you have to ponder long and hard to come up with such a wonderful opening line?*
GAINES: I don't think that I had to think too hard on that. I knew that Grant was going to tell the story, but I knew that he didn't want to be anywhere near it. He didn't want to be involved in it, directly involved in it, but he was always involved. He doesn't want to be there, but he's there.

Q: The women in your novels, as well as your short stories, are presented as strong, independent, and, in many cases, domineering figures. How reflective are these fictional constructs to the real-life women who were in your life in Point Coupee?

GAINES: My aunt, who could not walk, raised us. She cooked for us. We had to bring everything to her. We had a little wood-burning stove for food, for meat or vegetables or whatever it was that she was cooking that day, and we had to sit it right before her. She sat on a little bench by the stove, and another little bench in front of her, she used as a table. She'd cut up the vegetables and the meat, and then she could put it over in the pot on the stove. She washed our clothes. We had to bring everything to her. We had an old washtub at that time.

We brought the water, the old washboard, the soap, and everything, and she sat on the little bench there by the stove, and she would brace herself against the rim of the tub and wash the clothes on the board. Then she would rinse the clothes and the children would go out and hang the clothes on the line. She disciplined us. We had to bring our own switch and get down on our knees before her and take our punishment that way.

Q: *I'm sure she said, or, of course, you automatically knew that you shouldn't bring back the tiniest thing. You knew to bring back a switch "of substance" didn't you?*
GAINES: Oh, yes! [laughter] If you brought back a tiny switch, she'd send you back to get another one. I had a brother who'd bring back the tiniest one, and she'd say, "Go back, go back, go back!" And he'd go back two or three times to get the right size. She used to work in her garden, a little garden beside the house, and she would crawl over the floor and down the steps, across the yard right to the vegetable garden. Then she'd work in her little vegetable garden. There, she'd work. She had this little hoe, and she'd work among her vegetables, her cucumbers, or tomatoes, or beans, or peas, or okra, or whatever we had in the garden at that time of the year. She would work among that. She had to put her hand to the earth. She needed to put her hand to the earth.

During the pecan season she'd crawl over the back yard with a little sack, dragging a little flour sack or a little rice sack, and she'd find pecans under the tree and bring them back inside and crack pecans and make pecan pralines. With all those obstacles, she was the strongest person I've ever known in my life, and I think, most of the women in my books are, somewhat, part of my aunt. No one was based on her, but several people have said that Miss Jane Pittman is the story of my aunt, but Miss Jane Pittman is not. Miss Jane Pittman tried to do all kinds of crazy things, but my aunt could never do those things because she was crippled. So Miss Jane is not my aunt, but Miss Jane has a lot of the fortitude and strength of my aunt, letting nothing in the world get into the way of her continuing her life.

When it was cold in the winter, I would, because I was the eldest of my siblings, get out and start a fire in the fireplace to warm the floor by the time she'd get out of bed, because her bed was right by the fireplace. I'd have the floor warm by the time she got out of bed to crawl over the floor to the kitchen. I was raised by my aunt the first fifteen and one-half years of my life. She was religious, although she couldn't go to church. She would sing a little song and the minister would come by and talk to her, and the deacons would come by and talk to her. The women in my novels, I suppose, are based somewhat *around* her, not entirely, though. But her strength, I gave to them. I've known other strong black women. My mother was quite strong, I think, as was my grandmother. On that plantation there were very strong people.

Q: Your work graciously honors the spiritual lives of your ancestors on the Point Coupee Plantation. How strong a bearing does your ancestors' spirit have on you, not as a writer but as a man?
GAINES: My aunt, who raised me, made me what I am, both as a man and as a writer. It was my aunt, more than anyone else, the way she was and the way she raised me to be. She's the great role model in my life, more than my mother, or father, or my stepfather or the writers I've read or the people I've met. My aunt was a real role model in my life.

Q: Can you talk a little about the beautification ceremony that's held on the ancestral burial grounds every October here in Oscar?
GAINES: Yes. It's a Beautification Day, the Saturday before Halloween. It's in the cemetery back here, about three-quarters of a mile from where we are right here. We ask the people whose ancestors are buried back there to come around and cut grass or plant flowers or wash the tombs. But we [Gaines and his wife, Dianne] keep it up, year round. We keep the cemetery up, but we just want to get a gathering of the people, a kind of gathering of the masses, the descendants here, once a year. The rest of the time we try and do it ourselves.

Q: Are you satisfied with your journey from plantation scribe to the publication of Mozart and Leadbelly?
GAINES: Am I satisfied? Oh, I think I've done some things, but I think I should have done more. I should have done more. I could have done more. There are so many "ifs, ifs, ifs." If I could have gone to the library when I was six years old rather than when I was sixteen years old, I could have done much more. If I'd worked harder the last twenty years than I've been working,

I could have done more. I could have, and that's my only regret, that I didn't work quite as hard as I should have. Yes, I'm satisfied with some of my accomplishments, but I think they should be better.

William Hoffman ❧ 2001

CASEY CLABOUGH

William Hoffman, considered by many critics to be Virginia's finest living writer, was born in Charleston, West Virginia on 16 May 1925. He spent his early years in West Virginia, before attending Kentucky Military Institute. He graduated in 1943 and joined the army, serving as a Medical Corpsman in the 91st Evacuation Hospital. The bloody fighting he witnessed during the Normandy Invasion and subsequent allied drive toward Germany informed much of his early fiction. After the war Hoffman received his BA from Hampden-Sydney College (1949). He then enrolled in law school at Washington and Lee, only to discover his passion for writing and leave, spending a year at the Writers' Workshop, University of Iowa (1950–51). He worked briefly for a newspaper in Washington, DC, and a bank in New York before returning to Hampden-Sydney in 1952 as an instructor. Hoffman taught on and off at Hampden-Sydney for fifteen years, meeting his wife, Alice Sue Hoffman, there in the late 1950s. He is the father of two daughters and for almost forty years has lived at Wynyard, a historical house and farm in Charlotte Court House, Virginia. During a writing career spanning more than half a century (his first story was published in 1950 and his most recent novel, Wild Thorn, *will be released in December 2002), Hoffman consistently has written at a high stylistic level, producing twelve novels, four collections of short stories, and a play. This interview took place at Wynyard on 3 August 2001.*

QUESTION: *Who were your literary influences early on, when you were first publishing short stories, before the first two novels came out? Hemingway was an obvious stylistic and thematic source; who else?*
HOFFMAN: I went through a progression that drew me into writing and the first writer that really lit my fire was Thomas Wolfe. For a while I couldn't seem to read anyone else and I read everything he wrote. He really got me going. It took me a long time to get into William Faulkner. I would say I next

---

Originally published as Casey Clabough, "William Hoffman's Fictional Journey: An Interview," Vol. 41, no. 1 (2002), 80–86.

read Hemingway, largely because I was over in Italy [during World War II] and I bought a very cheap copy of one of his short story collections. Then I began to read his novels. This was a golden age of writing for a reader. Of course, I also got into Fitzgerald very deeply. Later on, I admired Robert Penn Warren a lot, especially *All the King's Men*. I read these people while I was branching out and trying to find my own way of writing, my own voice. I don't keep up with current writers as much as I should. I do like Cormac Mc-Carthy, for example, and there are certain books I like by some of the people I know. I like George Garrett's books and some by Fred Chappell, but I think by the time I got to those people I was pretty much set in the way I write. And I think what those early writers taught me was not so much a sense of style, I had to find my own style, but what I hoped would be a sense of integrity in what I was doing. And I was always conscious of this very fine writing that sort of set a benchmark on what I was trying to create myself.

Q: Has the kind of writing you admire changed over the years?
HOFFMAN: Yes, it has somewhat. It changed, of course, when I got into William Faulkner by reading a story of his called "A Rose for Emily." That made me see what he was really doing and the depth of his writing, all the various levels and what not. In fact, I was so taken with that story that when I taught at Hampden-Sydney I had my freshmen read it and we took up three classes on it. In fact, there are people today I taught in the 1950s who see me and say, "A Rose for Emily" [laughter]. I still like Thomas Wolfe, but he reads a lot differently now than when I was a young man.

Q: Days in the Yellow Leaf *(1958) was the first novel you wrote but* The Trumpet Unblown *(1955) was published three years before it. How did that come about?*
HOFFMAN: It came about this way as far as I can tell. I had an agent up there [New York City] who was just starting out and she sent *Days in the Yellow Leaf* around to two or three places and the last place she sent it to was Doubleday and there was an editor there who turned the book down but wrote me a very encouraging letter. I submitted *The Trumpet Unblown* to the same editor a month later and he accepted it, also agreeing to publish *Days in the Yellow Leaf* later on. That's how it happened.

Q: Although Days in the Yellow Leaf *was your first book, it seems to begin chronologically where* The Trumpet Unblown *ends. Both books take their titles from the poetry of Lord Byron and the respective protagonists, Tyree Shelby and Tod Young, are drained and largely apathetic as a result of their war experiences. Shelby goes through the war and is unable to connect with anyone afterward, and in* Days in the Yellow Leaf *Tod seeks refuge from the gaudy post-war economic prosperity with his hard-luck veteran buddies.*

HOFFMAN: I think there's a continuity of subject matter there. Certainly, that's the idea. It was this frame of mind I was in when I came back from the war and the first thing I had to write about was the trouble I had working my way back into civilized life. That's the thing a young writer would normally go to and that's what I did. And that was more important to me at that time than the actual war itself. The first two novels are autobiographical to a certain extent. As I progressed I was finally able to break away from the autobiographical stuff, but in the early days I was very much tied to the war. And I'm still . . . when people consider time they might mention AD or BC, but when I think of history it's almost automatic: I say, "Was this before or after World War II?" That was such a strong experience for me that sometimes I feel like I'm living on one side of the divide and everyone who wasn't there is on the other.

Q: *I've heard the so-called brutality of your first couple novels made you kind of unpopular in certain administrative circles on the campus of Hampden-Sydney College.*

HOFFMAN: Well, I doubt if teachers really know what it was like to teach at a place like Hampden-Sydney back then. The power of the president and the board was just overwhelming. The teachers had no union or whatever you might call it—they were kind of academic slaves to a certain extent. So when *The Trumpet Unblown* came out some of my colleagues got a little nervous about being around me because nothing had come down from the president's office.

Just to digress, there's an anecdote that goes with this. There was this prestigious visiting historian from the University of Virginia with the actual name of Thomas Jefferson Wertenbaker. As the name might suggest, he and his wife were very courtly and genteel and correct. They were sitting in their parlor one evening, he was doing some work and his wife was reading my book. All of a sudden she let out a loud gasp and Dr. Wertenbaker asked her what was wrong. She looked at him and said, "Is there a Mrs. Hoffman?" [laughter] But anyway, I received in my mailbox a notice to come see the president and I thought to myself that this might be pretty lively. The president was a Presbyterian minister of the severe old order and, yet, he had a side to him that was very progressive. I had no advanced degree when I was hired and the terms of the contract were such that I could only teach for two years, after which I had to get a degree. So here I was going to the president's office, having been there almost three years and with a controversial book just come out. I went in there and he stood for me and shook my hand and then he said, "Bill, I haven't read your book, but I notice it's getting a lot of attention. We're going to waive the rule that you have to go to graduate school." As soon as word got around that people weren't going to be smeared or polluted by being around me, everything was fine and smooth as can be.

Q: Violent acts often seem to be of great symbolic importance, even in several of your non-war narratives. Fred Chappell remarks that in your work "the violence brings to sharp focus truths that go generally unremarked in the course of daily events" (23). Do you agree with that?
HOFFMAN: I guess back when I first started writing I was considered by reviewers to be a pretty violent writer. I admit I was somewhat surprised by it since I was only portraying my experiences. It seems to me in light of today's fiction, that I'm not a very violent writer. I mean some of the recent writers I've read are really violent, perhaps excessively so. Now I do believe that life is violent. It's violent and it's tragic—that's my experience with it. If someone finds something symbolic or revealing in that, I'll take credit for it, but I don't sit down and write up violent acts in order to reveal character, even though violence often does reveal character—that's just a given.

Q: George Garrett asserts that your two wartime novels, The Trumpet Unblown *and* Yancey's War *(1966), belong "at the highest rank of the American fiction coming out of World War II" (88). In addition to the Hemingway influence, to what extent were those books indebted to other war fiction?*
HOFFMAN: I'm trying to think of the war novels I'd read. Of course, the one I like as well as any of them is *All Quiet on the Western Front.* Around the time I was writing I read Irwin Shaw and James Jones. I remember reading *From Here to Eternity* at Virginia Beach and becoming so engrossed I got a bad sunburn.

Q: World War II, especially in American popular culture, is lionized as the "Good War." Even supposedly realistic films like Saving Private Ryan *portray "good" American soldiers combating "evil" Germans. However,* The Trumpet Unblown *vividly portrays the rape, abuse, and exploitation of German people by American servicemen. Do you think that dynamic might inform the book's relative anonymity?*

HOFFMAN: I don't know. What I said to myself about war at certain moments while I was there was, "No war is worth this." I'm not a pacifist, to show you how contradictory that may sound. I was anxious to get to war, I couldn't wait to get there. I wouldn't trade the experience of war for anything, even though I think it's the most terrible thing to happen to me. I guess what it came down to in *The Trumpet Unblown* was that everyone became a sort of animal, or at least a lower form of human being and exploitation was the name of the game. You were being exploited by the army and what was going on, so you did it too. War does irrational things to people.

Q: Reviewers of Yancey's War *compared it to Joseph Heller's* Catch-22 *(1961), yet several of the events and figures in Heller's book seem drawn from scenes and characters in* The Trumpet Unblown. *Is there any connection?*

HOFFMAN: Well, I think there is a connection. I think there are specific scenes in books like *MASH* and *Catch-22* that come directly from *The Trumpet Unblown*. I'm not talking about military actions, which repeat themselves in most war novels, but in comic situations that I invented and were later mimicked in more popular war narratives.

Q: Your fourth novel, The Dark Mountains *(1963), is the epic story of the MacLauglin family. Twenty-seven years later MacLauglin descendants appear in* Furors Die *(1990). What is the relationship between those two books?*

HOFFMAN: That whole sequence comes from my great-grandfather who came from Scotland and made his fortune in the coal business. He was very much like James MacLauglin, very powerful, everyone felt a sort of aura around him. I remember people had a natural tendency to take off their hats when they talked to him. The book follows him and his descendants. Even though my father was a coal miner, I knew very little about mining, and actually went back to West Virginia while I was teaching at Hampden-Sydney. I drove back-roads and talked to mining people. A lot of them were very reluctant to talk to you, but I learned a lot about their lives and mining. Anyway, only half of *The Dark Mountains* was ever printed. It was twice as long as the published version. I sent it to Doubleday and they wanted to conclude the book with James MacLauglin's death. So there was this kind of lingering, amputated part of the book hovering around and I used material from that to flesh out part of *Furors Die*. What I had in that book was the so-called thin-ning of the blood, the old strong MacLauglin blood was running out. Now I'm going to switch to something you don't know. I have a book coming out soon (*Wild Thorn*, December 2002) in which another generation of MacLauglins appear. It takes place in the mansion James MacLauglin built in *The Dark Mountains*.

Q: *Your first two novels deal with men who have been beaten down and drained by their war experiences. In books like* A Place for My Head *(1960),* A Walk to the River *(1973), and* Godfires *(1985) your protagonists are older "dead men," men with talent and responsibility who have somehow underachieved and lost in life. What interests you about these kinds of characters?*

HOFFMAN: It seems to me I've always kind of come down on the side of men who didn't quite make it and I've wondered in these later years if it was sort of an egotistical thing, that I felt I was a failure too. I didn't really think of myself that way at the time when I was writing those books. But I've al-most always been on the side of the underdog. Now you might not think of a coal-mining tycoon like James MacLauglin as an underdog, but he was when he was a penniless immigrant and he was again when it came to fighting the United States government. I just feel more real affection for those kinds of people, who I think are tragic people. And of course there's the struggle for equality by the black community when all the schools are closing in *A Place for My Head*. It was just a damn hysteria in that town [Farmville, Virginia], and it was good material. I could use it.

Q: *The protagonist in* A Death of Dreams *(1973), Guy Dion, is sent to a Rich-mond-area substance abuse / mental rehabilitation clinic for therapy. Angus McCloud visits an almost identical facility in* A Place for My Head. *In the sto-ries "Dancer" and "The Secret Garden" (*Follow Me Home *[1994]), the female protagonists are threatened with being institutionalized. What interests you about that kind of milieu?*

HOFFMAN: That's an easy one to answer. My mother all of her life was in and out of places like that and her life ended in a place like that. When I was just a very small boy we would take these trips to see her wherever she would be. She went to a number of places, some very genteel, others not so nice. Sometimes she became so out of it, she couldn't really function . . . she ended up undergoing a lobotomy. By the way, I'm very fond of Ken Kesey's book

[*One Flew Over the Cuckoo's Nest*] for his treatment of that subject. When my grandmother died I looked after my mother and saw that she was being cared for. At times she could come out for a while, she would be alright, but then she would have to go back. So naturally this has been with me my whole life and it gets transformed in fiction. But that story "The Secret Garden" . . . that was my mother. And it's one of my favorite stories because I think I really put it all together there.

Q: The Land that Drank the Rain *(1982) strikes me as a biblical allegory, the title itself coming from a passage in the book of Hebrews (6:1–9).*
HOFFMAN: Yes, it is consciously allegorical; it's a little bit different from anything else I ever did. It's essentially a religious book and the great sin that Claytor is guilty of is a sin of the flesh. And it takes a great sacrificial act upon his part, the shedding of his own blood, to be redeemed. In the process he also saves the young man he's befriended.

Q: *Your two most recent collections of short stories,* Follow Me Home *and* Doors *(2000), contain several powerful first-person narratives by female characters. How do you go about writing from a woman's perspective?*
HOFFMAN: I don't particularly find it hard or difficult. You know I have an odd thing that happens to me and I don't know how to explain it. Sometimes when I take a shower somebody's name will pop into my head, male or female, and for just an instant I feel I'm that person and I see their face right in front of me. It's a spooky thing. Sometimes, too, when I've been writing hard in the morning I'll come out of my office and for a moment or two I'll have a conflict as to just who I really am. I don't know whether that's a gift or a curse. So maybe that's why it's not hard for me to imagine a female character. I guess "emphathize" is the best word for it.

Q: *The protagonists of "Night Sport"* (Follow Me Home)*, "Landings"* (Doors)*, and* Tidewater Blood *(1998) are bitter war veterans who in some ways resemble Tyree Shelby and Tod Young. However, their war was the Vietnam War. How do they differ from the World War II veterans in your earlier fiction?*
HOFFMAN: I really feel that war is a timeless universal. The only thing that changes are the cultural conditions and the outer accouterments: tactics, technology, uniforms, and so on. But the central truth of it is the same in all wars. The reason I use Vietnam now is the immediacy it has for readers, but the essence of war doesn't change.

Q: The suspenseful mystery narratives Tidewater Blood *and* Blood and Guile *(2000) have brought you to the attention of a new readership. However,* God-fires *(1985) was probably your first true mystery novel. These books stand out, structurally and stylistically, from your earlier material. Did you use a different approach in writing them?*

HOFFMAN: I think *Godfires* is the best hope of those types of books. When I wrote *Tidewater Blood* I never thought of it as a mystery novel. Then the publisher and critics started calling it a suspense novel, and of course I try to have suspense in every book. So I wasn't really trying to target a specific audience, but that's the way the publisher pitched it. I didn't care so long as they were trying to sell the book. So the response kind of blind-sided me. But when I wrote the sequel I was very aware of the mystery dynamic. Part of the reason for doing that is that I'm getting to the age where it's harder for me to come up with new material to write about. I still enjoy writing and by writing in this style I'm finally making a little bit of money.

Q: Tidewater Blood *and* Blood and Guile *take place in and around the fictional setting of King County with overlapping characters. Do you plan to write more King County mysteries?*

HOFFMAN: Yes, there'll be one more, the one that's coming out in December. I don't know after that. I've got one more novel out there that I wrote during the period between *Tidewater Blood* and *Blood and Guile*, which is more of a standard literary novel, but its fate is yet to be decided. One of these days soon I'll have to go down there and sit at the desk, and face the terror of the blank page. I don't have any idea what I'll do, but I'll do something.

Works Cited

Chappell, Fred. "Taking Measure: Violent Intruders in William Hoffman's Short Fiction." *The Fictional World of William Hoffman*. Ed. William Frank. Columbia: University of Missouri Press, 2000, pp.9–23.

Garrett, George. "A Life Without End: Two Novels About World War II by William Hoffman." *The Fictional World of William Hoffman*. Ed. William Frank. Columbia: University of Missouri Press, 2000, pp.88–97.

Robert Morgan ∾ 2000

PETER JOSYPH

For the documentary Acting McCarthy: The Making of Richard Pearce's "The Gardener's Son," *my collaborator Raymond Todd and I asked novelist and poet Robert Morgan to speak with us, on camera, about* The Gardener's Son. *Based on the murder of James Gregg by Robert McEvoy in the mill town of Graniteville, South Carolina, in 1876, the picture was co-produced by Richard Pearce and Michael Hausman on a budget of $200,000, which was provided by Public Television station KCET's Visions series. Directed by Richard Pearce from an original screenplay by Cormac McCarthy, it was shot by cinematographer Fred Murphy on 16mm film, using locations chiefly in North Carolina. The film aired on January 6, 1977, and was favorably reviewed by John O'Connor in the* New York Times, *Tom Allen in the* Village Voice, *and Alan Kriegsman in the* Washington Post. *It represents some of the best work by all of its participants.[1] It has never enjoyed a theatrical release.*

Our conversation took place in a small room at the Gramercy Park Hotel in Manhattan on February 12, 2000, when Morgan was in New York to meet with the publishers of his novel Gap Creek, *which had recently been chosen for the Oprah Book Club. Speaking about Algonquin, who published the book in hardcover, Morgan said: "Before this, the most copies they had sold of a book was 150,000. The day Oprah made the announcement, they had orders for 550,000 copies overnight."*

QUESTION: *You are one of the few people I know who saw* The Gardener's Son *when it aired in 1977.*
MORGAN: Purely by accident. I turned on the television to PBS. This film was already in progress. It grabbed my attention because of the voices, the accents. I realized: "My goodness, here's something from National Public Television where they really have the accents right and the dialect is right on the

Originally published as Peter Josyph, "Getting the Voices Right: A Conversation with Robert Morgan about *The Gardener's Son*," Vol. 40, no. 1 (2001), 121–131.

money." I remember the foreman in the cotton mill who says to the kid: "If I'm not mistaken you'll find a broom in there." My goodness—who has done this! So I kept watching, glued to the show.

I've never forgotten, after over twenty-two years, Ned Beatty coming to the door of that old tavern. He's told the mother is dead, and he says: "I didn't know that. C'mon in, honey, and get ye a drink. I'm mighty sorry t'hear that." That was so perfect. I was enthralled. Watched the whole thing. Very sad, very dark story. Credits came on, said it was directed by Richard Pearce, script by Cormac McCarthy. I, of course, knew about McCarthy, but I had never read him.

It was a very important thing for me to see that film because it showed me what you could do with the voices of that region. The cotton mills of upper South Carolina mostly employed the poor whites from the mountains. Many of my family members had worked in those cotton mills. My mother worked in a cotton mill when I was young. She supported us. So I was quite taken to see the anger in the character of the boy. It was a breath of fresh air to see that kind of realism. Particularly in terms of the voices, and the way in which those cotton mill workers were at such a disadvantage, but were, in a way, happy to be working there, to be making wages. They had come down from the mountains, having sold and abandoned their farms. I did not start writing fiction immediately after that, but within the next four years I did, and I believe that's one of the things that inspired me to start telling stories about Appalachia, about the mountains where I had grown up.

Q: Prior to that, had you not thought of using your native land as material?
MORGAN: I had published several short stories as a graduate student and they were all set in the area, but then I published only poetry for about fifteen years. The important thing for me in going back to fiction was learning to use voices. I had not done that in my earlier stories very much. It was a process of learning to let my characters tell their own stories, reveal themselves in the way they talk. The genius of Cormac McCarthy is partly in his ability to get the voices right. In all of his fiction and in the screenplay he has an amazing ear. That was a kind of revelation to me, to see that that's where so much of the life of the characters was, in the voices. This is certainly true in all of his books, especially in the Appalachian novels.

Q: Brad Dourif told us how he enjoyed watching McCarthy's delight in local speech patterns during the filming around Glencoe, North Carolina. Does one have to cultivate an ear?

MORGAN: I think you have to teach yourself to do that. Often the people who have the greatest trouble writing dialogue and dialect accurately are the people who have spoken it themselves. Because they do it, they are not aware of how to write it down. It can be an advantage to come in from the outside and consciously study it, listen to it. It probably begins for any writer, including Cormac McCarthy, with an ability to listen. My experience is that writers are often better listeners than talkers. Other people may talk better about fiction than its writers, but almost all the good writers I know listen and watch people.

They say Faulkner used to sit on the square in Oxford and listen to people tell stories. People often ask me: "How can you write so accurately about women? You're a man." My answer is, I have known a lot of women and listen to them talk. I used to listen to them as they strung beans or peeled peaches. I am sure McCarthy worked that way. I have heard he used to hang around a country store in Tennessee and talk to trappers, construction workers.

But *it is a made thing*, that's the answer to your question. It doesn't come naturally. Nothing about writing is natural. But if you work *really hard* at storytelling, at language, you can make it seem *perfectly* natural, as though it happened spontaneously. The best art does seem to be virtually spontaneous. I tell my students that you do not take a story from real life and transcribe it to the page, you *create* a sense of reality, one detail, one sentence, one image at a time.

Q: *In a lot of fiction that tries to capture a region, or a class or category of person, the writer assumes that once he gets the language the way he heard it, that's the prize, that's literature. But it has to attain a level of poetry, doesn't it? Often that's missing. It isn't missing in your books. It isn't missing in* The Gardener's Son. *McCarthy is a poet, is he not?*
MORGAN: He certainly is. His writing, his dialogue, is so compact. If you look at a page of *The Gardener's Son*, or *Child of God*, it's amazing to see the poetic energy there, the way he's caught the flavor of speech but *compressed* it. If you transcribed a conversation among people like that and printed it, it wouldn't be very interesting. McCarthy's writing is art. It is a made thing. He has caught those tropes, those expressions, and put them into a very compact form.

I believe a lot of people writing about poor people, people in Appalachia, may approach it with an agenda instead of trying to get inside the characters and let them tell their own story. I believe that if you write from someone's point of view, let's say Lester Ballard in *Child of God*, it can only be done if you really try to see the world as he sees it. This is the great thing that McCarthy learned, perhaps, from writers like Dostoevski. That you take characters who may be repellent to a lot of people, and who would be considered criminals or insane, but as a writer you try to get inside those characters and tell their story from their point of view, and that makes it live. It's very different from having an agenda, where you are going to show the world what poverty is like, or what the criminally insane are like. It's the difference between fiction and nonfiction, perhaps. The fiction writer is not writing an argument. You want to show real people.

Q: Were there elements of place that rang true to you in the film?
MORGAN: The scene that I remember most vividly is the tavern scene. That was just astonishingly real to me. You have a tavern that was really just a shack, a barn, with these men sitting around passing a jug of moonshine and slicing off a bit of potato as a chaser. Also, the house where the mother is lying in state was particularly well done. I think the script mentions black cloths hung over the mirrors. That was a particularly good detail. But beyond the detail, the tone of the piece, the realism, the hardness of it impressed me. This was not a romanticization of cotton mill life, and it was not an essay. Here was a filmmaker, a writer, and actors who were willing to look at poor people as they were.

Q: James Cagney used to have an expression, "dropping the goodies," for some actorial touch that, even if he were playing the bad guy, would charm the audience, warm them up to him. Most of the performances in this film don't attempt that. Certainly Dourif's doesn't. Were your sympathies with the kid? He is a murderer.
MORGAN: I certainly sympathized with him. Because you know that had he had a good lawyer, and if he had had money, he might have been convicted but he probably would not have been hanged.

The story is about moral ambiguity to a great extent. You don't know, finally, why he is so angry. It may have been almost an accident. In modern times it would have been judged differently—he was unbalanced, he was angry, it happened spur-of-the-moment, it was not premeditated, it would have been Murder Two instead of Murder One—so you have to be sympathetic to a character like that.

One of the great things about the story is that it's not a story of moral judgment. You do feel Gregg, the mill owner, taking advantage of people. He's propositioning his women employees. I know that happened all the time. I've been told stories about that. McEvoy certainly knows the owner does that, so that even if Gregg didn't proposition his sister, McEvoy knows he might have. It was considered more or less a right of the cotton mill owner.

I guess my greatest sympathy is for the sister, the female characters. I really wish more of the script had been kept in the movie. Some of the greatest writing McCarthy has ever done, probably, is in the later scene where the sister is in the hospital in Columbia, that monologue where she keeps circling back to the horse called Captain, who they sold and who she sees in the streets of Greenville later.[2] *That* was a *very* telling detail, that the horse had a name, that they remembered the name of the horse, that the horse was important. The loss of that horse symbolized the loss of their farm and their identity as a rural people. They had moved to the cotton mill and they had lost their horse. The loyalty of the horse, the fact that the horse recognizes them years later on the streets of Bringle, that's a wonderful detail.

I think McCarthy thought his way very deeply into that story.

Q: *It's also poignant that the horse is named Captain. It's a boss's name—"Cap'n"—plus Gregg is "Captain Gregg"—but here it means something different.*
MORGAN: Yes, it's her memory of the farm, which is probably viewed as a kind of Eden lost. It certainly was not when they were living there. But living in a cotton mill town with all the problems they've had—the father's alcoholism, the son's murder conviction, the mother's death—she certainly looks back to that mountain farm as a much better place and time, and the horse is symbolic of that.

Horses are so close to the people in rural life. You work with a horse. That's why it fascinates me so much. I worked with horses when I was young. The horse has a name, it's not just a *horse*. It's Captain.

Q: *When Raymond and I went to Graniteville, I spoke to a girl who was working in a convenience store just outside of town. She said: "What d'you want to go there for?" I told her we were doing some research. She said: "Well I live there. You don't want to go there." I told her we needed a place to stay. She said: "There's nowhere you can stay in Graniteville." She just didn't want me to go there. It's still a mill town, still a company town, there are company houses all in a row, and the stench is, at times, overwhelming. In the cemetery on the outskirts of town, where you can still hear the mill, still smell it, I said to Raymond: "Having been here, I could see where a guy would commit a murder just to get out."*

MORGAN: They paid *very* low wages before the year of the minimum wage. My mother, on her first job, made nine dollars a week. She was the only person in her family employed. This was 1931, when she graduated from high school. In the nineteenth century they paid even less. The same people who had owned the plantations, after the Civil War, in the Reconstruction period, built cotton mills. They had lost the slave labor and they replaced it with the poor whites of the Piedmont and the mountains. They could pay them almost nothing, because these are people who were not used to a cash economy. They had practiced subsistence farming. They were attracted to the cotton mills because, hey, they were making wages, they could live in town and buy things. But it was a pretty bad system.

Yes, I could see where somebody would be so angry. Yes. But the brilliance of the film is partly that it's never explained. McCarthy is a writer who doesn't *explain* his characters. They do what they do and you can interpret that however you want. I think that's part of the fascination of his stories. They're not stories of moral judgment, they're about people.

Q: Raymond and I would like to see the film re-shown. How would you answer someone who says: "Why bother? It's an old film, it's about a very small region of the country, it's the nineteenth century, it's not like that any more, it's a murder by an unknown guy no one cared about then and no one cares about now. It's important to you, Bob Morgan, because it influenced you, but does it have any importance beyond that?"
MORGAN: The first answer is the artistic quality of it. Works of art are important not only because of the subject, but because of the way they are made. It is so brilliantly written, directed, and acted, that it should be brought back. But it's also about a very important issue and a very important time in history. I believe that fiction and film are the main ways people know about history, and to know who you are you have to know something about history. I think there would be a real audience for this movie, because we are, now, looking more into our roots than we have in the recent past. If you want to know something about this country, you have to know what happened in the nineteenth century and the early twentieth century.

Often the best stories are set way off in places nobody's ever been, about incidents they've never heard of, and this is a particularly interesting story because it's about one of the great transition periods in American history. Most viewers of films and television know more about the Civil War than they know about the period just after it, when the upper South, the Piedmont

South, was in a *terrible* period of poverty. I've heard stories in my family about this period. There just wasn't *anything*. There was no way to make a living. The land had been devastated. That was one reason why these people went down to live in the cotton mill towns and were enticed to work for wages, because everybody was having such a hard time. So I would say it's important for people to know about this period and these kinds of people.

What makes a story accessible to a general audience is the artistry. We like stories that are real, that are detailed, that are local. Oddly enough, what would make a story set in an exotic place accessible is the specificity. Paradoxically, it's that local color, that local detail, that makes it accessible to any audience. Instead of *stripping that away* to make it accessible, you do exactly the opposite: you get the dialect right, you get the details right, and that makes it understandable to somebody in Russia or Japan, or to somebody a hundred years later.

Q: *You gave a talk in which you referred to something that you, certainly, achieve in your own work. You said that it's in the detail that a story achieves a cosmic element. You said: "The greatest writers evoke a sense of the poise and scale of eternity in their work." That's a fascinating phrase,* the poise and scale of eternity.

MORGAN: I believe that's one of the things that makes a writer a poet.

To bring into play a very local story, in the foreground you have a character, you have a very angry young man, McEvoy, in South Carolina, who inadvertently—or with a plan, we're not sure—commits a murder. It's an engaging story, partly because the detail is so specific to the time and place, so it seems real, we get involved in it. But the *effect* of a story such as that, one that is really well done, is that it seems universal, it seems to fit the way we view humanity, history.

It's a tragedy. Cormac McCarthy is a tragic writer. When you pull back from a story like that, you feel that it fits into the larger world and into the larger human condition. It isn't *just* a local story. Viewed from a distance, it seems even more tragic, these individuals caught up in the great processes of history, economics. And it's that combination of double vision that's one of the marks of a great writer. They see the local this story, but you also feel it connects to the larger patterns of nature and history.

In some ways, McCarthy is a great naturalistic writer. You can feel the forces of nature as well as of the characters' personalities. You see this in a novel such as *Child of God*. You see it particularly in *Suttree*. The story's all about the city, but at the end, as Suttree's leaving the city, you expand to the countryside and then to a mythic sense of nature and destiny.

Q: *Where would you rank McCarthy among American writers, particularly those of the twentieth century?*
MORGAN: My sense is that some of the writers of the last half of the twentieth century and the beginning of the twenty-first are as good as the great writers of the earlier twentieth century. In the future, writers like Cormac McCarthy, Tim O'Brien, Louise Erdrich, Lee Smith, Doris Betts, Reynolds Price, Alice Walker, will be seen as great writers the way Faulkner, Hemingway, and Fitzgerald are. Academia has canonized certain modernist writers, talked and talked about them so long that we think of them as deities, and nobody can ever be that great. I suspect that that is just a myth created by academia, as I suspect modernism is a myth created by academia.

In the longer context, you can see that Cormac McCarthy links up with Melville and Dostoevski and it has very little to do with modernism, it has to do with these great tragic stories, with the drama and power of them. Perhaps some of the great modernists are not as good as the great contemporary novelists. It would be hard to find a writer about war better than Tim O'Brien, for instance, even considering Tolstoi and Stendhal and the writers about World War II. Of course we don't know how these people will be ranked because we don't know what the tastes of the future will be, but I suspect that McCarthy will be thought of as one of the great American writers a hundred years from now.

Q: *I used to say to academics: "I don't acknowledge post-modernism because I don't acknowledge modernism. There are things in Laurence Sterne that are every bit as postmodern as Pynchon!"*
MORGAN: [Laughs] Absolutely. All the elements of fiction seem to have been present at the beginning, in the eighteenth century. Nothing has happened that's entirely different from what Sterne, Richardson, Fielding, and Defoe did at the very beginning. The great dramas, the historical epics, the ironies, the experimental tongue-in-cheek writing in Sterne, the comedy of Fielding—it was all there at the very beginning.

Q: *Can you think of other films about the South that have struck you with comparable force to* The Gardener's Son?
MORGAN: So many films about the South have been romanticized. One

of the most realistic films I have seen recently is *Sling Blade*, by Billy Bob Thornton. That seemed to hit that note of the real. The voices have that sense of discovery. A character says: "Are you going to carry me over?" Meaning, am I going to ride with you. Hollywood *can* get the South right, but it rarely does. In television and film they usually rely on stereotypes. The first major American movie was about the Civil War, and the most famous movie of all time is about the Civil War, so around the world that's the audience's view of the South. What you get in *The Gardener's Son* is the smaller picture. You get down to the finer details, and it has a realism and a toughness that's very special. I would like to see more films like that.

Q: *To get such fine performances, it does seem to help, doesn't it, to have good writing?*
MORGAN: It's a lot easier to be a really good actor if you have really good lines to say and a really good character. I'll never forget that when he was given a lifetime achievement award, Cary Grant thanked the writers, and he named half a dozen.

Q: *Billy Bob Thornton directed* All the Pretty Horses.
MORGAN: He has a wonderful sense of characterization through voice, both as an actor and as a writer. I noticed this in *The Apostle*. He's the man who tries to run the preacher off. That just seemed *absolutely* right. That anger—he got that anger right, and the fear of religion, of the spirit—and the way he changes on camera. *That* was an awfully good movie, also. But both as a writer and as an actor, Thornton has such a feeling for the complexity of characters who are poor, or are not well educated. He doesn't think of them as simple. He sees their complexity.

Q: Sling Blade *has something in common with* The Gardener's Son *in that there are no easy answers there, either. Even in the way it is lit, you get the sense that Karl has vast areas of personality that will remain dark to the viewer and, perhaps, to anyone that knows him.*
MORGAN: Well, the good writer and the good actor will find the character often through the paradoxes, the contradictions that will make him or her most real. Nobody is either all good or all bad. The challenge is to include those contradictions and yet, at the same time, to give the character an overall unity, and I think Thornton is one of the best at doing that.

Q: In my own work, I have allies who support me by what they do. I look at them and say: "someone else is aiming at the same sort of thing." They're with me every day. I couldn't get by without the touchstone of knowing that they've done it, or are doing it. Is there any sense in which McCarthy has been an ally to you?

MORGAN: Yes. He is one of the writers who showed me the possibilities of working with the region, with characters who are at the fringe of society, as it were. I believe it was easier to get back to fiction writing after having discovered his work, encountering the power of the language, the way in which he will look at the world in its contradictions and pain. He is one of several writers I rely on for a sense of encouragement and of possibility.

My first writing teacher was the novelist Guy Owen, who planted seeds I'm sure he never realized, talking about dialect, learning the terms local people used, that sort of thing. Owen was a great influence on me. Not at the time. Later. And certainly Cormac McCarthy. Lee Smith, another writer about Appalachia. Fred Chappell was one of my teachers. I've learned a lot from Fred. He's been very encouraging over the years. A short story that has meant a lot to me over the years is Alice Walker's "Everyday Use," which is about a family of farm women in Georgia. The older woman brags about how she can kill a hog all by herself. [Laughs] She can run the place all by herself! That has a wonderful realism and toughness to it.

It is easier to write knowing that there are writers like Cormac McCarthy who are successful, that great writing is not something of the past, but also of the present.

Q: What will you do when they come to you and say: "It's not enough that Gap Creek *is a novel, we're going to film it—will you do the screenplay?"*

MORGAN: I would like to have a shot at it. Screenwriting is very different from fiction writing. I believe literary people don't realize how hard it is to adapt something for film. It seems easy, perhaps, because it's not about writing but about visualization and drama. I think it would be a great challenge. I would like to try it.

I love movies. I had never seen a movie in a theater until I went off to college. I grew up in the country and my parents wouldn't let us go to see movies, but when I moved off to college I just went wild going to see movies and loved them. I believe that film has had a lot of impact on fiction writing. We have learned a lot from film, particularly about pacing and compression.

So I would be thrilled if somebody made a film of one of my books, and yes, I would enjoy at least trying to write a script.

Q: *I won't ask whether you'd feel a loss of power being stripped of your prose. As a poet you work very sparsely, don't you?*
MORGAN: I believe film and poetry do have a lot in common, and film and the short story. But I'm in awe of film and its power. It's different from language. Often the hardest novels to adapt are the best written, the novels that live in their language, in the narration, in their descriptions. That's very hard to adapt. It may be easier to adapt novels that are not that great.[3] The way you tell a story in film is somewhat different. I tell my students that film is, oddly enough, more a medium of *reaction*. To know what something means, the camera turns to the face of the actor, and we know, by their expression, if it's moving or mysterious. Since you don't have that actor or the camera in fiction writing, you have to show what happens and the reader responds to that. Paradoxically, film is more the medium of reaction, and fiction the medium of action. You tell the reader *what happens* and you don't have to explain what it means.

Q: *Your face is very congenial to the camera. Have you done any acting?*
MORGAN: No. I sort of wish I had. I believe fiction writing is very similar to acting. The great pleasure of writing fiction is that you don't have to be yourself. You can get into your characters. You can forget your own troubles for a while and think of the troubles of your character Julie, or Jimmy, or Hank. I feel there's something very close to acting in writing. I often wish I had tried acting, but I never did.

Q: *When they film* Gap Creek *they'll probably find a part for you.*
MORGAN: [Laughs] I can be the old guy!

Q: *James Dickey tells the story of playing the sheriff in* Deliverance, *"Well, they just had a costume that fit me . . . " But when you look at the size of Dickey . . . [Laughter] When Raymond and I make our own dramatic films, we might have to put you to work for us.*
MORGAN: Okay. That's a deal.

Notes

1. In *The Gardener's Son*, Kevin Conway plays James Gregg, who is shot in the office of his mill by Robert McEvoy, played by Brad Dourif. Robert's father, a gardener at the mill, is played by Jerry Hardin; his mother is played by Penny Allen; his sister, from whom Gregg tries to buy sexual favors, is played by Anne O'Sullivan. Nan Martin plays James Gregg's mother, and Ned Beatty plays Pinky, a good ole boy with whom Robert takes a drink when he returns to Graniteville to see that his mother is *not* buried there. Paul Benjamin plays the attorney hired to defend Robert, who is hanged at the end of the film.

2. The shooting script and the script published by Ecco Press contain a framing device—a contemporary scene preceding, and another succeeding, the historical narrative—which is not in the finished film. Fred Murphy is fairly certain that this frame was shot, and Anne O'Sullivan vaguely recalls seeing it. "I was an old lady who never married," she told us. "It was a real woman of that age, it wasn't me in makeup. It informed how I played the character, because it made me think: 'This is somebody that takes something in and each day it lives in her.'"

3. A similar view on adaptation was expressed to us by Michael Hausman, whose subsequent credits include Richard Pearce's *Heartland*, *No Mercy*, and *Family Thing*, as well as *Amadeus*, *Ragtime*, *Silkwood*, *Things Change*, *Nobody's Fool*, *The People vs. Larry Flint*, *Man on the Moon*, and *Gangs of New York*.

    "I have an axiom," he told us, "which may or may not be true. I have examples of pictures I've made myself that prove it either way. Good underlying material is not necessarily good for either the screenplay or the movie. *Ragtime*, for example. Wonderfully written book by Doctorow. A wonderful movie on its own that Milos Foreman directed and I helped produce. The complaint I got all the time: *it wasn't the book*. I don't know how to answer that. It *wasn't* the book. If you wanted the book it'd be much cheaper, you could photograph the pages, flip em, we could probably make it for $25. Sometimes good material can't ever be translated to film. There's too much meat on the bone, there's too much fleshing out. I'd rather have a lousy book with a good idea and get a good screenwriter, rather than a tremendously popular book. That's a producer's bank, the popular book. Producers want to have successful Projects so if the picture goes bad, they can say: 'But it was a great book!' I would rather pay less for the book and make it into something."

Del Shores ❧ 2007–2008

ANDREA POWELL WOLFE

Actor, playwright, director, and producer Del Shores was born in Winters, Texas in 1957. He resided in Texas throughout his childhood and much of his early adult life until he moved to Los Angeles, California, to pursue acting. He has published five plays, Cheatin' *(1984),* Daddy's Dyin' (Who's Got the Will?) *(1987), and* Daughters of the Lone Star State *(1992), which comprise his Lowake, Texas series, and* Sordid Lives *(1998) and* Southern Baptist Sissies *(2001), which treat the suppression and denial of gay identity in small Texas communities and the struggles of gay men to overcome the oppression of cultural and religious values. A recent work,* The Trial and Tribulations of a Trailer-Trash Housewife, *is currently unpublished but enjoyed a successful six-month run in Los Angeles in 2003.[1] Shores's plays have earned numerous awards, including the GLAAD Award for Outstanding Production of the Year for* Sissies *in 2002. Shores also wrote the screenplay and executive-produced the 1990 film version of* Daddy's Dyin', *which starred Beau Bridges, Tess Harper, Judge Reinhold, Keith Carradine, and Beverly D'Angelo.[2] In 1999, Shores wrote and directed the big-screen version of* Sordid Lives, *featuring Beau Bridges, Delta Burke, Olivia Newton-John, Bonnie Bedelia, Leslie Jordan, and Beth Grant, a film that quickly became a cult classic.[3] Shores has also written for television, including several episodes of "Queer as Folk." Currently, Shores is working on a film version of* Southern Baptist Sissies *and "Sordid Lives: The Series" for MTV's LOGO Network. As his many critical and commercial successes demonstrate, Shores's writing seems to resonate with the concerns of mainstream America as well as within the gay community. I first met Del Shores at a question-and-answer session following a production of* Sissies *at the Theatre on the Square in Indianapolis, Indiana. The following interview was conducted through email exchanges beginning in August 2007 and continuing through February 2008.*

Originally published as Andrea Powell Wolfe, "Queering Texas: Interview with Del Shores," Vol. 47, no. 1 (2009), 104–20.

QUESTION: *I thought that I would begin by asking you how you feel about labels. Do you consider yourself a Southern writer, for instance? Do you want to be known as a gay artist? Do the two terms, "southern" and "queer," fit with how you identify as an artist or even with how you see yourself as a human being?*
SHORES: It seems I'm referred to in press these days as "openly gay writer/director" or something like that. I don't mind it although there is much more to me than just the "gay" part. In fact, I think that embracing that part of who I am has been a huge part of my later career. Hey, as long as they are talking about you, right?

Q: *What about the "Southern" part of the label "Southern Queer"?*
SHORES: Most of my work, yes, is set in the South, Texas mainly. I do identify with the South and Southern culture. I write what I know. I have, of course, had some nice success with characters based outside of the South (Ty's LA friends in the upcoming series "Sordid Lives: The Series" [and with characters in] "Queer as Folk" and "Dharma & Greg"), but I think I'll always be remembered for my quirky Southern characters.

Q: *I know that you grew up in Texas and that all of your plays are all set in Texas. How is being a Texan different from being a Southerner, or is it?*
SHORES: Some Texans seem to think that they are not a part of the South. However, I think our cultures are pretty much the same. I find that there is a Southern/Texas sensibility that is pretty similar.

Q: *In* Sordid Lives, *Ty has to leave his Texas hometown and family to come to grips with his own identity, his relationship with his mother, and his role in the larger community. How has your own journey for understanding compared to Ty's?*
SHORES: When I first moved to LA, it was just amazing. I came here to act, and the mentality was just so different. I'm not saying that many of the values [and] morals that I was raised with were thrown out the window. But my mind did open to all people, all religions, and a lot of what I was taught, what was engrained (if you will), started evaporating. In other words, my mind opened and I realized that God wasn't sending Jews or homosexuals to hell and that I had to reevaluate many of my beliefs—and ultimately changed them.

Q: *Can you talk more about how your perspectives on yourself, your family, and your background have changed throughout your life?*

SHORES: Well, a lot actually. I tried being straight for many years. Even married a woman, had two children. Stayed in the church for awhile. But my life was in turmoil, in chaos, and I had to go through a lot of therapy to learn to love who I was, how I was created. Coming out really has had an effect on how my family sees me. Also, my work has been judged pretty harshly by the conservatives, the Baptists and fundamentalists. But I've also been embraced by so many and feel very fortunate to have intense, loving, and loyal fans and friends.

Q: As you've noted, the progression of your career seems to parallel your personal growth in many ways: your later plays, Sordid Lives and Southern Baptist Sissies, differ from your Lowake, Texas, series plays in that they feature gay characters and confront issues related to gay identity in the South. Can you talk a little bit about how you see Sordid Lives and Sissies as different from the plays that preceded them?
SHORES: When I decided to write about being gay in Sordid Lives, I made a promise to myself—I would write from my soul and not censor myself, not think about what my family would think [or], for that matter, anybody. So, I think that my journey as a writer, as a true artist began when I accepted the truth about my sexuality to the world—and to myself.

Q: How did the process of writing your later plays differ from the process of writing the first three?
SHORES: The structures were less traditional, the stories bolder, braver, and, with Sissies, I feel that I hit that stride that I'm known for—a blend of tragedy and intense comedy.

Q: How did you know when you hit that stride?
SHORES: I think I knew I could mix tones and get away with it when Daddy's Dyin' opened on stage. I saw tears and laughter within the same scene. Of course, the tragedy got more intense in the last two plays, but there is still lots of laughter.

Q: How do you see your newest play, The Trials and Tribulations of a Trailer-Trash Housewife, fitting into your canon of work?
SHORES: It certainly was my most critically successful. That play astounds me. I honestly felt like some abused woman found my spirit and channeled her story through my pen. Sounds weird, I know, but where did she come from? She found me.

Q: *Looking back on* Daddy's Dyin', Cheatin', *and* Daughters of the Lone Star State, *do you see any manifestations in these plays of the struggle with sexual identity that you may have undergone during the period of your life in which you wrote them?*

SHORES: I was ready for that, so, no, not even in my writing. Of course, I did write guys in *Cheatin'* with their shirts off and in underwear.

Q: *I'm thinking specifically of the relationship between Clarence and Teddy Joe in* Cheatin'. *Certainly, the two men are clearly marked as heterosexual, but the exchange that takes place between them after their physical altercation is surprisingly intimate and tender.*

SHORES: Hmm . . . Never thought about it. I always just saw them as straight friends who found themselves in a hotel room together after one of them had screwed the other one's wife.

Q: *I find it interesting that, also in* Cheatin', *Clarence's disparagement of homosexuality is presented as comical. In a sort of drunken rampage, he labels the weatherman on Channel Five a "sissified, plaster-haired homosexual." Later, after Bo Bob makes several attempts to pull him out of his depression, Clarence calls him "homasexual," too (emphasis added). How can we interpret Clarence's ridiculously homophobic behavior?*

SHORES: As how those straight boys are in the South. I grew up with a few too many "Clarences."

Q: *Can you say a little bit about how and why you used recurring characters and a single setting in the three Lowake plays?*

SHORES: I loved Preston Jones's *Texas Trilogy*.[4] He inspired me greatly, so I decided to pay homage to him (since he died at such an early age) with my own Texas trilogy. Plus, I just couldn't let go of the town and those characters. I still just love them. Mama Wheelis (in *Daddy's Dyin'* and *Daughters*) is based on my great grandmother, and every time I see the play or watch the movie, it's like having her back, having my entire family back.

Q: *How do you see the Lowake plays as paying tribute to Jones's work?*

SHORES: He wrote a trilogy, as did I. He wrote plays that stood alone without seeing the other ones, but some of his characters cross[ed] over and told a completely different story. I loved that and did the same with my first three plays.

Q: Why was it important to you to continue writing about the folks and the cultural climate of Lowake, Texas, after you finished Cheatin'?

SHORES: My grandfather was dying while we rehearsed *Cheatin'*. I would tell stories to the cast about what was going on, and our director, Sherry Landrum, said—"there's your next play." I didn't feel finished with Sara Lee, so I decided to make her the "added" sister in my mom's family. It worked out well.

Q: How was it for you to see characters in the Lowake series, like Sara Lee, develop over the course of several years?

SHORES: I loved it. I sometimes think I'd like to write a series of monologues re-visiting the characters in my plays, my favorite ones, to catch up with them.

Q: I'd like to return to an earlier comment that you made. You said that you were ready for my question about the connections between your early plays and your later focus on homosexuality. Are you asked to talk about the Lowake, Texas, series in relationship to your other plays frequently? Do you feel like it is important for critics to make connections between your plays, or do you see them more as separate, or self-contained, entities?

SHORES: Well, they work as solo pieces, but I do believe the body of work should be acknowledged, and a good critic will always comment on your early work, your last play, a similar character, etc. I'm not sure if "important" is the right word, but I think it's pretty damn smart when they do it.

Q: In the second and third Lowake, Texas, series plays, Daddy's Dyin' *and* Daughters of the Lone Star State, *you include an author's note stating, "These people are real, not cartoons. It's easy to go for the laughs, it's harder to strive for the truth." The line between cartoonish comedy and tragic truth seems a fine one. How do you see comedy and truth working together in your plays?*

SHORES: At its very best when performed by the right actors. That's why I use the same actors over and over. They "get" me. They get the tone. They know how far to push without spilling into cartoons. I can hardly watch other productions of my plays because so many times, there is too much chewing of the scenery.

Q: Do you think that this has anything to do with the fact that you use Southern settings and Southern characters? How do you see the stereotyping of Southerners as backward or unintelligent as getting in the way of honest portrayals of Southern culture on the stage?

SHORES: Sure, that's some of it. And of course, it's the comedy, too. Actors love to get laughs, and some think that that is more important than truth. I do think that many people outside of the South see my characters as caricatures because they truly don't know them. I love it when my Southern fans say, "I have an aunt just like Sissy." Or, "My Mom IS Latrelle."

Q: *What is the importance of comedy in such a tragic story as that which you tell in* Sissies, *for example?*
SHORES: Comedy helps you get through the tragic parts. The blend makes it more entertaining, easier to digest. If there were no Peanut and Odette, I'm afraid the audience would just slice their wrists right there in the theatre.

Q: *How would you say that your early focus on truth, even within the genre of comedy, has guided your career?*
SHORES: It's all I know how to do, really. It's certainly allowed me to have choices in TV. I have written on dramas and comedies and nobody seems to pigeon hole me into one or the other.

Q: *Several of your plays, including* Daddy's Dyin', Sordid Lives, *and* Sissies, *revolve around funerals or at least include funeral scenes. Can you say more about the recurring theme of death in your body of work?*
SHORES: It's there, isn't it? I don't know. It just seemed to be a part of the stories I wanted to tell.

Q: *Another theme that seems to recur throughout your body of work is that perhaps most clearly expressed in* Daddy's Dyin'. *Evalita insists that although she drinks and cusses and lies, she lives, while her more conventional family members are dead. This theme of living life to its fullest appears in* The Trials and Tribulations of a Trailer-Trash Housewife *as well, as the line "I am not going to shrivel up and die" sort of becomes Willi's mantra throughout the play. What is your advice to people regarding how to truly live?*
SHORES: Whatever makes a person happy. Evalita liked the worldly life and was judged for it. I think judgment is a bigger part of the themes in my plays. I guess I'd love, in a perfect world, for everybody just to let people do what makes them happy and not try and impose their own beliefs or religion or whatever.

Q: *What are the markers of good living, in your opinion? Which of your characters, if any, come to sound conclusions as to how to live well?*

SHORES: Olivia Newton-John, my dear friend, just wrote a song for the series "Sordid Lives" called "It's None of My Business What You Think of Me." I
think we would all be happier if we could live by that. I guess I love Benny in
Southern Baptist Sissies for that reason. He has found a place where he can be
himself, do what he loves, and doesn't care what the world thinks.

*Q: Yet, at the same time that the achievement of individual subjectivity is pre-
sented as crucial, the formation of community seems to play an important role
in many of your plays. In* Sordid Lives, *for instance, the community finally
comes together in the end, despite individual differences, around Peggy's coffin.
And in* Trailer-Trash Housewife, *women of diverse backgrounds join together
in a pivotal gesture of solidarity against an abusive man. Can you talk more
about the tensions between community and individuality that occur in your
body of work?*
SHORES: Well, so many things affect an individual and how the community
[and] his/her family relates, responds. Skin color, sexual orientation, actions,
religion. I think that love and acceptance for everybody is ideal, but we're
not there, are we? I'm not saying that "Benny" should just retreat from the
real world, but I'm also not saying he should not either. So, I write about the
conflict, and it's always nice if you can have that moment of community or
family coming together, even if you know that after "The End" there will
always be more struggle and conflict. I always joke that after the family sings
together at the end of *Daddy's Dyin'* that a big fight will take place when they
get home from the funeral.

Q: When Sordid Lives *was released as a film in 2001, it quickly became something of a cult classic. And, as you mentioned, "Sordid Lives: The Series" is
slated to air on MTV/LOGO in 2008. Why do you believe that this story has
remained popular throughout the past several years?*
SHORES: I think it's because of the intense comedy and those brilliant actors.
Also, I hear over and over how someone has an "Aunt Sissy" or a mother like
"Latrelle." As crazy as they are, I think people really relate to the characters.

*Q: Can you say more about why you think that it has come to mean so much
to so many people?*
SHORES: Different reasons, I suppose. I get a lot of letters from young
men—even older men—gay—who have told me the movie helped them
come out to themselves and their families. "Ty's" journey really resonates

with so many gay men. Plus, it gives people theme parties, costumes, lines to repeat, you know?

Q: *How has it been for you to see this story become so popular and affect so many people's lives?*
SHORES: Just amazing. I'm still blown away by the response. We went on tour last year with much of the film cast and to see those audiences howl and shout out the lines. We were like rock stars.

Q: *You mentioned during the question-and-answer session in Indianapolis that* Sissies *is going to be produced in film version in 2008 as well. Do you foresee a similar reception to this film as the one that* Sordid Lives *received?*
SHORES: It'll be different. *Sissies* is my most personal play, and it is the journey that I share with so many others. Honestly, I get more letters about *Sissies* and the profound effect it has on people. I want the film to do the same. The word "healing" is used a lot.

Q: *What do you feel that you were able to achieve in* Sissies *that makes the play feel more personal to you and perhaps even to audience members as well?*
SHORES: The church was a huge part of my childhood. My dad was a Southern Baptist preacher; my brother still is. So all the teachings were engrained. Being gay was something I did not want to be—because of the church. I finally decided to write about the pain, the struggle and the anger—and, ultimately, the hope.

Q: *You also said in the question-and-answer session that you wrote a part of yourself into all of the sissies. Of your major gay characters, with which do you most identify and why?*
SHORES: All the sissies are part of me, but "Mark" really is me. He's a writer. He's got "issues" and is fueled by rage. He feels he has to change the world.

Q: *Is that why Mark, and not one of the other three main characters, is presented as the central consciousness in* Sissies?
SHORES: He's the storyteller. He's telling the story because he has to fight. He has to purge. And he is on a quest to be happy and find answers.

Q: *Mark is definitely the sissy who is most able to eloquently express his anger toward and disillusionment with the Southern Baptist Church. He subverts the biblical message that homosexuality is wrong by quoting other outlandish bible verses throughout the play, and he shares his most anguished and angry poetry with the audience in a couple of scenes. Was it gratifying for you to, through the character of Mark, "talk back" to the biblical and institutional doctrine of the church that, often, systematically silences the voices of those who don't conform to it?*

SHORES: Oh, it made me so happy. I can quote the Bible to this day and debate. My mom was the high school speech and drama coach. My brother was a state debate champion. We were taught to think, to take both sides of an issue and defend them both. I love the moment in *Sissies* where Mark and T.J. are fighting after Easter service and Mark says "I know everything you know—and more!" My reason for that is that I have done research on both sides, whereas I believe fundamentalists just take the Bible, or a few scriptures, and never look at the humanity, the studies, the truth.

Q: Although Mark and the other sissies do respond to the doctrine of the Church with their own stories and opinions, the play does not portray Christians, God, or Christianity unsympathetically. In fact, I was absolutely impressed, when I first saw the play, with your ability to so powerfully challenge the anti-gay stance of the Church expressed by the preacher and the mothers throughout Sissies *and simultaneously show these characters as basically good people who want for the boys that which they think is best for them. How did you manage to treat each of the characters in the play, even those who indirectly cause so much anguish for the boys, with respect and dignity?*

SHORES: I always try to paint a picture. And thanks for pointing that out. I do believe there are very good people, with very good intentions in the church. I wanted to show these characters as good, caring people because they are the good people I grew up with.

Q: After his suicide, toward the end of Sissies, *Andrew tells Mark that he has learned the truth about God and that the real God accepts and loves him just as he is. Can you talk a bit about your spiritual beliefs? Do you envision God as a being who accepts each of us unconditionally? You mentioned during the question-and-answer session in Indianapolis that your own father was a preacher and that other close family members remain conservative Christians. How has your personal background in the church impacted your spiritual journey?*

SHORES: I'm still on a journey. I'm at peace with who I am and I'm a believer that we are all a part of a collective universe that is God, so yes, that God is one who loves me unconditionally because He is part of me. Learning to love myself, how I was created, was a huge part of my quest into a spiritual realm that I finally "got." Having been raised in the church, it was so hard to separate spirituality and religion. I was so angry at religion, yet I loved the church, many of the teachings, so the struggle was intense, painful, and not easy. Still isn't sometimes. I mean, you saw *Sissies*. I always say if you really want to understand me, fourth monologue, second act.

Q: Both Sordid Lives *and* Sissies *end with hope. In* Sordid Lives, *Ty learns that his mother has known that he was gay for years and that she loves him anyway. In* Sissies, *Mark is able to at least envision a world "of acceptance and understanding and love." You mentioned hope earlier. Do you feel hopeful about the future of the gay community? What markers of change do you see?*
SHORES: Oh, my God, yes. We're in the news. We are fighting for equal rights and starting to get them. We have out gay celebrities. We have straight people fighting for us. Politicians are supporting us, fighting about our rights. And we have churches changing their views. Let's just take Ellen [DeGeneres], for instance. She is loved, her ratings are high, her audience is primarily straight, and she is OUT!

Q: What challenges do you foresee for the future of the gay rights movement?
SHORES: I went to Spain a few years ago with my husband and was shocked at how open and accepting the people were towards "gay." They have legalized gay marriage, but that happened way after "acceptance" was just the normal way of life. The only people who stared at us when we would hold hands were Americans. For us to continue to be "out," continue to be a presence will help get us to what other countries have. The challenge is for us to stay strong, stay proud, and be known—and everything else will fall into place.

Q: I'm interested in your representation of sexual promiscuity in Sissies. *The play seems to present the club lifestyle as appealing but dangerous for young gay men searching for places to fit in and to feel loved. I'm thinking specifically of Peanut, an older gay character who admits to a lifetime of loneliness despite his many sexual encounters. Peanut goes on to disparage the club lifestyle and even to warn Andrew against it. What did you hope to convey with this portrayal of Peanut?*
SHORES: First of all, you can't just take one character, or two, and think that that is my philosophy, my view of clubs or the gay community. Those are two

very different characters, at very different walks of life. I've known them both, and, yes, there is tragedy in our gay community. But there is also happiness and celebration. In the movie version of *Sissies*, I have a scene where Andrew goes to the club for the last time, and it is one big celebration of gay! A live performance by Debby Holiday, boys dancing and having the time of their lives. I've had nights like that. I live a very happy gay life—sometimes going out in clubs, and it never feels tragic. So, there was no negative message I was sending about gay club lifestyle. Again, I was just painting a picture. The club was my canvas and I was painting Andrew and Peanut and Odette.

Q: I'm also wondering about your portrayal of drag. Drag is presented somewhat ambiguously in both Sordid Lives *and* Sissies. *Through his adoption of the persona of Tammy Wynette, Brother Boy, in* Sordid Lives, *has clearly lost touch with his own identity. But, as Brother Boy points out to his therapist, doing drag is the only thing that has gotten him through the hell of institutionalized life. And, in* Sissies, *drag seems to offer Benny a way of understanding himself as a gay man. What are your thoughts about the role that drag plays in the lives of these characters and for gay men in general?*
SHORES: Well, I do feel that it is a way that Brother Boy and Benny feel completely comfortable. Mark really gives it to Benny, telling him how he hides out behind the drag so he doesn't have to face reality in a real world. But you know, what's wrong with that? If it makes him feel safe, happy, a star, good for him. As for Brother Boy, well, it is the only thing that gives him joy in a miserable situation. And again, in a twisted way, he does feel like a star. We all love to be adored, you know?

Q: I've noticed that in several plays you examine important social issues through the interactions that take place within communities of Southern women. This occurs perhaps most obviously in Daughters, *which is comprised entirely of dialogue between women. In this play, the Daughters of the Lone Star State club members, all white, middle-to-upper-class women, wrestle with issues of race and class that affect not only their club but the entire community of Lowake. Even in* Sordid Lives, *a play so focused on a gay character, much of the action takes place within traditionally female spaces like Sissy's kitchen and living room. Why did you choose to feature female space and interactions so prominently in this play?*
SHORES: Well, for me, the women I grew up with, my mom [and] my aunts were the ones who I felt comfortable around. The men, I just couldn't connect with. So, naturally, I love writing Southern women. And, my God, they are

funny, right? I adore the women I've written so much. I believe that the first chapter of *Sordid Lives*—"Nicotine Fit"—is still perhaps my strongest work from start to finish. Those four women (when cast with the right actresses)—well, it's just magic for me.

Q: *How do communities of women offer you opportunities to explore issues related to sexuality?*
SHORES: I think Southern women certainly are more tolerant of homosexuality. You rarely hear of a Southern boy who came out to his mom who rejected him. They figure out a way to accept them.

Q: *Can you say more about the roles that women play in Southern communities?*
SHORES: They are just so strong, so important. Of course there are all kinds of women in the South, but I find that they are very opinionated many times and the backbone of many families.

Q: *Of the women in your plays, mothers in particular often play crucial roles. Mothers seem to have a unique kind of power to impact their sons' perceptions of themselves. Ty's crisis, for instance, revolves largely around his fear that his mother will not accept him once she learns that he is gay. Similarly, in* Sissies, *Andrew's suicide is prompted by the knowledge that his mother knows that he is gay. Can you talk a bit about the mother/son relationships in these plays? Why are these relationships sites of such anxiety for your gay characters?*
SHORES: I think that many of us gay boys have such a special, close relationship with our mothers. And we are petrified of losing that (if we were to come out). Like I said before, it almost always turns out just fine, but the relationships are so strong, so special, that I just think there is fear of losing that—so coming out to your Southern mama is very hard sometimes.

Q: *Although you problematize race relations in your Lowake, Texas, series plays, you feature racial issues more prominently in* Trailer-Trash Housewife. *Why did you decide to include a major black female character in this play so much about "white trash"?*
SHORES: I wanted to show how friendship can transcend the teachings of racism. Put a face on a person and gay, black, Mexican—whatever you were taught were less than you—simply goes away when you get to know someone. I love LaSonia and Willi's friendship. I love how comfortable they are with each other . . . that black/white does not exist until someone else brings it into their relationship.

Q: Since you are a Southerner, do you feel compelled to deal with racial issues in a particular way?

SHORES: I was brought up with a very open-minded liberal mother who started the first Negro Baptist Mission in Winters, Texas, when I was a kid. So I worshipped with all blacks, yet I would hear that "n" word a lot, because ignorant people say it in Texas. Still. Prejudice is alive and well today as it was when I was a kid. I wanted to expose that and to show how utterly foolish and ignorant bigots and racists look. Two of my most cherished awards are my NAACP Image Awards for Best Writing and Best Production of *Trailer-Trash Housewife*.

Q: Do you feel that the Southern legacies of slavery and segregation, which still prompt much literary exploration among Southern writers, have affected your work?

SHORES: How could it not, right? It's part of our history so it certainly comes into play. Leslie Jordan and I once wrote an unproduced screenplay with a wonderful black character who gets fed up with being ordered around by a co-worker and she says, "I need to remind you, Abraham Lincoln done freed the slaves!"

Q: Speaking of Southern literature, how do you feel that you fit into the distinct tradition of Southern writing? Who, if anybody, do you identify as your literary forbears?

SHORES: I'm about to go to a Tennessee Williams play as I answer this question. First and foremost, he is my literary hero, my biggest influence. I love Horton Foote, Pat Conroy, Eudora Welty, Fannie Flagg, Preston Jones, Rebecca Wells, Robert Benton—such great story tellers. Southerners are story tellers. We can spin a yarn. When I was a little boy, my mother used to let me tell big whoppers and instead of saying "that's a lie," she'd ask, "what else happened?" When I read articles where I am mentioned as an important voice in Southern writing, grouping me with many of my heroes, it is very humbling.

Q: How do you see your work as unique within the context of contemporary gay drama, like that of Tony Kushner, Terrence McNally, and Larry Kramer, for instance?

SHORES: [My] work is funnier. My stories come with humor as well as drama. But you just mentioned some of the greats, and I am humbled by their work.

Q: What do you envision for the future of gay theatre?
SHORES: Great plays that can be seen and appreciated by mainstream audiences. Gay theatre crossed first, I believe. I have a feeling gay theatre is going to get even more political with what Bush has done!

Q: You've had a diverse career: you've done acting, writing, directing, and producing of stage, television, and film. How have all of these experiences helped you to develop as an artist?
SHORES: I've always written, but [I] came to LA to be an actor. I always feel that everything I've done and do is an extension of acting. I started writing so I could act in scenes in class, then I starred in my first play. I then started directing because I had a vision and didn't want anybody else to screw it up—plus, I adore actors!

Q: Do you enjoy all of these roles—actor, writer, director, producer?
SHORES: Love them all!

Q: Do you have a favorite?
SHORES: I guess I'm most at home when I'm directing something I've written.

Q: Which do you want to do more of in the future?
SHORES: I would like to direct more film and continue the series "Sordid Lives" for several seasons. And of course, theatre is my passion, so I'd love to see one of my plays open in New York.

Q: What projects are you doing currently? I know that you are working on the film version of Southern Baptist Sissies *and the television series "Sordid Lives," and I assume that you have plans for publishing* Trials and Tribulations. *How is each of these projects going? Do you have other projects in the works?*
SHORES: I'm about to leave to go to Shreveport to shoot 12 episodes of "*Sordid Lives: The Series*" for LOGO. After that (sometime around April 2008), I will shoot the film version of *Sissies*. I'm holding out on the publishing of *Trailer-Trash Housewife* because I'd love to see it open in New York first before regional theatres start producing it. I also have a new play I've been circling a long time called "Transitions," so I'd love to get that finished and produced. Then there is a screenplay that I adore that I'm also focusing on that I wrote a few years ago with Leslie Jordan called *When Fleeta Goes Marching In* that I plan to direct. Lots of stuff. I like being busy.

Notes

1. I would like to thank Del Shores for so generously allowing me to review the un-published manuscript of *Trailer-Trash Housewife* in preparation for this interview.
2. *Daddy's Dyin'—Who's Got the Will?*, DVD, directed by Jack Fisk (Culver City, CA: MGM/UA Home Video, 2004). Orig. Release VHS, 1990.
3. *Sordid Lives*, DVD, directed by Del Shores (United States: 20th Century Fox Home Entertainment, 2003). Orig. Release VHS, 2000.
4. Preston Jones, *A Texas Trilogy* (New York: Hill and Wang, 1976).

Lee Smith ༈ 2008

LINDA BYRD COOK

*In mid-May 2008, after completing the necessary tasks to conclude a busy spring
semester of teaching, I made a journey that will be imprinted forever in my
mind and on my heart. I traveled to Hillsborough, North Carolina, to visit Lee
Smith at her home, and together we drove to her cabin nestled in the Appalachian Mountains. Sitting out on the front porch, in this breathtaking setting that
transported me to Lee's fictional world, we talked extensively about her writing
and her spiritual vision.*

*QUESTION: You've often commented on your attraction to the more intense
forms of religion, the letting go that characterizes the more ecstatic religious or
spiritual experiences. And you've compared the passion of religious conversion
to the passion of sex, to the passion of writing. Would you say that you still have
these same feelings, or have they changed?*
SMITH: Well, I think that as you get older, they do change. The younger you
are, the more intense your feelings are. That's why, for instance, the lyric poem
is the perfect artistic expression of the young writer, or the short, tense story.
As you get older, you start writing novels. Then they start getting longer, because you're more interested in the long view, the long haul, in how things
play out overtime, and that brief ecstatic moment sometimes almost comes to
seem the province of youth. I think that's really true. It's not to say that there
are not consolations, you know, of age and of the long view, and I still have
these intense moments, these intense flashes and so on. Really, it seems to me
more and more the writers whose work I really love speak of having this too.
Writing is a way to just get completely out of your head.

I remember Annie Dillard telling me that she feels more alive when she's
writing than at any other time. Once when she and I were talking about

Originally published as Linda Byrd Cook, "A Spiritual Journey: An Interview with Lee
Smith," Vol. 47, no. 1 (2009), 74–103.

prayer, I asked, "What would you say prayer is exactly?" She said, "It's like writing." Another time she called me and said, "Well, I think prayer is just when
you think real hard." I asked her, "Is that all there is to it because I wonder if
I'm doing it right." She said, "No, that's all there is; just think *real* hard." It's like
a concentration of daily life, of average thought or feeling, like a distillation.
Just like I think poetry is a distillation of prose thought. And with sex, it's the
same thing, of course. It's wonderful, but when you're married for forty years
or something, a certain kind of affection, and just knowing somebody this
well over this length of time comes to seem very important too. When you're
twenty-two, whoever even thought of that? [laughter] It's not that the intensity goes away; it's just that it becomes more a part of one's whole life, whether
it is with religion or whether it is with something else.

Writing *Saving Grace* was a very intense experience for me when I was
attending those churches and doing the actual writing. Anyway, as I've gotten older, in terms of actual religion, I think that my religious feelings have
occurred more outside the church. This is interesting because many people I
know are moving more toward the regularity of church and the support of a
church family. Although I love this church here—the Episcopal church—and I
love the minister, I think I have been feeling, in general, more "religious," more
intense, perhaps, out in nature, or reading—reading poetry, reading Thoreau,
reading the kinds of things that put you in nature.

*Q: I think what you're saying reflects what the contributors and editors of the
book that you recommended to me,* All Out of Faith: Southern Women on
Spirituality, *communicate.*[1] *They point out what they perceive as the dramatic
difference between religion and spirituality.*
SMITH: It's just more spirituality that I am feeling now and less attachment
to any particular church or ritual. And in fact, for the last several years, Hal
and I have been really very active participants in the Unitarian church when
we're in Maine because we just happen to really like it. All our neighbors go
there and it's really close; it's a deeply spiritual, very philosophical approach.
Every time I go, I find something that I think deeply about, something I
haven't heard necessarily before. Finally, there's a comfort from the Bible, but
there's also a familiarity. It's hard to hear those Psalms and hear them new, in
a certain way. So, I have loved the Unitarian service, as well as that of the Episcopal Church. But what touches me most is just the getting out into nature
and thinking about things this way.

Q: You once said that you felt if you loosen up, let go too much (and this goes way back), that there's always that fear of becoming too religious or too spiritual—even going nuts.

SMITH: Yeah!

Q: Whenever I teach your novels and students make remarks about a character like, "Oh, she's crazy," or "he's crazy," I say, "wait a minute." Then we talk about definitions and what "crazy" actually means and we discover that your characters have often been damaged. Oftentimes, these characters seem very spiritual (or rather, I see them as being very spiritual), and I think with the progression of your novels, the damaged characters become more spiritual. Juney, of course, is an example. I'm sure it's the damage that was done to him that has created in him this great gift. I mean, he's divine in that way. Do you see your damaged characters as being spiritual? I'm just curious about how the two go together. Have the characters "let go" to the extent that they've suffered? Can you comment on this?

SMITH: Well, I can. I just saw again the one-woman show of *Fair and Tender Ladies* this weekend, and in that book, there are two characters I want to mention.[2] One is Garney, who's the revivalist and the minister, who has so much religiosity, as well as greed, and lots of other problems. Then there's Ivy herself, and Oakley, who is really spiritual and loves his church, and works with wood and so on, and finally manages forgiveness. And there's Ivy herself, who seems to me to be a deeply spiritual person, but so many of her most spiritual moments arise from the domestic impulse, like when she's made biscuits that time, or when she's looking at the clothes flapping on the line and it's like she sees her whole family dancing in the wind. Or the time with Honey Breeding, which is definitely a sort of union with the ineffable, with the sexual, but it also has to do with the top of the mountain and nature and the cave and the natural world. There's a real spiritual element to it. So I don't see Ivy as damaged, and I don't see Oakley as damaged. I would see Garney as not mentally ill or damaged, but as the worst of that kind of religious impulse.

Q: I wouldn't even call Garney spiritual. I think I'd call him a religious fanatic.

SMITH: I wouldn't call him spiritual at all. Yeah, he's just a fanatic.

Q: I know Faulkner has been a tremendous influence on you, and Garney reminds me of all the religious fanatics in, for instance, Light in August.[3] *Every*

one of the religious characters is a fanatic. I think Oakley Fox is probably, for
me, the only example of a good Christian in the novel.
SMITH: He's a good man.

Q: *It's just so often that the self-proclaimed or acknowledged Christians are*
hypocrites.
SMITH: Or they're very narrow. Or they're out for their own good, like Sam
Russell Sage.

Q: *Or Virgil Shepherd.*
SMITH: Now, Virgil Shepherd was a very interesting character for me. When
I started writing that book, *Saving Grace*, I really wanted to make a real villain because somebody had said to me, "you're just terrible at creating villains since you like all your characters too much." And that rang true for me.
[laughter] So I thought, I'm going to make a real villain, and he's going to be
awful, but the more I got into it, he didn't seem . . . I mean, by his own bizarre
lights, I don't think he meant to be bad.

Q: *I think that's part of it, Lee—the no villains thing. This is something that*
comes up with my students when we look at any one character; for example,
with Jacky (On Agate Hill), as a reader, you want to say, "Damn, Jacky, you've
got this wonderful wife you're madly in love with, you've got the intensity, the
passion. Why do you have to do this?"
SMITH: Yeah, settle down!

Q: *That's who he is! And Molly knows that, she understands it, she never ques-*
tions it; the whole thing is just beyond judgment. Your characters are beyond
judgment. You don't judge them.
SMITH: No, I don't judge them.

Q: *So, it's very difficult, although readers will. But my students won't after I teach*
them. [laughter] They will say, "It's okay. All these characters are flawed human
beings."
SMITH: But readers get so mad at me. I had an entire book group not long
ago somewhere right outside Winston-Salem that called me up and I could
hear them all buzzing in the background. They said, "we just want you to
know we were reading your book, *Fair and Tender Ladies*, until we got to the
part where Ivy ran off and committed adultery and we put it down and we

have not finished it." [laughter] I mean, there's a lot of judgment and particularly in certain areas where people haven't been exposed to as many different kinds of people or kinds of religion or thought.

Q: This makes me want to go back to Joline B. Newhouse of your story, "Between the Lines." She says basically, "Such is life. All of that is life." We can leave areas out, but they are still part of it.
SMITH: They are!

Let me say something about Juney in *On Agate Hill*. To me, that book is sort of inextricably linked with Josh and Josh's death.⁴ And Josh, in the latter part of his schizophrenia, really did become a deeply feeling, empathetic, and understanding person. I mean, whole areas of his brain had been blown out in these various psychotic breaks. He had lost many IQ points and so on. But all the time he'd spent in the hospital in the groups and the different kinds of things he experienced left him with a real feeling for people. He was so empathetic and he had an absolutely unerring instinct about people. You know, because of his illness, he hadn't been able to go to college or anything, but he was the kind of person who could really understand other people. He would meet somebody, and I would say, "Well, how'd you like so-and-so?" And whatever he would say would be absolutely just so perceptive. It was really interesting, and he was so big by the end, he was like the bodhisattva; he was a man like a mountain, a mountain that you could rest against.

I remember too somebody who was also schizophrenic, less damaged than Josh, an older musician who could take gigs and travel and have more of a regular life. He said to me one time, "You know, my illness has left me with certain gifts." I use this line in *On Agate Hill*, and I think in a way these are not gifts you want necessarily, because the illness is terrible, terrible, but Josh had certain gifts and he certainly did have that kind of spirituality. I had no idea that Juney would show up in that book; he just appeared like a blessing for me and he somehow seemed to embody all those really dear and deep and moving qualities that Josh had. And you know, when Josh died, over four hundred people came to his funeral, people that he had touched. In my study I have a laundry basket of letters that people wrote to me, you know, just people all over town, a lot of people I didn't know at all, people that Josh had known from the hospital the different times, people who came to the restaurant, people that knew him. You know, he also hung out at several different coffee shops and he talked to everybody. It was really remarkable.

Q: *So, for all those people, he already would exist in their hearts forever because of how he had affected their lives.*

SMITH: And a lot of them hadn't known him earlier. I mean, there are a lot of people still in town who did know him when he was a boy, but a lot of the people who came to the funeral and wrote letters had only known him in the last ten years of his life when he'd been able to be out of the hospital. He was a real character around town, you know, talking to all kinds of people and touching all kinds of lives. So I guess you could see Juney as a damaged character, but you could also see him as a person with certain gifts. So it's both. I saw Silvaney as more damaged.

Q: *Like Tennessee, same kind of thing.*

SMITH: Something had been done *to* them.

Q: *By someone, or society, or a representative of society. Even though Josh was enduring in the minds and hearts of all those people, because writing for you is a spiritual experience, creating Juney was your own personal way of grieving through the writing of that book, but also preserving Josh's presence because your writing, your novels, are forever. They are always alive and open.*

SMITH: Yes, that's true of writing. That's why it's so helpful—for all of us. It really is. So although he was definitely different, I didn't think of Juney as being so damaged as just being outside our order.

Q: *I guess I see the damage as his having been left by his mother just to be raised by the wolves or whatever, in that sense.*

SMITH: Oh yeah. That's true.

Q: *But when you look at it in some ways, we all are damaged. We've all been damaged in some way.*

In All Out of Faith, *some of the writers' comments about their spirituality really stand out for me. Some of them echo what I see in your writing. I know that your interview with Susan Ketchin was done back in 1994, but other essays in the collection were written much more recently. I'd like to get your response to some of the comments in the book. For example, in her essay, Dorothy Allison says, "Art should provoke more questions than answers and make us think about our lives and our journeys." That struck me.*

SMITH: That strikes me too, and I believe that is absolutely true. I think that real art always provokes more questions than answers because the more generic kinds of fiction, for instance, provide pat answers to things, you know, the great questions are wrapped in a little bow at the end. I think that's the difference between generic fictions and literature. It's that whole worlds are opened, questions are asked, and they're not necessarily answered.

Q: *That makes me think of* The Last Girls, *which was marketed as a woman's book, and some readers got kind of upset because everything wasn't neatly tied together with a bow, like you said. I couldn't help but chuckle because I thought, that's the whole point—that it's not, that there are unanswered questions and that this brings up all these questions for us to think about. Everybody doesn't live happily ever after.*

SMITH: It's the journey and it's different in each case. It's not just quest and conquer and nab it and wrap it up, you know, complete the quest and it's all spelled out. It's *not* all spelled out, and I think actually women are kind of better than men often at . . . [laughter].

Q: *Right, because men are more linear in their thought—that there's a goal.*

SMITH: Yes, men are more linear and there's a goal, and I think women really are more open to the journey itself, to serendipity, and to the gifts that surprise turns in the road can bring.

Q: *I'd like to talk to you about another powerful statement that Allison makes. She says, "In art, transgression is holy, revelation a sacrament, and pursuing one's personal truth the only sure validation."*

SMITH: Oh, yeah.

Q: *You've said that you're interested in crossing the line/the boundary and in where the lines are, what it means to be good or bad, what's expected, and whether to be contained or to escape, all of these things. And Allison says that to transgress is a holy experience, and in so many of your characters' "transgressions," they have their most spiritual encounters.*

SMITH: Well, it certainly can be. Yeah, I think that is very, very interesting.

Q: *You've mentioned to me Sue Monk Kidd specifically. And I've read a good deal of her work too.[5] She talks about giving birth to her new female self and she says that a huge part of that birthing process was writing in her pink journal. When you finally sit down and put into some kind of form all your notes and journaling, do you feel that, through your writing, your creation, your art, you're giving birth to a part of yourself?*

SMITH: Often, yes, I feel like I'm expressing or giving birth to, a certain self that doesn't have any life in my own real life. I think a lot of times it's like Anne Tyler's wonderful quote when she said, "I write because I want to have more than one life." Much of the time when we write we're giving birth to another possibility. This is the person I've never been and will never be, but now I'm going to get to experience his feelings and thoughts for awhile or walk in her shoes for a little while. And I certainly do enjoy that.

Q: *Several other women writers have remarked on the parallel between the literal giving birth to a child and the creation of a literary work. I think of Sylvia Plath and Alice Walker, even Anne Bradstreet, in her poem, "The Author to Her Book" (c.1666). The pain of creating, whether it's giving birth to a baby or a book . . .*
SMITH: Right, and then the emptiness, the post-partum depression, like, my God, what do I think about now? You know, you're pregnant with a book for six years or something. You've lived with this character, these characters, this set of problems and ideas and givens for so long that it leaves you empty, and like a child, it takes on a life of its own. And like a child, you don't know quite what you've created. [laughter]

Q: *Right, and you can't go around telling people how to treat your child or what to think about it.*
SMITH: No, you can't. You have to let it go, and you can't tell people how to read it or what this means or whatever. You can't say, "this is a very nice child"—you cannot do that! I think there are many parallels. I do think probably for women it's different than writing for men. I mean, men don't have this parallel. They don't have this sense. It's a more abstract enterprise. When they create a novel, they haven't given birth. It's a different kind of metaphor and a different sort of process. It is a more abstract, intellectual process; it really is.

Q: *I keep going back to your comments about your very first short story that you wrote as a child, about Adlai Stephenson and Jane Russell. You've commented that the same things that were there in that first story have repeated themselves in your fiction. Sue Monk Kidd refers to consistent themes in women's writing. She quotes Clarissa Pincola Estés's book,* Women Who Run with the Wolves.[6]
SMITH: Yes, oh yes. I like that book. I read it a long time ago.

Q: *In that book, what Estés says connects strongly with your writing. "When a woman is cut away from her basic source, she is sanitized."*
SMITH: That is good!

Q: You've often talked about your work in this light. For instance, about The Last Girls, *you said you realized it couldn't be true to life because it would be too sanitized. And you also said that you wanted to get to the "source" of these women.*

SMITH: Yeah, particularly after interviewing five or six of them and hearing their real life stories about tragedy and illness and death and divorce and mental problems and money problems and just all kinds of things. They wouldn't really want those put in a book, so I would have had to write about it in a much more distant sort of tepid way. But as fiction, if I made up my characters and put them through some of the same kinds of things we were all really going through, I could explore their emotions and not embarrass the real women.

Q: And it got to the heart of the matter. It got to the essence of who they are, just not in that way.

SMITH: Yeah. It's always been a lot easier for me to tell the truth in fiction because there are too many people you can hurt if you tell the truth in nonfiction. And they're all still right there.

Q: So oftentimes, we don't tell the truth in real life because of that.

SMITH: I know. We usually don't and sometimes we don't tell it because we can't stand to know it ourselves.

I want to get back to the issue you mentioned concerning your students' looking at writers and asking why all these women have such severe problems.

Q: Yes, they say, "can we read somebody that's normal?" [laughter]

SMITH: Well, I think it's true, having taught writing for so long too. I think the need to express oneself, the need to create some sort of order with words and expression, often does come out of great unresolved conflict, traumas and dramas of one's life, and it's old hat to say that every writer has an unhappy childhood. Yet there is something in the circumstances of one's life, whether she starts writing as a child or later where she feels a little bit "outside," she feels a bit the outsider in her own family or in the world in which she finds herself. She has something to say about it. If she felt that she were entirely of it, part and parcel, she wouldn't have become a writer. I'm actually writing a little essay about this now for an Appalachian Writers' Workshop that I'm going to this summer that Silas House, my student, is directing. But, I think that by the very act of writing, we make ourselves outsiders too, by objectifying elements of our life, putting them down on paper. Suddenly we're outside of our hometown or our family—we're outside of it by writing about it, and this produces feelings of guilt and estrangement. It's very complicated, but it's not that I think that writers are crazy so much as that they are sensitive and they always feel a little bit at odds with something in their life, something that they want to comment on. You know, a lot of times they want equality. Many black writers, for instance, really wanted to comment on things that had been deeply disturbing about their youth and the lack of equality, the prejudice they had faced. Appalachian writers, too, you know, have felt stigmatized. Women writers have often felt that they were thrown into roles that were so rigid and they could not express their true selves, and I mean, there are all kinds of us, and it's not that we're crazy. When we mention Dorothy Allison . . . , homosexual writers have certainly felt that it was so hard for them to be authentic. I think in a certain way, you could almost characterize all of it as a search for authenticity, for the real self, the true self, and where we can find it, whether we're writing nonfiction or fiction. That's kind of what it is, but writers are sensitive people that feel the need to do this, so they are not crazy, but artistic, sensitive, more tuned in, more fragile in a way, more open to possibility.

Q: *Lee, I know you had a happy childhood.*
SMITH: Yes, I had a very happy childhood, but I also had both parents who were institutionalized, you know, in mental hospitals. But they were so kind. They were so kind to each other, they were so kind to me, but yet there were months at a time, many times, when both of them had to be in the hospital, and then there was that one year when they were in the hospital at the same time for nine months.

Q: *What was your age at the time?*
SMITH: Thirteen. And I think that's one reason, in a certain way, that I keep writing about thirteen year-olds. People have asked me why I do that, which is real interesting to me because I wasn't realizing I'd done it so much. Like this most recent book, Molly's thirteen when she keeps her diary. Everybody's thirteen!

Q: *And Karen, in "Tongues of Fire," is thirteen.*
SMITH: Yeah. And there's been a nervous breakdown, too. And I don't know, maybe it's just the age where you're enormously open to everything. It's a pivotal age. You're as smart as you'll ever be, and you haven't really become

either boy or girl necessarily. It's before you have to be a girly girl. You can be a tomboy.

Q: Your life hasn't been determined.
SMITH: No, no, and it hasn't been taken over by society and any sort of expectations. But the year I was thirteen, I was living with my Aunt Millie up in Maryland because both my daddy and my mother were in the hospital at the same time. Then I went back to Grundy and lived with my Aunt Lois and Uncle Bob and some of my cousins. I think I was in kind of a crisis, although I didn't really perceive it as a crisis then. But things were very intense. And thirteen is a very intense age anyway.

Q: You mentioned that for every individual writer, there's something that is driving him, and for some, like you said, it's some kind of extremely painful experience.
SMITH: Yes, that they have to just deal with through their writing.

Q: Yours though, seems to be more of a sustained, gradual process because I think it has been the spiritual part. You have said that your writing is a spiritual search. So, maybe not even a conscious effort on your part, but through your writing and through your characters, you're searching, finding that these organized kinds of religions, and as you said, the ritual at one point, deadened the passion and killed any kind of spirituality that you had at that time. Your writing itself has become a religion.
SMITH: It really has. It's become a search. And it's through writing that I feel I have come to articulate my own questions and feelings and so on. The writer Peter Taylor once said, "I never know what I think until I read what I've written." [laughter] I think the very act of writing causes us to focus upon what we are feeling and to put our own experiences and thoughts and feelings into a certain context, and when you go back, you can see exactly what is going on. When I needed a divorce real bad but was not articulating that, even to myself, I was writing *Black Mountain Breakdown*, where Crystal becomes literally paralyzed. She's literally lying in bed being fed red Jell-O by the neighbors. Now anybody ought to say, wait a minute. [laughter] What's going on here? And when I go back and read that novel, it's very clear to me that things had come to a certain point and that's sort of how I felt psychologically, you know, within that marriage.

Q: Crystal is a perfect example. Talking about things that contain and restrict, a couple of times she has experiences where . . .
SMITH: Where she expresses herself.

Q: She's not strong enough yet to break through.
SMITH: She doesn't have an adequate sense of self, so she just models herself into whatever these people, first her mom and then these various partners, want her to be. Thus, the tragedy. . . .

Q: So many of us do that.
SMITH: Yes, we do, especially us good girls.

Q: Right, and it all goes back to that comment in Women that Run with Wolves *about cutting away. Lots of things—circumstances and people—contribute to cutting women away from our basic source, which I think is the case with Crystal although there was not much of a source to begin with. But she is so much cut away . . .*
SMITH: Absolutely.

Q: In your writing, it seems that all your protagonists are trying to escape somehow, even in your earliest story, as I mentioned, with Adlai Stephenson and Jane Russell—religion and flight, the sense of being confined. At this point in your writing and in your personal life even, are you still aware of that tendency toward escape in your writing?
SMITH: *Yes, absolutely!* And it's not so much at this age. It's not so much wanting to escape my own life, but it's just wanting to experience more than we can experience if we remain really within the confines of our own lives. Why not explore a different time, a different part of history, a different kind of person that we will never be? So there is escape in that sense. It's not being unhappy, but it's the desire to have more. I think that finally the religious impulse is also the desire to have more, the desire to feel as much as you possibly can and understand as much as you possibly can and you know, break free of finally this body and this life into whatever is there, if you can. I mean, that's part of that same desire.

Q: But with your characters, often that breaking through comes in a very physical, bodily way, which is what sets it apart from other writing that may do the same thing. It's because it's through the physical; the flesh is part of it.

SMITH: That's right! Yes, for me, it's through the body. The body is the only way. And in my writing, I have to know all the time what my characters are smelling and what they're seeing and what they're feeling and what they're touching. I have to know the scene. I have to know what they're hearing. I just have to physically experience their world, and they therefore have to experience their world very intensely, you know, in their bodies, very intensely, because in my own work, in my own self, I think it's only through the body that you can get there.

Q: *And do you think that the block, for so many of us females having grown up in the South and really other parts of the country too, is that training that we receive early on about the body being bad, you know, the flesh is bad, you need to escape that. Nothing of the flesh is of God, etc.*
SMITH: Absolutely.

Q: *That's why we have so much trouble in reclaiming our bodies, as Ivy does. You know, she reclaims her body and her experience.*
SMITH: But it's not only reclaiming. I walk three miles a day, and I know so many other women who are really active. And they go canoeing for miles and they do all these things, and I just think we have a sense that we can reclaim our bodies also. We can do all kinds of things. It's funny, I wrote Honey Breeding, and now the only people I know who are actual bee-keepers are women. [laughter]

Q: *Well, he's kind of androgynous. Many of the male characters that are a part of these spiritual experiences seem to be somewhat feminized.*
SMITH: They seem like the other half. There's a lot of twinning going on. They are like the other half, and when I wrote them, I didn't know that, but being a professor too, I can step back, you know, and see that. So many of us do not get to express those parts, you know, the decision-making, adventuresome parts of ourselves. I was lucky. I got to. You know, I went to those girls' schools where they encourage you, and this was very good for me. They didn't make me so much of a lady but encouraged me to go down the river on a raft, or try things, whatever I wanted to try.

Q: *Unlike you personally, those experiences for so many of your characters, like Grace with Lamar, for instance, the swimming, and Ivy's desire to ride the logs like the boys are doing. It's that males get to do these things and we don't. And that kind of limitation parallels the traditional orthodox religion that was being forced on them that women cannot do these things.*

SMITH: Absolutely. It's funny to be at this advanced age of my life, still feeling the results of this and struggling with it. I don't know if I told you that there was this huge move to ban all my books in southwest Virginia this year.

Q: No, you didn't tell me.

SMITH: Oh, I've got a whole file on it. It's very interesting.

Q: What was the reason for this?

SMITH: The reason was that they promote adultery. This is right up your alley, Linda! And it was a former minister, a fundamentalist, right-wing minister who had been elected to the School Board up around Abingdon. He got in and then he said the reason he had run was because his daughter had shown him a list of choices of books to read for her AP English class, and *Fair and Tender Ladies* was on the list, and he said the book promotes adultery. Then he either got somebody to make a list or he made it himself, of every single word and line in the book that he felt promoted adultery and was unfit for children to read. He wrote them all out and published the whole thing in the newspaper, out of context, and this huge controversy erupted.

Q: Oh my word! No, I knew nothing about this.

SMITH: Oh, there was this huge exchange of letters in the paper. Then a group of people took up for me, and it went on and on and meanwhile, I had scheduled, right then, a tour of southwest Virginia and three community colleges, UVA extension colleges. I went right into a firestorm! You know, I'd go to this little college and there'd be all this media.

Q: Did you know ahead of time that you would be facing this?

SMITH: No. Well, I knew sort of about it, but I didn't know what a big deal it was until I got there, and you know, I was on TV. I was on the front page of the paper. The books were selling like crazy. [laughter]

Q: That's what I was thinking. That's as good as being an Oprah choice. Probably better.

SMITH: Well, they voted it down. But it was a huge to-do, and really, it's the kind of thing . . . I told someone if my mother hadn't been dead . . . (you know, my mother was so conventional herself), she would have died. She would have been so embarrassed to see my picture on the front page of the paper for this reason. [laughter] I mean, the huge front page! This just happened a few months ago, so these things are still going on, I guess, because of the sexual openness in my books. But as Hal said, these people have never read another book, obviously, because my books are just the safest books in the world compared to what's being published, compared to what's on the Internet, compared to what is on television. It's crazy.

Q: *That's what I'm thinking.*
SMITH: I guess because it's on the school list.

Q: *I thought maybe you were going to say that the complaint was not only about the sexuality, but also about the treatment of traditional religion.*
SMITH: Well, I think probably that too.

Q: *Of course, because my whole reading of your work is going outside, the search for, you know, spirituality.*
SMITH: Well, it certainly was a minister that got undone by it. So . . . [laughter] It was so interesting. It got to the point where they were planting people in the audience at these schools. I mean, the whole freshman class at UVA-Wise [University of Virginia, Wise Campus], had been required to read *Oral History*. There was a whole gymnasium full of freshmen that had read *Oral History*, and so I got up and talked about why I wrote the book. Then this man who was obviously not a student stood up and they handed him the microphone for questions and answers. He said, "I have noticed that all your women have no sexual morals. Is that based on you and your own real life? Would you like to comment on that?" Everybody just went (inhalation) . . .

Q: *What did you say?*
SMITH: I said, "No, of course it's not." And I went on and said, "If you are referring to Dory she was really meant to represent the mountains themselves and the outside interests who came in and took advantage of them, so there's a real reason there." And I went on, blah, blah, blah. But I was so nervous! And then when I was signing books, there was this big-haired woman who was in the line and she got up to the front with *Oral History* open to where Parrot Blankenship is telling a dirty joke.

Q: Oh, yes, I remember that one. The cave and . . . [laughter].
SMITH: And she thrust the open book at me and said, "I bet you wouldn't dare to sign here, you hussy." She did! [laughter] And by then I had people from the President's Office with me wherever I was going and the President of the College himself coming in to introduce me and stuff like that. It was so bizarre. But all of this was really recent; it just happened. It was right after Thanksgiving. I was four days up there. And I was getting over the flu or something, so I didn't feel well to begin with.

Q: Oh yeah. This sounds like something from the 1950s.
SMITH: It was weird. I felt so weird. And people who had invited me were so embarrassed, but it was big, you know. It was serious, and you feel weird leaving one of those little schools and then just driving to your motel or something. I was really glad that I had taken my secretary Mona with me.

Q: I guess it was like being right in the middle of one of your own stories.
SMITH: I was thinking about that, and this is a big claim of country music. It's like all our little hometowns of the heart and everybody's singing about 'em but you ain't livin' there! [laughter] Because you know, you couldn't live there anymore, so this is really authentic. You don't ever think that, though. You do romanticize it, and you think of how you love to go back and so on, but there *is* that underside, which is what you're writing about too. In that sense, my writing does and always has transgressed absolutely, because I have expressed untraditional kinds of spiritual searches and you know, an open sort of sexuality and an openness to different kinds of adventures that life holds for women, not necessarily falling into women's traditional roles. You know, I'm not writing a moral lesson.

Q: It's the incongruity of some of the characters that appear to have a traditional kind of life and yet they have experiences that are non-traditional, and these kinds of experiences where they really grow and they become better at "life" (whether they're by themselves, or whether they have a family or whatever). I think if readers sensed some sort of punishment for these characters for not going to church, or for not praying, for not being faithful to one's spouse or whatever, it would all be fine and good. But it's the idea that these kinds of experiences can broaden a person, that going outside in some way is almost necessary because otherwise, we're stagnant in this little container.
SMITH: Yeah. I know. I think so too.

Q: And I think that your characters have to discover that they are divine within themselves and that nature holds divinity; they don't have to depend on something outside themselves. Barbara Kingsolver talks so much about nature and Appalachia.⁷ In particular, I remember her comments about the divinity in nature, particularly in mountains. I think you said at one point that the mountains and God were one to you and I think it's important that that's where your characters discover themselves.

SMITH: This reminds me of a little exchange I had one time with a real good friend of mine, Roy Blount, an old friend. He was introducing me to somebody, and he had just finished reading I forget what book, and he said, "This is Lee Smith and I just finished reading her book such and such, and she'll do anything." And I said, "Roy, I will not. My *characters* will [laughter], but precisely because I won't." [laughter] You know, I like to entertain many possibilities in my fiction that I would probably be very chicken to follow through with in my life.

Q: In On Agate Hill, *I noticed one of the first mentions of homosexuality in your novels. Correct me if I'm wrong, but I don't think that there's any other novel that you've written . . . It's great—Tuscany's father that has the sex change and becomes Ava, and his lover . . .*

SMITH: I've had some homosexuality in my stories, though. But I guess that is the first novel.

Q: And I was so pleased because I thought again, that's my whole argument that it's all okay, that all these things are okay. Again, there's no judgment.

SMITH: Yeah! Exactly!

Q: In fact, Tuscany re-establishes contact and a relationship with her father, and I think her last statement is something about "she," talking about her father.

SMITH: Right! Yeah.

Q: I wondered if you ever resisted this before, if you ever had a story going in your head that homosexuality could have been a part of and you edited it out.

SMITH: I don't really think so, I guess because of my sense of my own sexuality and so on. I haven't ever had any lesbian experience and therefore I have felt unqualified to really write about it in depth and the way I like to do my characters. Several times in short stories, I have had lesbian characters and gay characters, but in terms of major characters for these long novels, I just haven't felt like I knew enough exactly.

Q: *Of course, with Miss Torrington* (Fair and Tender Ladies), *that's never developed, but that's a good example.*
SMITH: Yes, she is definitely a lesbian character.

Q: *You know, her comment to Ivy that there are kinds and kinds of love, and Ivy, of course, doesn't understand that until she's much older.*
SMITH: And then Ivy *does* understand that there are kinds and kinds of love. But *I* believe that there are kinds and kinds of love.

Q: *And I think an example is when Molly goes back to live with and take care of Simon.*
SMITH: Exactly!

Q: *He had been in love with her, but she's always been like a daughter and also an extension of her mother. But when she goes back and she's talking about sleeping beside him, it's so clear that it's not sexual at all. There's a kind of love there.*
SMITH: Yes, there's something there. There's a kind of love. There are all kinds of love that we don't even have a name for. And I think the older you get, the more you understand that.

Several weeks ago, I went up to Richmond to do a talk, and I got with several of my oldest friends from St. Catherine's. We were all boarding students, and we sort of had a pajama party. [laughter]

Q: *These were high school friends, right?*
SMITH: Right! And one of them, Sally Richardson, is still a real good friend of mine. We even went to camp together. We go way back. We stayed at her house and several other women came. You know, here we all are at this age, but we got to talking about that, about various women that we had known at St Catherine's as teachers. We had many quote "old maid" teachers. You know, we just decided that. But it was so radical at that time to be actually physically lesbian. I think probably most of them were not; they were just something that didn't have a name.

Q: They couldn't have acted on it.
SMITH: Right, they couldn't have acted on it. They were totally devoted to us girls, did not abuse girls or anything like that, but they were just, maybe what my mother used to say, "asexual." They were just different; there was something that wasn't a name there, and they were the loveliest women, people that devoted themselves to the school and to us and so on.

Q: And I think we just don't understand something like that that doesn't fit into a certain "role."
SMITH: And many of them were lifelong friends but didn't live together. It's very interesting—more things than we understand are out there.

Q: You said you think that writers have felt at odds with something in their lives. That was one of your comments that struck me. You said there seems to be with most writers something that they have felt at odds with, so the writing comes from that. Would I be correct in assuming that for you, the something that you have always felt at odds with since you were a child is traditional patriarchal religion?
SMITH: Yes! You would be absolutely correct! I also felt at odds with "place." I know I'm deeply rooted to place. I was, as Mike Mullins told me one time, being "raised to leave" because my parents were so much interested in sending me off to college and really not even wanting me to live in Grundy. Mama was from the Eastern Shore. She had ideas of gentility and so on. So there was conflict because I loved Grundy so much, but I think I was also somehow very conscious of everything, somehow aware that I might not always have that—my place. I do think every person who's going to become an artist of any kind does feel a little bit the outsider, the outsider in your own family, the only one in that church that didn't feel a certain way, the person who knows she may not live here all her life. And that makes it possible for you to become a writer because if you're in the middle of the story and totally immersed in the story, you don't see the story. It requires a slight distance and you often have a certain conflict, and that's what makes for a story; that's what makes for a writer. If there's no conflict, there's no story. I mean, I had a real happy childhood, but still there were conflicts and I did feel a little outside, not quite like everybody else. My parents were so old, for one thing, and they'd had me so late in life, and I was an only child.

Q: *Would you say that your spiritual search (because clearly that's what your writing has been, conscious or unconscious) has led you to a sense of the sacred, the divine, outside of organized religion?*
SMITH: Absolutely, and I think I have more and more decided that the sacred is to be found in the everyday, not only in transcendent moments, you know, moments in nature when you're at a peak, but also in the cup of coffee and sunlight coming in a window on a page that you're reading.

Q: *And just sitting here in this beautiful place and hearing the birds?*
SMITH: Yeah, and just being smack in the middle of your life.

Q: *Would you say that for a woman who is struggling, such as some of your characters are, and you yourself did, as so many of us in the South do, to be in touch with herself and searching for something that speaks to her, something that accepts her, validates her, would you say that she could very well be drawn to a sense of the feminine divine? When I say feminine divine, I'm suggesting the sacredness that's there not only in the female body, but in the female experience?*
SMITH: Absolutely! That's what I was just saying. I have often found a real sense of the divine in moments that seem sacred to me and mean so much within domestic life, within the feminine experience, with roles—with smelling bread cooking or fixing flowers, or whatever, digging, you know. These are the moments that seem sacred to me, and increasingly as I get older, I think I have moved away from the real organized patriarchal kinds of religions toward a more organic spirituality.

Q: *And the mountains are a huge part of that?*
SMITH: Yes. Absolutely. There's a more feminine sense of that, and the role, the most important role really for me, where I felt more in touch with myself and with whatever else is out there, was being a mother. It's *still* being a mother. Also, there are moments, you know, in romantic relationships too, where you do feel such communion and such a sense of things outside yourself, but there's nothing quite like being a mother. [laughter] So it is a very feminine sense of things.

Q: *Because those things are the most sacred for us, as women, and because we're so early conditioned and taught that sacred, divine experiences do not come from those feminine experiences at all. Divine experience occurs inside some*

walls and there's a white male God somewhere who is watching and judging
everything we do.
SMITH: And who's judgmental. The distant father.

Q: *Right. Because of this, it takes us longer.*
SMITH: Yeah, it took me a long time to not feel guilty because I couldn't really be the "church lady" like my mother and all the women I knew growing
up. I wasn't going to do that; I clearly wasn't, and I never really did. I went to
MWF [Methodist Women's Fellowship] because I loved the emotional things,
you know, MWF camp where you'd all be out under the stars, singing a hymn
and all, but not the church lady.

Q: *It provided the occasion for you to make that trip to the outdoors and to*
the campfire and have experiences that weren't available inside the walls, both
metaphorically and literally, I guess.
SMITH: Oh, yeah.

Q: *Since sexuality as being in touch with the body is an integral part of your*
characters, they are extremely sensual. So many of them feel the roughness of
a surface, or the texture of a fabric, or the warmth of the concrete and are so
aware. Their senses are just so awakened.
SMITH: Yeah. The senses are really important to me, and there is a whole
lot of sensory imagery in my writing, most of it even not sexual, but sensory.
In a certain way, I feel that I should have been a poet because it does seem
to me that the way to the mind and the heart is only through the body. It's
only through the senses, and I know when I'm teaching, one thing I really
try to stress to my students is that our whole aim as fiction writers is to have
our readers *be there* in the world of the story and the only way they can get
there is if we give them sensory images. You know, they have to be able to see
something. They have to be able to touch something. They have to be able to
smell something. Those kinds of things, you know, *are* through the body. The
way to the mind and the way to the heart is through the body. The way to the
soul is through the body.

Q: *That's all we know, right?*
SMITH: Yeah, and it goes with my theory of writing realistically, to give those
kinds of details.

Q: *That being the case, that this is integral to the characters in their lives, in their journeys, in their relationships, would you describe your own spirituality as one that's rooted in ideas that encompass the feminine divine?*

SMITH: Yes, absolutely! But I would say, in the same way that I don't really read from the Bible and fixate on passages about God and the nature of God, I also don't read mythology for the ancient goddesses. I mean, my idea of the divine is, I think, a more feminine divine, but it's still completely outside the box, just like my idea of religion as a whole is more outside the box.

Q: *The feeling I get is that it's not mutually exclusive and that's what many feminist theologians suggest.*

SMITH: I have no doctrine.

Q: *It's not either you believe in a male God or you believe in the Great Mother Goddess. It's not one or the other; it's almost asexual and androgynous. It's a being that's . . .*

SMITH: Beyond that. It's really beyond that. But many of the ways and times that I feel most in touch with spirituality, with this being, with whatever is beyond us, *is* when I'm involved in things that have to do with a woman's role, with the feminine role.

Q: *And that seems to be true with your characters too.*

SMITH: That's true.

Q: *And it seems to me in reading the characters and living with the characters and loving the characters and seeing their developments, that their experiences—having their own feminine experiences—often involve getting outside the boundaries that you've always talked about, the letting go to some extent, whether it's running to the top of the mountain, rolling through a field, feeling like you're tumbling down a hill, whatever it is that allows for that perception.*

SMITH: Yeah, that's right!

Q: *Whereas Sue Monk Kidd refers to her experience as one big huge awakening, that doesn't seem to be the case with your writing. It's a gradual kind of thing with the characters as they progressively develop during the course of your writing. But Kidd sees her experience as being an awakening and she calls this the birth of her self, her new self. Kidd says, "Bringing forth a true, instinctual, powerful woman who is rooted in her own feminine center, who honors the sacredness of the feminine and who speaks the feminine language of her own soul is never easy."*

SMITH: And I would love to be exactly that! I mean, that's a description of what I would certainly hope to be. But it has been gradual, and there wasn't some huge break. I mean, I know there are other people who had to leave their minister husbands or make a huge change or something like that, and I didn't. I wasn't that rigid growing up. But I came from a very traditional family in a very traditional part of the country. And so, it's been a while.

Q: You know, what Kidd says about "feminine" language resonates particularly with your writing, I think, because of your interest in language, not only the language you're using as you're creating these worlds, but the interest the characters themselves have. Oftentimes the female characters, but sometimes the males also, feel the inability of language to capture experiences.

SMITH: Yeah.

Q: Often feminist critics have suggested strongly that women need to have a complete separate language because the language we use is male. You haven't openly acknowledged anything like this, but so many of your characters can't find the words to express an intense experience. I mean, they love language and they want to hear language and it's like food and it's satisfying, but there's always this sense of finding a language that speaks to their experiences.

SMITH: Lucinda MacKethan, who's been my good friend since we were eighteen, once wrote that I am more of a "speakerly writer" than a "writerly writer." And I think that this term is feminine. I mean, I think *talk*, you know, talk—gossip, an informal kind of storytelling—is my language. I have been accused of being anti-intellectual and anti-education because so many times the very educated characters are so out of touch with themselves.

Q: Like Richard Burlage?

SMITH: Right. Again, I guess I feel that those kinds of disciplines that they have gone through and are acting out of are like the box.

Q: You know, I hadn't thought about it, but it takes a tremendous effort for a character to break through that, and Richard does, with Dory. All of his senses tell him that he is experiencing something divine with Dory, here in the mountains.

SMITH: He knows all this, but he cracks up! [laughter] Because it's too scary—for him to have all that.

*Q: Yea, it's too scary for him . . . About all the characters and their searches . . .
interestingly, they are all (and I'm making a generalization here) searching for
validation, which I think we all do.*
SMITH: Yes, which all people are.

*Q: And they seem to start with the natural route. Most of them try traditional
Christianity; they pray to God; they listen for some guidance; they try every way
they can, but it seems that most are left unsatisfied and they may or may not
find something else. I think of the earlier, younger characters—they have these
mystical kinds of experiences but they can't ever put that together, or integrate
that with their everyday lives.*
SMITH: Yeah.

*Q: The spirituality that most of these characters eventually embrace is one that
has to be a broader experience, it has to encompass their own experience, and
their own experience oftentimes includes the sexuality, so anything that says this
is bad and wrong can't work for them.*
SMITH: Yeah. I think that's true.

*Q: Lee, is there anything else that you would like to share with me or talk about
that relates to your own spirituality?*
SMITH: No, there's really not, but I do think that *place* is tremendously important in my work. Because I grew up completely surrounded by mountains;
the little town of Grundy was in the bottom of a teacup, or a bowl. So, when
we would be going home from college, we would say, "when are you coming
in?" It was always "coming in," like you were going *into* something, and there
was very much a sense of almost a womb. I mean, it was a basket, a womb,
you know, a place of safety, and it was a sense of community, the whole ma-
trix, which I think of as feminine. One reason is because both my parents
did suffer from depression and anxiety and were hospitalized from time to
time and I was always staying with another relative. It was always fine; you
know it really does take a village, and that *was* a village, and I think of that
as a very feminine sense of community. I was cared for, taken care of. There
were men in my father's family involved too, but it's the sense of community,
of everybody sort of mothering you and looking out for you. That's really the
sense I had growing up. And I think that may be one reason I put too many
characters in my books all the time because I have this sense of, you know,

the community. Also, I read a long time ago a story about something called the "basket theory of fiction" (and I talked about this a little bit in *The Last Girls*) from Ursula Le Guin. The theory says that with men, so often the plot is linear, the plot of boys' books. And with girls, it's the journey that counts and it's who you meet along the way. My writing follows more the basket theory of fiction; it's a whole group and it's what happens and it's not linear, it's not quest and conquer. It's a very storytelling, discursive, talking kind of thing. I think of it as a feminine way of telling a story. And for me, it is inextricably tied to place, a feminine sense of community, as opposed to living in isolation, which I think of as a very male thing. Although some of my women do it . . . [laughter]

Q: One of the things that is so interesting about The Last Girls *is that we have the river journey, which we think of as linear, but the story is almost spinning in circles because all the women's lives are circling and looping and catching parts of each other's lives as they're all centered on Baby's life.*
SMITH: Yeah. It has not been a straight progression for any of those women or one that followed expectations. Theirs all depended on what happened to them and who they met along the way and all that kind of thing.

Q: When you talked about all the community nurturing you, I jotted down the word "mothering"; then, you used the word yourself.
SMITH: Yeah, absolutely.

Q: It makes me think so much of other women writers who see mothering as not exclusively a biological experience, but rather a communal one in which several people work together to nurture and raise a child. In The Color Purple, *for instance, there are no female characters that actually literally raise their own children.[8] Everybody's raising everybody else's children and they're all moved around and switched around. This is a whole new idea of mothering.*
SMITH: Right. That's true.

Q: And it's almost a utopia that Walker creates in a lot of ways. But it's interesting that that's all okay. It's a woman's world there, and the men, in that case, are left out because they're not part of it.
SMITH: Yes, and there's a lot of villages and tribes and so on where it's a real communal thing too. You know, it's an older way of looking at things, I think.

Q: With the whole import of the mountains, and you made a comment many years ago that until you started working the mountain material, you couldn't give women a mythic role. I think it was in an interview with Dorothy Hill. But as you've moved away from the mountains in some of your fiction, like The Last Girls, *for instance, I see these women as also having a mythic role.*
SMITH: Yeah, I do too.

Q: So it originated here in the mountains and then it continued. And with On Agate Hill, *we come back here. I think this is such an important point, in the sense of your own journey, but then Molly's is totally different than previous characters.*
SMITH: But still we come back. [laughter] That's why I had to bring you up here!

As we left the cabin and drove back down the winding, steep roads to re-enter civilization and the twenty-first century I realized what a gift Lee had given me.

Notes

1. Wendy Reed and Jennifer Horne, eds., *All Out of Faith: Southern Women on Spirituality* (Tuscaloosa: University of Alabama Press, 2006).
2. "Ivy Row," One-Woman Show by Barbara Bates Smith. Original production co-adapted and directed by Mark Hunter, Musical accompaniment by Jeff Sebens, Off-Broadway, First performed 1990.
3. William Faulkner, *Light in August: The Corrected Text* (New York: Vintage Books, 1990; orig. publ. 1932).
4. Lee's son Josh Seay died October 26, 2003, at age thirty-three, having spent half his life confronting the brain disorder schizophrenia. For Lee's account of her son's illness, see "Goodbye to the Sunset Man," *The Independent Weekly* (Oct. 2004), available online at http://www.leesmith.com/works/sunsetman.php.
5. Kidd's best-known works include *When the Heart Waits: Spiritual Direction for Life's Sacred Questions* (San Francisco, CA: Harper & Row, 1990); *The Secret Life of Bees* (New York: Viking, 2002); and *The Mermaid Chair* (New York: Viking, 2005).
6. Clarissa Pincola Estes, *Women Who Run with the Wolves: Myths and Stories of the Wild Woman Archetype* (New York: Ballantine Books, 1992).
7. Barbara Kingsolver, *Animal, Vegetable, Miracle: A Year of Food Life* (New York: HarperCollins, 2007).
8. Alice Walker, *The Color Purple: A Novel* (New York: Harcourt Brace Jovanovich, 1982).

Literary Interviews Published in the *Southern Quarterly*

1981

"**Harry Crews**: An Interview." David K. Jeffrey and Donald R. Noble. Vol. 19, no. 2, 65–79.

"Interview with **Erskine Caldwell**." Jac Tharpe. Vol. 20, no. 1, 64–74.

1982

"Kingfish of American Opera: An Interview with **Carlisle Floyd**." R. L. Cowser, Jr. Vol. 20, no. 3, 5–18.

"**Harry Crews** on the American Dream." Larry W. DeBord and Gary L. Long. Vol. 20, no. 3, 35–53.

"A Conversation with **Eudora Welty**." Martha Van Noppen. Vol. 20, no. 4, 7–23.

1983

"**Madison Jones**: An Interview." David K. Jeffrey and Donald R. Noble. Vol. 21, no. 3, 5–26.

"Interviews with **Seven Contemporary Writers**." Laurie L. Brown. Vol. 21, no. 4, 3–22.

"The World of **Lee Smith**." Anne Goodwyn Jones. Vol. 22, no. 1, 115–39.

1985

"Rites, Masks, Light and the Poet's Craft: An Interview with **Peter Cooley**." Caroline Barnard Hall. Vol. 23, no. 4, 77–89.

1987

"Interview with **David Madden**: On Technique in Fiction." Jeffrey J. Folks. Vol. 25, no. 2, 24–38.

"A Conversation with **Shirley Ann Grau**." John Canfield. Vol. 25, no. 2, 39–52.

"An Interview with **Jane Reid-Petty** of New Stage Theatre." Philip C. Kolin. Vol. 25, no. 4, 39–46.

"**John O'Neal**: An Interview." Elizabeth A. Barron and Donald R. Mott. Vol. 25. no. 4, 75–84.

1988

"'Waiting at Dachau': An Interview with **Reynolds Price**." Ashby Bland Crowder. Vol. 26, no. 2, 12–26.

"An Interview with **Bobbie Ann Mason**." Albert E. Wilhelm. Vol. 26, no. 2, 27–38.

"An Interview with **Tennessee Williams**." Jere Real. Vol. 26, no. 3, 40–49.

"What It Means to Be a Southern Writer in the '80s: A Panel Discussion with **Beverly Lowry, Reynolds Price, Elizabeth Spencer** and **James Whitehead**." Austin Wilson. Vol. 26, no. 4, 80–93.

1989

"Interview with **Helen Caldwell Cushman**." Harvey L. Kievar. Vol. 27, no. 3, 86–98.

"An Interview with **Virginia Caldwell**." Edwin T. Arnold. Vol. 27, no. 3, 99–110.

"Interview with **Robert Amberg**." Ken Bloom. Vol. 27, no. 4, 25–30.

"An Interview with **Judith McWillie**." Stephen Flinn Young. Vol. 28, no. 1, 25–39.

1990

"An Interview with **Lee Smith**." Dorothy Combs Hill. Vol. 28, no. 2, 5–19.

"An Interview with **Bruce Childs**." Steven T. Ryan. Vol. 28, no. 3, 89–96.

"An Interview with **James Seay**." William Walsh. Vol. 28, no. 4, 99–115.

1991

"A Conversation with **Seven Fiction Writers**." Peggy Whitman Prenshaw. Vol. 29, no. 2, 69–93.

"A Conversation with **Clyde Edgerton**." Kenn Robbins. Vol. 30, no. 1, 58–65.

1992

"An Interview with **Bobbie Ann Mason**." Dorothy Combs Hill. Vol. 31, no. 1, 85–118.

1993

"**Will Campbell** by the Fire." W. Dale Brown. Vol. 31, no. 2, 165–86.

1994

"Interview with **Lee Smith**." Elisabeth Herion-Sarafidis. Vol. 32, no. 2, 6–18.

"A Conversation with **Lee Smith**." Rebecca Smith. Vol. 32, no. 2, 19–29.

"Interview with **Lee Smith**." V. Hunt. Vol. 32, no. 2, 30–36.

"An Interview with **Larry Brown**." Susan Ketchin. Vol. 32, no. 2, 95–109.

"Interview with **William Christenberry**." Peter J. Brownlee. Vol. 32, no. 3, 89–95.

"**Gail Godwin** Talks about Southern Storytelling." Jocelyn Hazelwood Donlon. Vol. 32, no. 3, 11–24.

"An Interview with **Daphne Athas**." Michael Parker. Vol. 32, no. 3, 25–42.

"Interview with **Eve Shelnutt**." Felicia Mitchell. Vol. 32, no. 3, 43–50.

"With Wings to Fly: A Conversation with New Orleans Novelist **Nancy Lemann**." William A. Francis. Vol. 32, no. 3, 51–66.

"Interview with **Tim McLaurin**." Donnalee Frega. Vol. 32, no. 3, 67–88.

"Interview with **Herbert Singleton**." Deborah Gilman. Vol. 32, no. 3, 96–110.

"A Conversation with **Dixon McDowell**: The Horton Foote Documentary." Stephen Flinn Young. Vol. 32, no. 3, 147–57.

"Talking with **Josephine Humphreys**." Alphonse Vinh. Vol. 32, no. 4, 131–40.

"An Interview with **Richard Marius**." Carroll Viera. Vol. 33, no. 1, 113–25.

1995

"Interview with **Mary Lee Settle**." Jennifer Howard. Vol. 33, nos. 2–3, 79–83.

"'Parts of a Novel That Will Probably Never Get Written': An Interview with **Elizabeth Spencer**." David Hammond. Vol. 33, nos. 2–3, 85–106.

"Interview with **David Madden**: 'The Theatrical Image.'" Peggy Bach. Vol. 33, nos. 2–3, 215–26.

"Interview with **Ellen Douglas**." Christine Wilson. Vol. 33, no. 4, 15–21.

"'I'm in That Secular World, Even Though I Keep Looking Around for Someplace Else To Be': Interview with **Ellen Douglas**." Betty Tardieu. Vol. 33, no. 4, 23–59.

"An Interview with **Lewis Nordan**." Blake Maher. Vol. 34, no. 1, 113–23.

1996

"Interview with **Doris Betts**." W. Dale Brown. Vol. 34, no. 2, 91–104.

"Go Ahead On: An Interview with **Gurney Norman**." J. W. Williamson. Vol. 34, no. 3, 9–20.

"Interview with New Orleans Novelist **Chris Wiltz**." William Francis. Vol. 34, no. 4, 109–19.

1997

"An Interview with **Minnie Bruce Pratt**." V. Hunt. Vol. 35, no. 3, 97–107.

"An Interview with **James Conaway**." Marsha Hurley and Brian Isbell. Vol. 35, no. 3, 109–15.

1998

"'I Still See with a Southern Eye': An Interview with **Jill McCorkle**." Charline R. McCord. Vol. 36, no. 3, 103–12.

"'I Have to Know Where These Characters Have Walked': An Interview with **Carolyn Haines**." Charline R. McCord. Vol. 36, no. 4, 130–40.

"An Interview with **Harry Crews**." Erik Bledsoe. Vol. 37, no. 1, 97–117.

1999

"**William Styron**: An Interview." Virginia Gunn Fick. Vol. 37, no. 2, 158–62.

"Fishing from the Poetry Boat: A Conversation with **David Bottoms**." Alice Friman and Bruce Gentry. Vol. 37, no. 3–4, 93–105.

2000

"Late-Night Rambles with **Richard Marius**: An Interview." Jeffrey Folks. Vol. 38, no. 4, 124–32.

2001

"A Conversation with **John M. Barry**." Huey Guagliardo. Vol. 39, no. 4, 67–81.

"Getting the Voices Right: A Conversation with **Robert Morgan** about *The Gardener's Son*." Peter Josyph. Vol. 40, no. 1, 121–31.

"Losing Home: A Conversation with **Ted Tally** about *All the Pretty Horses*." Peter Josyph. Vol. 40, no. 1, 132–46.

2002

"An Interview with **Donald Harington**." Larry Vonalt. Vol. 40, no. 2, 69–85.

"**William Hoffman**'s Fictional Journey." Casey Clabough. Vol. 41, no. 1, 80–86.

2003

"An Interview with **Lewis Nordan**." Edward J. Dupuy. Vol. 41, no. 3, 95–108.

"An Interview with **Richard Marius**." Randall K. Brison. Vol. 41, no. 4, 96–104.

2005

"'He Liked to Call Me Padre': **Bishop Duncan Gray** Remembers William Faulkner." Sally Wolff King. Vol. 43, no. 1, 80–106.

2006

"The Scribe of River Lake Plantation: A Conversation with **Ernest J. Gaines**." Anne Gray Brown. Vol. 44, no. 1, 9–31.

2009

"A Spiritual Journey: An Interview with **Lee Smith**." Linda Byrd Cook. Vol. 47, no. 1, 74–103.

"Queering Texas: Interview with **Del Shores**." Andrea Powell Wolfe. Vol. 47, no. 1, 104–20.

Index